RUNNING BOOK DISCUSSION GROUPS

A How-To-Do-It Manual

Lauren Zina John

HOW-TO-DO-IT MANUAL FOR LIBRARIANS

NUMBER 147

NEAL-SCHUMAN PUBLISHERS, INC.

New York   London

Published by Neal-Schuman Publishers, Inc.
100 William Street
New York, NY 10038

Printed and bound in the United States of America

The paper used in this publication meets the minimum requirements of American National Standard for Information Sciences—Permanence of Paper for Printed Library Materials. ANSI Z39.48-1992. ∞

Library of Congress Cataloging-in-Publication Data

John, Lauren Zina.
  Running book discussion groups: a how-to-do-it manual / Lauren Zina John.
    p. cm. — (How-to-do-it manuals for librarians ; no. 147)
  Includes bibliographical references and index.
  ISBN 1-55570-542-1 (alk. paper)
 1. Book clubs (Discussion groups)—Handbooks, manuals, etc. 2. Group reading—Handbooks, manuals, etc. 3. Books and reading. I. Title. II. How-to-do-it manuals for libraries ; no. 147.
  LC6619.J64 2006
  374'.22—dc22
                                                          2006000704

For California George

CONTENTS

List of Figures   vii

Preface   ix

Acknowledgments   xiii

Part I. How to Launch a Successful Book Discussion Group

1. Exploring the Great American Book Discussion Group   3

2. Recruiting Members   19

3. Choosing the Right Books   29

4. Planning When and Where to Meet   49

5. Generating Publicity   55

Part II. How to Run a Successful Book Discussion Group

6. Talking the Talk   81

7. Booking an Author and Planning an Event   103

8. Organizing an Online Library-Sponsored Book
    Discussion Group   113

Part III. Ten Guaranteed Crowd-Pleasing Book Discussions

Overview   131

September   *Travels with Charley: In Search of America*
            by John Steinbeck   133

October   *In Cold Blood: A True Account of a Multiple
            Murder and Its Consequences* by Truman Capote   139

November   *The Namesake* by Jhumpa Lahiri   149

December   Holiday Book Discussion Overview Sample Selection   159

December   "The Dead" by James Joyce   163

January   *Friday Night Lights: A Town, A Team, and A Dream* by H. G. Bissinger   169

February   *Dreams from My Father: A Story of Race and Inheritance* by Barack Obama   179

March   *Charming Billy* by Alice McDermott   187

April   *Nickel and Dimed: On (Not) Getting by in America* by Barbara Ehrenreich   195

May   *Snow Flower and the Secret Fan* by Lisa See   203

June   *The Kite Runner* by Khaled Hosseini   211

Part IV. Resources for Book Discussion Groups

Resource A: Annotated Bibliography of Books and Magazines for Book Groups   225

Resource B: Online Tools for Choosing and Evaluating Books   231

Resource C: Professional Organizations /Subcommittees: Support for Librarians Who Run Book Groups   235

Resource D: Partnership Strategies: Checklist for Getting Help from Bookstores, Schools, and Community Groups   237

Index   241

About the Author   250

LIST OF FIGURES

Figure 1–1 Press Release: The San Francisco Reads Program, San Francisco, California   16

Figure 1–2 Press Release The City of Santa Ana/Cal State Fullerton One Book One City Program—2002, Santa Ana, California   17

Figure 2–1 Sample Survey: Starting a Group for the First Time   27

Figure 3–1 Web Site: Downer's Grove Public Library Get Real — Nonfiction for Fiction Lovers, Downer's Grove, Illinois   37

Figure 3–2 An Annotated Bibliography: Mystery Reference Sources   44

Figure 4–1 The Shrewsbury Public Library Book Group Schedule for Fall 2004   51

Figure 5–1 Poster: Promoting *The Bridge of San Luis Rey*   59

Figure 5–2 Sample Flyer: Author Program   61

Figure 5–3 E-mail Press Release: The Menlo Park Almanac Weekly Community Newspaper, Menlo Park, California   64

Figure 5–4 Sample Correspondence: Writing to an Interested Patron   67

Figure 5–5 Book Group E-Mail: Slide Talk Based on John Steinbeck's *East of Eden*   69

Figure 5–6 Book Group E-mail: Book Discussion of Thornton Wilder's *The Bridge of San Luis Rey*   70

Figure 5–7 Web Site Page: Book Groups of Boone County Public Library, Kentucky   72

Figure 5–8 Web Site Page: Book Group of Bettendorf Public Library, Bettendorf, Iowa   75

Figure 6–1 Web Site: The Internet Public Library Literary Criticism Collection   88

Figure 6–2 Book Discussion Kit: Stephen Dobyns' *The Church of Dead Girls*   97

Figure 6–3 Book Discussion Kit: Instructions for Patrons, Boone County Public Library, Kentucky   99

Figure 7–1 Sample E-Mail: Author Invitation   111

Figure 7–2 Sample: Thank-You Note to the Author   112

Figure 8–1   Roselle Public Library Book Bloggers FAQ, Roselle,
              Illinois   116
Figure 8–2   Rules for Participating in the Tippecanoe Public
              Library's Online Book Group,
              Lafayette, Indiana   119
Figure 8–3   Hennepin County Readers Online Book
              Group Message   121
Figure 8–4   Recruitment Ad: the Halifax Public Libraries
              Online Book Club, Halifax,
              Nova Scotia, Canada   124

PREFACE

As anyone who has attempted to launch or lead a book discussion group can tell you, it's much more complicated than gathering a group of people to read and discuss the same title. I wrote *Running Book Discussion Groups: A How-To-Do-It Manual for Librarians* to provide my colleagues with community outreach ideas, time-saving book selection tips, suggestions for member recruitment and publicity, and ready-made book discussions. The bottom line? This guide may actually let you enjoy your role as group director and organizer and give you time to read and savor your selections!

I knew that I had to write a guide to book groups the day that a patron approached the reference desk, whispering, "Help me . . . I am the *victim* of a book discussion group." Her choice of words initially startled me, but as her story unraveled, I came to understand her use of the term.

This particular patron was struggling through her group's monthly selection—a long historical novel set in eighteenth-century New England from which she took little pleasure. Worse still, she was constantly intimidated by the other people in her group, many of whom were better educated, better read, and better traveled. She desperately wanted to impress them, at least once. It would have been easy to pass judgment on this patron, or simply try to talk her out of continuing with the group, but reference librarians are there to help—not to judge. Being a book group leader as well as a reference librarian, I knew how to prepare for group discussions. I helped her find reviews of the book, author biographies, and the publisher's reading guide. I encouraged her to stick with the selection—or at least skim it and read the last chapter to see how things turned out. Last but not least, I suggested that before completely souring on book groups, she might want to join the public library's group. I introduced myself as the leader. "The people in this discussion group are wonderful," I said, "and they have a wide variety of educational backgrounds." I mentioned that we sometimes host an author and keep connected via e-mail between meetings. At our meetings we help members find other books and films to round out their appreciation of the title. Most importantly, we select books that people actually enjoy reading, not books that people think that they *should* read in order to impress others.

My encounter with the *victim* of a bad book group reaffirmed for me just how strongly I believed in the power of good book groups. After seeing how unpleasant a poorly planned book discussion could get, I realized that I had knowledge to share with other librarians.

ORGANIZATION

Running Book Discussion Groups is organized into four parts which guide you step-by-step through the tasks and responsibilities you will face as a book group leader. Part I: "How to Launch a Successful Book Discussion Group" will help you get off to the right start—learning about the background of these literary gatherings and the groundwork that must be done in order to launch your own group.

- Chapter 1, "Exploring the Great American Book Discussion Group," traces the evolution of book discussion from Bible study on the Mayflower to today's "One Book, One City" discussions. You will discover that then as now, the keys to success include easy access to affordable books, publicity, and cooperation with social institutions like schools, centers, businesses, and churches.
- Chapter 2, "Recruiting Members," offers strategies to attract your very first members and to keep them once they have joined. This chapter advocates active involvement: going to bookstores, speaking at schools, and enlisting other advocates. When it comes to getting new members, networking is key.
- Chapter 3, "Choosing the Right Books," features general guidelines for how to select books and more specialized suggestions to navigate the classics, nonfiction, best-sellers, and genre fiction. Because most people who attend discussion groups expect to get the books for free, this chapter suggests that you select what you can get easily. Smaller, private groups with the luxury of external funding may be better positioned to tackle more obscure choices.
- Chapter 4, "Planning When and Where to Meet," explores the essentials that might easily be considered trivial—how to select a place to meet, pick a time, arrange the space, serve snacks, and more. You would never host a dinner party without establishing these basics, so why would you host a discussion group without putting in the same amount of planning?

- Chapter 5, "Generating Publicity," is filled with sample flyers, press releases, and e-mail announcements that you can use as a model or launching pad in the creation of your own versions. You will also find ample guidance to create effective public relations materials.

Part II: "How to Run a Successful Book Discussion Group" guides you through the steps of successful management. The chapters cover the elements of the actual meeting—from ways to break the ice to how to move your discussions online.

- Chapter 6, "Talking the Talk," will help you lead with confidence. You will find tips for how to make introductions, sustain conversation and avoid silences, develop engaging questions, handle "problem" members, utilize resources, and more.
- Chapter 7, "Booking an Author and Planning an Event," takes your meetings to the next level. You will learn how to entice authors to your meetings, build a successful program, and publicize this special event.
- Chapter 8, "Organizing an Online Library-Sponsored Book Discussion Group," brings your group to a whole new audience of readers. This chapter sorts through available technologies—blogs, chat rooms, software packages—and shares best practices for moving into the electronic arena.

Part III: "Ten Guaranteed Crowd-Pleasing Book Discussions" gives a head start to programming your first few meetings. These ten ready-to-use book discussion programs feature fiction and nonfiction titles that have proven successful in discussion groups. Many book discussion groups meet for the ten-month period that follows the pattern of the school year and take off the summer months of July and August. I suggest some titles to tie in with seasonal and annual celebrations—the haunting and terrifying *In Cold Blood* is perfect for October, while *Dreams from My Father* is a touching memoir for February's celebration of Black History Month. Other selections highlight popular nonfiction (*Friday Night Lights* and *Nickel and Dimed*); classics ("The Dead" and *Travels with Charley*), and best-sellers (*The Namesake* and *Charming Billy*).

There are numerous discussion group guides already available both online and in print; but the guides in *Running Book Discussion Groups* are unique in that I designed them for use in a library setting. They contain a mix of "hardball" and "softball" questions engineered to appeal to the wide range of users in your library. Each discussion guide provides the following essential information:

- how to get this book (pricing, editions, and publisher information)
- plot summary
- author biography, including information from interviews, reviews, and other relevant sources
- explanation for why this book has been popular with book groups
- suggestions for using props or other media to support/ enhance the discussion
- at least ten discussion questions with proven "icebreakers" for getting the conversation rolling

These programs often bring users into the library for the first time, and they can be a powerful tool for stimulating further usage of the institution's resources. Accordingly, they highlight film adaptations of books; large-type and audio editions of titles; additional titles by the author; and travel guides and other materials that relate to elements of the book.

Finally, Part IV: "Resources for Book Discussion Groups" contains materials for starting a new group or for making a good group better. You will find an annotated bibliography of books and magazines for your group, a list of online resources for choosing and evaluating titles, a guide to professional organizations that support librarians who run book groups, and a checklist for partnering with other organizations.

Throughout *Running Book Discussion Groups: A How-To-Do-It Manual for Librarians* you will see highlighted Web sites, templates for creating your own materials, helpful tips, interviews and anecdotes from librarians across the United States and Canada, and more. In writing this guide I came to realize our colleagues share a wealth of information in daily exchanges. Through online bulletin boards I communicated with a wide range of librarians—from ones who work in quiet rural libraries open only a few days a week to bustling city libraries, some open until midnight. The common thread is a troupe of book group discussion leaders who generously shared their wonderful suggestions and revealed their enormous enthusiasm. I hope that *Running Book Discussion Groups* sparks your interest in this unique service and helps to create your own success stories at your library.

ACKNOWLEDGMENTS

I gratefully acknowledge the support of my friends and colleagues at the Menlo Park Library. I would like especially to thank the Friends of the Menlo Park Library and Roberta Roth, the outreach/literacy coordinator.

Thanks to well-read and thoughtful book group members like Susan Huch and the historian of Menlo Park Presbyterian Church, Bill Russ.

Thank you to Dr. Al Jacobs, literary performer and professor emeritus of Menlo College. Al taught me everything I know about lifelong learning and community building. I love to listen to him read out loud.

I am grateful to Michael Lambert, branch manager of the East Palo Alto Public Library; Alison Anson, public services librarian at the San Carlos Public Library; and the librarians and technical support folks at the California State Library's Infopeople Project for providing input and encouragement.

Many thanks to the people at the Town and Country Club of San Francisco: Barbie Geisler, librarian and author; Lynne Stevens, Renaissance woman and fellow bookstore browser; and to all the ladies of the book selection committee. They all share my love of books and book discussion and inspire me with their insights.

The San Francisco Bay Area is blessed with talented authors, generous with their time. I would especially like to thank Ron Hansen and authors Laura Fraser and Ethan Watters, and members of the San Francisco Writer's Grotto.

On the days when I'm not in a library, you'll most likely find me in a local independent Bay Area bookstore. Three great ones are Keplers in Menlo Park, Cody's in Berkeley and San Francisco, and Book Passage based in Corte Madera. Their staffs, selection, programs, and book discussion groups are first-rate and an inspiration to readers and librarians everywhere!

Last but not least, thanks to Neal-Schuman Publishers and editor Michael Kelley for transforming a long-time librarian into a first-time author.

Part I

How to Launch a Successful Book Discussion Group

1 EXPLORING THE GREAT AMERICAN BOOK DISCUSSION GROUP

"Book groups are the graduate seminar, the encounter group, and the good old-fashioned village-pump gossip session, all rolled up into one . . . Library-sponsored groups are perhaps the most democratic book groups around—they're free of charge and open to everyone, even those who snooze through the discussion or don't read the book." (Slezak, 2000)

Are you running a book discussion group at your library? Are you thinking about running a group? Either way, I hope that this book will provide some valuable ideas and tools.

I hesitate to begin with an overused metaphor, but I can't resist observing that book discussion groups are like snowflakes. No two are alike. You won't find one single, foolproof methodology here. But you will be able to take a look at some of the challenges and opportunities found in the public library setting, and discover "best practices" from librarians around the country.

If you are holding this book in your hands, you most likely have participated in at least one session of a book discussion group, whether at your library, a bookstore, or a private home. Perhaps you prefer to talk about books online and participate in "virtual" discussions. We'll talk about these groups in Chapter 8. If you have not yet attended a group, however, please make plans to do so *soon!* As helpful as this book will be, this is an activity that you need to learn by doing—both as a leader and as a participant in groups led by other librarians.

I have just completed my second year of leading a monthly book discussion group at Menlo Park Public Library, located in an affluent suburb in the heart of Silicon Valley. Most of my members are women ranging in age from forty-five to eighty-five. We have a core group of twenty members and a combined e-mail and snail mail (postcard) list of over one hundred—with anywhere from eight to twenty people showing up at one time. Author events draw larger crowds. Obviously my book group experience is going to be very different from that of a leader working in a large urban public library or a small rural one, but this book will contain case studies from a wide range of libraries. We hope that you will be inspired by their success.

BEFORE THERE WAS OPRAH

These days, book groups are a popular American pastime, with people meeting regularly in living rooms, libraries, and even the local Starbucks to share ideas. With book groups now sponsored by radio and television programs, as well as online clubs and bookstore promotions, you might think that we are at the dawn of the book group age. In fact, many people believe that the person most responsible for introducing book groups to Americans is daytime television talk show host Oprah Winfrey, who in 1996 introduced the concept of a nationwide reading program to her viewers.

See Oprah's Web site (www.oprah.com/books) for more information. But the truth is that formal and informal book discussion groups began just as soon as there were books!

To chronicle book discussion group history thoroughly, you would have to start with ancient Egypt and the first library in Alexandria and move on to ancient Greece up through the Gutenberg printing press that brought us printed versions of the Bible. In the interest of time, however, I'll briefly focus on the history of the book group in the United States. I present this mini-history lesson to show that, then as now, Americans formed book groups for many of the same reasons:

- to make sense of the world around them
- to understand themselves better
- to feel less isolated and develop a sense of community
- to become more educated and/or fill the gaps in their education

Another less altruistic reason for establishing and participating in book groups is to coerce people into thinking the same way. For example, Adolf Hitler was known for promoting literary discussions of his treatise *Mein Kampf,* but it is hard to imagine that there was much room for disagreement in his living room. On the other hand, the book *was* a best-seller in the United States in 1938 and was most likely a catalyst for a wide range of opinions. In a public library setting open to all, you will have to be prepared for readers from all walks of life. We will talk about ways to hone moderating skills in Chapter 6.

COLONIAL READERS

Many historians credit the Puritan religious leader Anne Hutchinson with establishing America's first literary discussion group in 1634. Technically speaking, the group wasn't even in America yet, because the discussions were held on the boat that sailed from

England to the Massachusetts Bay Colony. Women passengers gathered each week to talk about that Sunday's sermon. Once they were settled in Boston, the women's group continued. However, when the male religious leaders found out that the women were debating rather than simply reading religious tracts, they decided it was an unsuitable way for women to occupy their time. That's one of the reasons that Hutchinson was banished, and she fled to establish what eventually became the state of Rhode Island.

MIDDLE-CLASS READERS

The next boom in book discussions happened in the 1800s when literacy increased and more books were printed in this country or imported from Europe. After the American Civil War, declining birth rates and improvements in home appliances, such as stoves replacing fireplaces, gave Americans—especially women—more free time. Middle-class Americans of both sexes became more interested in educating themselves and began to attend lectures on the arts and sciences. Literary groups and book clubs also flourished. Classes and discussions were less formal than their elite European counterparts—the salons. However, they were still far more formal than they are today, as participants spent hours preparing notes and commentaries that would resemble today's college term papers. For many members—especially women who lacked access to higher education—book groups were a place to attain such an education. Some women probably saw such groups as a duty or social obligation rather than an enjoyable activity. In modern times, however, more people are having fun with book groups, although some persist in the notion that fine literature should not be fun.

It is important to note that while today public libraries strive to serve all citizens, and book programs often stress diversity, most of our country's early book discussions were segregated by race and religion. African-American women and men had their own discussion groups in Philadelphia as early as the 1830s, including the Female and Literary Society's book group, which hosted abolitionist William Lloyd Garrison as a speaker. Richard Kleim, a recent graduate of the Library and Information Sciences Program at Florida State University, discusses this segregation in a 2003 paper on the history of book discussions, available on his Web site (www.kleim.org).

THE CHAUTAUQUA MOVEMENT

One nationwide book discussion group, founded in 1878 and still in existence today, is the Chautauqua Literary and Scientific Circle (CLSC). Chautauqua was originally founded by the Methodist Church headquartered near Rochester, New York. Today it is open to all faiths and run as a more secular organization. The Literary and Scientific Circle was specifically organized to send out books to rural readers. The members would read together in small home-town discussion groups that would meet for summer "graduation" sessions at Chautauqua headquarters. Most of the students were women, and rather than focusing on fiction, as today's book groups tend to do, the Chautauqua groups focused on such topics as world history, science and nature, philosophy, and comparative religion.

In 1904, the Chicago branch of Chautauqua decided to do further rural outreach by organizing tent lecture shows to tour the Iowa cornfields. The purpose was as much to entertain as instruct. There were often magicians, musicians, and motivational speakers along on the tour. Still, reading continued to be a popular activity. By 1914, the program had enlisted half a million readers in twelve thousand circles in every U.S. state, with forty-nine thousand graduates of the four-year program.

Before 1890, half of the ten thousand Chautauqua circles were in small towns and villages with populations of between five hundred and thirty-five hundred people. Few of those towns had public libraries, but programs like the CLSC inspired citizens to start funding and building public libraries. In fact, some of these communities, with the help of local Chautauqua circles, lobbied for and received funds from the Carnegie Foundation for library buildings. CLSC membership gradually declined after the late 1890s—with the organization partly a victim of its own success. Competition came from home libraries, correspondence schools, universities, and various other reading circles.

Today, the Chautauqua Literary and Scientific Circle is the oldest continuing book club in America. Its Web site at www.chautauqua-inst.org/clsc.html includes the entire reading list, from 1878 to 2004. It is interesting to note how the reading selections reflected national interests and attitudes over the years. In 2002–2003, members were reading Karen Armstrong's book *Islam: A Short History*. In 1960–1961, members read Rachel Carson's *The Sea Around Us*.

THE GREAT BOOKS MOVEMENT

The first book discussion boom of the twentieth century happened just after World War II with the Great Books program that had its roots in academia as part of the curriculum at Columbia University and the University of Chicago. The Great Books course was originally intended to introduce college students to the major thinkers in Western culture. The authors selected were those traditionally featured in American college classes in the 1950s—Greek philosophers, Founding Fathers, Shakespeare, and Dickens—authors who came to be known in the less traditional 1960s as the "Dead White Males."

Eventually, however, the Great Books program caught on in continuing education courses that were opened to the general public. Housewives, businessmen, soldiers returning from World War II, and bright high school students flocked to these programs, with a lot of publicity done by word of mouth. After all, television had yet to be invented when the Great Books program got started. By the late 1950s, the seminar had attracted fifty thousand registered participants across the United States, with many of the meetings held in public libraries. Since then, participation has dropped considerably, but there are still some 850 groups meeting around the country. About a third of these groups meet in public libraries, though not all are run by librarians. Leaders are trained in a discussion method called "shared inquiry" that focuses on the actual text rather than on personal experiences.

Over the past five years, capitalizing upon renewed interest in book groups, Great Books has set up a Web site (www.greatbooks. org) and begun offering more contemporary programs. For example, a workbook written in English, *A Latino National Conversation*, contains essays and short stories by Hispanic authors, including Julia Alvarez, Martín Espada, Oscar Hijuelos, and Richard Rodriguez. You can order a free Great Books "starter kit" with tips on how to lead a discussion by calling 1–800–222–5870 or sending an e-mail to gbf@greatbooks.org. If you are thinking about running a program aimed at the Latino community, you can ask for a free review copy of A *Latino National Conversation* workbook, which has some great individual program ideas.

THE OPRAH ERA

While one goal of this chapter is to let you know that book groups do not begin and end with daytime television talk show host Oprah Winfrey, she does have a huge influence on American book buyers and readers. Her book club "on the air" began in 1996, when she recommended the novel *The Deep End of the Ocean* by Jacquelyn Mitchard. Periodically after that, Oprah would announce a new selection to viewers, and follow it up with one or more televised segments during which the author would be interviewed and an in-studio book group would meet and talk about the book on the show. When Oprah chose the novel *Cane River* about a family of slaves in Cane River, Louisiana, she interviewed author Lalita Tademy on location in Cane River, toured the ruins of the plantation Tademy had described, and even offered viewers a glimpse of the river itself.

Between 1996 and 2002, Oprah's Book Club promoted works by contemporary authors. Choices included *Black and Blue* by Anna Quindlen, *Daughter of Fortune* by Isabel Allende, *The Poisonwood Bible* by Barbara Kingsolver, and *Sula* by Toni Morrison. Often, due to huge customer demand, publishers would issue special paperback editions of "Oprah Books," complete with an Oprah-endorsed seal of approval on the cover. But while the publishers were happy, the readers signed on, and most authors were thrilled, not everyone agreed on the quality of Oprah's choices or on the wisdom of her audiences. On the one hand, some critics applauded her for bringing contemporary, well-reviewed American and international fiction to national and even international attention. On the other hand, there were critics who said that her selections were too depressing and filled with pathos aiming to appeal to middle-aged, middlebrow women.

Patti Thorn, writer for the Denver *Rocky Mountain News*, observed, "They couldn't agree on much about this newcomer: She was a miracle worker, bringing fine literature to the masses. Then again, she was a snake-oil salesman pushing schlock on middle-aged women." (Thorn 2005) Either way, her selections sold. When Winfrey selected Toni Morrison's *Song of Solomon*, the book had 360,000 copies in paperback. Soon after, 730,000 copies were reprinted. "Winfrey provided a bigger boost for Morrison's commercial clout than the 1993 Nobel Prize for Literature," said Kathleen Rooney, a creative writing teacher at Boston's Emerson College and author of *Reading With Oprah: The Book Club that Changed America*. In her book, Rooney points out that in an industry where few novels sell more than thirty thousand copies, Oprah's picks regularly sell a million or more. According to Rooney, Oprah believes "there's not just one right kind of person or one kind of book. That gets rid of a lot of elitism and snobbery. You don't have to be a college professor to love literature." (Keller 2005) This message resonated with Oprah's huge audience. In 2002, Rooney reported that the *Oprah Winfrey Show* had "a domestic audience of an estimated twenty-six million viewers per week, plus a foreign distribution in 106 countries ranging from Afghanistan to Zimbabwe." (Rooney 2002)

Despite its popularity, Oprah temporarily canceled her on-air book club in 2001. The cancellation came in the wake of an incident in which novelist Jonathan Franzen, author of *The Corrections,* very publicly expressed his disdain at his novel being chosen as an "Oprah book" and was disinvited from appearing on the show. Oprah did not specifically refer to Franzen when she told her audience that she was disbanding the club, instead claiming that the task of selecting great books on a regular basis had simply become too much for her. She said she needed a break. But she revived the club in 2003, switching to discussions of classic literature ranging from Steinbeck to Tolstoy to Faulkner. Readers who signed up for the club on the Oprah.com Web site could log in to read specially prepared lectures by college professors and participate in online book discussions.

On September 22, 2005, Winfrey switched gears again, announcing that the next selection for her television book club would be *A Million Little Pieces* by James Frey, a memoir of addiction and recovery. *BusinessWeek* reported that within four days club fans had bought eighty-five thousand copies. An additional 615,000 books with the Oprah Book Club seal on the cover were available at stores. (Green 2005)

BusinessWeek columnist Hardy Green observed, "What publishers want is what Oprah invariably delivers: unconditional praise . . . she also creates communities of readers, ensuring that no one need face brain benders like William Faulkner's *The Sound and the Fury* all alone." (Green 2005)

THE ELEMENTS OF BOOK GROUPS

So what can we, as library leaders, learn from Oprah? Although she is using techniques that successful book group leaders have used throughout time, she can reach a much wider audience far faster than Anne Hutchinson could on the Mayflower. You don't have to be a television personality or founder of the state of Rhode Island, however, to use these techniques. Here are the elements of successful book groups:

> **A charismatic founder who likes books *and* people.** Yes, it's hard to beat Oprah at this game. But, Great Books was developed in the late 1940s by the University of

Chicago's well-liked, collegial president Robert M. Hutchins, who was just thirty when he assumed his post. He wanted to extend the world of literature beyond the "ivory tower" of academia, and he brought Great Books to high schools, church groups, and libraries. Make sure that your library group is led by a "people person" who can share a love and enthusiasm for books with others. Above all, choose a leader who knows that he or she is not teaching a college literature class or performing on *Masterpiece Theatre*. A learned yet friendly approach will work better than an elitist one.

An accessible, affordable, selection of books. Anne Hutchinson started with the Bible—the one book that most families had a copy of. Great Books leader Hutchins arranged for the books to be printed in cheap paperback editions—and then got the business and academic community to buy them for and distribute them to Great Books readers. Today, the Great Books Foundation continues to supply readers and leaders with inexpensive paperback copies of books, sample discussion questions, and leader training. Oprah has also served as a catalyst for publishers to do so. When you choose books for your group, it helps to have the books readily available at the library for free or to be able to purchase them cheaply, perhaps at a group discount, at your local bookstore.

Business and community partnerships. To build support, Great Books partnered with the business community, gathering together a group of Chicago businessmen interested in self- and community improvement and in keeping up with the educational attainments of the Europeans they encountered during the war. The members, who were enthusiastic about all aspects of Great Books, as well as fine dining, became known as the "Fat Man Group," a name they were quite proud of! (Laskin and Hughes, 1995) Oprah has partnered with authors, book groups, bookstores, and publishers who bear her seal of approval. On her Web site, she has partnered with professors and scholars who lead online lectures and contribute content. As a library book group leader, you need to reach out to your community, whether asking a local professor or civic leader to address your group, or requesting free coffee from Starbucks.

Programs and booklists that evolve to meet community needs. Many people think that the Great Books program has not evolved quickly enough to meet public library needs, as participants can still choose modules of "Dead White Males." But, at the same time, the Great Books module on Politics, Leadership, and Justice selected by Albany Public Library in Northern California includes Lincoln's "Second Inaugural Address," Martin Luther King's "Letter from Birmingham Jail," and Isak Dinesen's "Sorrow-Acre." Although Oprah's picks have broadened across the years, her original fiction choices were said to appeal to her viewers—women between the ages of eighteen and fifty-four—who, by the way, purchase most of the fiction in America. (Rooney 2002)

In response to reader interest, book group leaders across the United States are now expanding their reading lists to include books about the Middle East, Latin America, South Africa, and the American immigrant experience. California's Fremont Public Library, located in a community with the largest Afghan population outside of Afghanistan, sponsored a reading program based on *The Kite Runner,* a novel by Afghan writer Khaled Hosseini. San Francisco Public Library's community-wide reading program in 2005 featured local author Gus Lee, author of the novel *China Boy,* speaking about growing up in Chinatown in the 1950s.

COMMUNITY-WIDE READING PROGRAMS: THE "ONE BOOK" CONCEPT

Building upon Oprah's discovery that entire television audiences could be motivated to read books together, community-wide reading programs supported by public and private organizations are once again popular in the United States. The most recent trend is the "One Book" concept founded in 1996 by Nancy Pearl, a librarian with the Seattle Public Library's Washington Center for the Book. At the local level it often works something like this. Your library or a local bookstore or even your City Council polls local readers and "adopts" a book that people in your city will read together over a period of a few months. Then these groups, perhaps with some help from the publisher, the author, or a grant-making organization, distribute free and/or low-cost copies of the books (usually in paperback), as well as free reader's guides. Some communities even create promotional buttons or posters with the name of the book and the program. To support folks in their reading efforts and to promote the idea that reading is fun as well as educational, cities generally plan public readings, moderated discussions, literary festivals, and (if the author is alive) in-person author appearances all over town. There have even been literary singles mixers. Certainly a library can play a central role in the festivities, but there can be book discussions and related events at the town square, the local beach, coffee shops, schools, houses of worship, and even before a screening at the local movie theater.

What are communities reading? The book generally has a strong social message or local angle. It may be a well-loved classic or a more contemporary book. And it can be a national best-seller or a regional favorite. Here are some picks from the city of Austin, Texas, which sponsored a community-wide reading program called "Keep Austin Reading," managed by the Mayor's Office and Austin Public Library:

2002 – *Bless Me, Ultima* by Rudolfo Anaya
2003 – *Holes* by Louis Sachar
2004 – *All the Pretty Horses* by Cormac McCarthy
2005 – *Writing Austin's Lives: A Community Portrait* by the People of Austin

Although you'll see the term "One Book" often used to refer to these programs, there is no one official way to present them and no one official trademark. Sometimes a city will adopt a book and sometimes the program will be promoted by an entire state. For example, in 2004 the state of Alaska sponsored a program centered on the book *Endurance: Shackleton's Incredible Voyage* by Alfred Lansing, the tale of British explorer Ernest Shackleton's abortive 1914 attempt to reach the South Pole. Sometimes everyone in a school or religious organization may choose to read a book together. If this happens in your community, let people know how your library can help out!

STARTING IN SEATTLE

In 1998, the first book that residents of Seattle read together was the novel *The Sweet Hereafter* by Russell Banks. This story of a tragic accident involving a school bus full of children is narrated by four people: the driver, a father, a lawyer, and one of the children who survived. In 1999, Seattle readers explored the novel *A Lesson Before Dying* by Ernest J. Gaines, which had been chosen by Oprah Winfrey in 1997. Set in a small Louisiana community in the 1940s, this novel tells the story of Jefferson, a young black man condemned to die for a murder he didn't commit, and the teacher Grant Wiggins, who is sent to teach Jefferson how to die with dignity. Critics have compared the themes in this book to those expressed in *To Kill a Mockingbird*. Author Gaines visited Seattle, giving readings and joining discussions at several libraries and at Town Hall. Readers were also invited to attend a panel discussion by lawyers and experts on the death penalty, which figured prominently in the book. In 2004, Seattle read a variety of works by Isabel Allende. Here's how the event was announced in the "What's Happening" section of the *Seattle Post-Intelligencer* on May 21st:

> The Washington Center for the Book's citywide reading program, now renamed with a much simpler moniker ("Seattle Reads Isabel Allende"), launches its most ambitious version yet, with Allende events aimed specifically at attracting teen readers as well as those who speak Spanish. Allende is a perfect author for such outreach since she has written books for both adults, including *The House of the Spirits,* and recent books for young adults, including *Kingdom of the Golden Dragon.* The bilingual writer, who was born in Peru and raised in Chile, also is well known for her ability to mix both English and Spanish responses in her public appearances, often translating her own responses for those who speak the other language. Allende's Seattle appearances range from large venues to small and include the new Central Library on Tuesday. (Marshall 2004)

For the first three years, the Seattle program was funded by a grant from the Lila Wallace-Reader's Digest Fund. Today, thanks to private gifts to the Seattle Public Library Foundation and a major grant from the National Endowment for the Humanities, this annual series is offered by the Washington Center for the Book. If you are thinking about creating a program like this in your city, it is important to consider where your funding will come from and whether you are planning for a one-time-only event or for discussion of multiple books over time.

CALIFORNIA READING

Thus far, John Steinbeck novels remain a favorite choice for Californians participating in "One Book" programs. However, more contemporary choices have included *The Tortilla Curtain* by T. C. Boyle and *The House on Mango Street* by Sandra Cisneros. In

2005, the city of San Francisco adopted Gus Lee's autobiographical novel *China Boy* (see Figure 1–1 for the press release). All of these books examine ethnic identity and immigration issues in current times.

Short stories have been adopted, too. In the summer of 2002, the Pasadena Public Library initiated a "One City One Story" program with writer Mark Salzman's short story "The Soloist."

One of the most imaginative California city reading programs that I came across when I began studying the "One Book" phenomenon was offered in October 2002 by the City of Santa Ana in cooperation with California State University at Fullerton. The community chose to read John Steinbeck's novella *The Pearl* (see Figure 1–2 for the press release, which has a complete program description). Paperback copies of the book were distributed in both English and Spanish versions. Cal State students went to local high schools and junior high schools to read the book with kids, and a singles mixer was planned. But perhaps the most unusual event scheduled was a bilingual interactive puppet performance based on themes from *The Pearl*.

NEW YORK STATE OF MIND

Puppet shows aside, community-wide reading programs are not without their controversies. In New York City, for example, residents argued for weeks over whether it was even appropriate to assign just one book in a city where readers have so many diverse interests and backgrounds. In 2003, comparing New York City's stance with that of her own city of St. Petersburg, Florida, columnist Sandra Thompson wrote, "New York wanted to read one book, but since it's New York, they couldn't agree on a title. Deadlocked over *Native Speaker* by Chang-rae Lee and James McBride's *The Color of Water*, a memoir of an interracial family, in both cases someone was afraid of offending someone . . . Political correctness shouldn't be a criterion . . . and besides, there's always next year to pick another book." (Thompson 2003)

Meanwhile, Marta Segal Block, a columnist writing in *The Common Review,* the magazine of the Great Books Foundation (Volume One, Number Four, 2002), complained that many of the community-wide reading choices are too depressing.

In an article entitled "Reading Melancholy in One Book Cities," Block criticizes:

> California is attempting "One Book, One State" and has chosen the laugh-a-minute novel *The Grapes of Wrath.* Knoxville, Tennessee, has joined in the depress-a-thon with their Steinbeck pick *The Pearl.* As if *The Grapes*

of Wrath weren't enough for the Los Angeles citizenry, they've added the dystopic *Fahrenheit 451* to their assignment sheet.

Why are our libraries and civic groups trying to depress us? Is it our country's Puritan background that makes us think if we enjoy something it can't be good for us? Is it our cultural moment of renewed seriousness? Our effort to reconnect with tragedy at every level? Or is it just that many of the people on these committees are would-be teachers eager to dole out the punishment of a tear-jerking assignment? (see talk.greatbooks.org/tcr/block14)

THE INDIANAPOLIS INITIATIVE

In December 2004, *The Bondwoman's Narrative* by Hannah Craft was chosen out of 155 literary works as the selection for the city of Indianapolis "One Book, One City" program. Set in the 1850s, the novel is a first-person account of a Virginia woman who was born a slave, but later escapes to freedom in New Jersey. The book was first published in 2002 after Harvard University professor Henry Louis Gates, Jr. attended an auction and purchased Craft's original manuscript. It is believed to be the only known novel written by a slave and the first ever to be written by an African-American woman. Library officials chose to announce the selection in front of a crowd at the African Methodist Episcopal (A.M.E.) church in the town of Bethel, established in 1836. Linda Mielke, library CEO, told the audience, "While there is much to learn by simply reading Hannah Craft's story of freedom . . . we can also learn about some of the anti-slavery movement from this historic congregation." The program, a collaborative effort between the City of Indianapolis and the Indianapolis-Marion County Public Library, included discussions of the book held at difference library branches in January 2005. The grand finale was a special presentation of the popular Conner Prairie interactive freedom program "Follow the North Star," which took place at the Glendale Branch Library during Black History Month in February. (Perry 2005)

STARTING YOUR OWN PROGRAM

If you would like to know more about community reading programs, the Library of Congress keeps a centralized database of "One Book" projects across America. The Library of Congress Center for the Book state-by-state listing of past and current "One Book" projects can be found at www.loc.gov/loc/cfbook/one-book.html. Use the following link to see the same listing by author: www.loc.gov/loc/cfbook/onebookbyauthor.html.

Figure 1–1   Press Release: The San Francisco Reads Program, San Francisco, California

---

For Immediate Release: May 3, 2005 Mayor's Office of Communication

Mayor Newsom Announces New Reading Initiative
Author Gus Lee to Launch One City One Book:
San Francisco Reads

San Francisco — Citing the importance of reading and literacy, Mayor Gavin Newsom today announced a new reading initiative, **One City One Book: All San Francisco Reads**. The selected book is Gus Lee's moving 1991 novel *China Boy*, about a six-year-old Chinese immigrant named Kai Ting who attempts to make a life for himself in San Francisco's Panhandle neighborhood during the 1950s.

"San Francisco prides itself on its strong literary and cultural traditions," said the Mayor. "It is essential that we as a city continue to foster a climate that encourages reading, especially among our young people, the future leaders of tomorrow."

In *China Boy*, the young Kai saves himself by learning how to box at the local YMCA, whose multi-ethnic instructors become both a surrogate family and a symbol of how a civic institution can improve the quality of people's lives as it brings people of all backgrounds together.

While Lee's poignant description of the homes in Kai's poverty-stricken neighborhood recall books like Frank McCourt's *Angela's Ashes*, his evocation of Kai – a boy desperate to know what his friends eat at home, ignorant of the fact that he is almost blind, and certain that he can feel his mother's presence in the cold foam of the Pacific surf – is utterly unique. Lee's evocation of San Francisco, from the dense shopping districts of Chinatown to the soaring, whitewashed Central YMCA, turns the city into a character in and of itself.

One City One Book launches this June just in time for summer vacation reading. Now is the time for book groups and classroom teachers to put *China Boy* on their reading list for early fall. Reading and discussion groups, author visits to schools and libraries, and public programs will take place in September and October. Current partners in the One City, One Book program include Mayor Newsom, the San Francisco Public Library, and Friends of the San Francisco Public Library, the Northern California Independent Booksellers Association and the National Foundation for Jewish Culture.

In searching for a compelling title, the six-person selection committee for San Francisco's first **One City, One Book** program searched for a book that met as many of the following criteria as possible: of high literary quality; reflective of universal issues facing San Franciscans; mirrors the diversity of San Francisco; connects to San Francisco either through the content or perhaps because the author is from San Francisco; available in key languages; currently in print and available in large quantities; appeals to adults and teens; available in paperback; capable of sparking provocative discussions; lends itself to engaging public programs around the book.

One City One Book is funded by Friends of the San Francisco Public Library, the Gerbode Foundation, the Maisin Foundation and other donors. **One City One Book** discussion materials and Gus Lee's *China Boy* will be available in libraries and bookstores in June 2005.

Figure 1–2   Press Release: The City of Santa Ana/Cal State Fullerton One Book One City Program—2002, Santa Ana, California

One Book, One City to Promote Community Involvement in Reading

What: In a spirit of community collaboration to promote reading, Cal State Fullerton will join the city of Santa Ana and other educational institutions to kick off the One Book, One City program, which will feature the John Steinbeck classic *The Pearl.*

When: Noon Monday, Oct. 7, 2002

Where: Civic Center Plaza of the Sun, Santa Ana Boulevard and Ross Street

Program: Rob Richard, Santa Ana Public Library director, will emcee the festivities, which will include Santa Ana Mayor Miguel Pulido and special guests; the presentation of colors/pledge of allegiance by Santa Ana High School Junior ROTC Color Guard; student speakers from Santa Ana College and area high schools; and entertainment by students from the Orange County High School of the Arts.

More: One Book, One City posters will be given away and from a bookmobile, librarians will be on hand to loan up to 300 copies of *The Pearl* – 200 in English, 100 in Spanish. Plus, representatives from participating groups/institutions will provide information about upcoming events and programs featuring *The Pearl.*

Background: Joining other cities across the country that have initiated similar projects – originally conceived and launched in Seattle – Santa Ana's One Book, One City campaign not only encourages residents to read *The Pearl,* but is designed to broaden and deepen an appreciation of literature through reading and discussion. *The Pearl* was selected in honor of the centennial of Steinbeck's birth.

Something for Everyone: Children, parents, students and singles will find something to whet their appetites for Steinbeck's classic in a variety of offerings from Cal State Fullerton: Secondary Schools

Assisted Reading: Beginning in mid-October, teachers' aides from Cal State Fullerton's community services program will work with small groups of junior-high and high-school students to improve literacy and assist in reading *The Pearl.* The two-hour, weekly sessions will continue through March.

Interactive Puppet Theater for Children: Based on themes from *The Pearl,* special puppet performances will be presented at the Grand Central Theater – free – to children and their families. This bilingual production, designed, written and performed by Puppets Café Group, will feature local Santa Ana students who will participate in the performance and interact with the puppets. Sundays at 2 p.m. on Dec. 15, Jan. 19, Feb. 16 and March 9

Singles Mixers: Combining literature, art and food, singles of any and all ages are invited to come together at the Grand Central Art Center to read *The Pearl* and dine at one of the center's cafes, then peruse the nearby galleries and/or enjoy an art film. Every Friday in January.

Celebrity Reading and Fundraiser: Guests at this February event will have an opportunity to spend an intimate evening at the Grand Central Theater listening to and watching a noted celebrity read passages from *The Pearl.* Proceeds from the event will be donated toward the purchase of books for students. Drawing *The Pearl:* Presented at Grand Central Theater, narrators will read selected passages from the book while artists illustrate the scenes on large paper for the audience. Thursdays at 7 p.m. on Feb. 13, March 13 and April 17.

REFERENCES

Green, Hardy. "Why Oprah Opens Reader's Wallets: She offers the guidance and sense of community bookstores no longer provide." *Business Week* (10/10/2005), p. 46.

Keller, Julia. "Author reads Oprah loud and clear." *The Bergen County (New Jersey) Record* (4/18/2005), p. F.04.

Kleim, Richard. www.kleim.org

Laskin, David, and Holly Hughes, ed. *The Reading Group Book*. New York: Plume/Penguin, 1995.

Marshall, John. "Allende Expected to Bring In Wider Audience for Book Club." (What's Happening) *Seattle Post-Intelligencer* (5/21/2004), p. 26.

Perry, Brandon A. "Slavery era author might have ties to local church." *Indianapolis Recorder*; (1/28/2005). Available: www.indygov.org/eGov/Mayor/PR/2005/2/20050207a.htm

Rooney, Kathleen. *Reading With Oprah: The Book Club That Changed America*. Fayetteville, Arkansas: University of Arkansas Press, 2005, p. 56.

Rooney, Kathleen. "Oprah Learns Her Lesson (Oprah Book Club ends)." *The Nation* (5/20/2002).

Scott, John C. "The Chautauqua Movement: revolution in popular higher education." *Journal of Higher Education,* Vol. 70, No. 4 (7/1/1999), p. 389–412.

Slezak, Ellen, ed. *The Book Group Book*. Chicago: Chicago Review Press, Inc., 2000.

Thompson, Sandra. "City Needs More Mature Choices on Arts Scene." *St. Petersburg Times* (3/15/2003), p. 1B.

Thorn, Patti. "Author covers prose, cons of Oprah's club." Available: www.rockymountainnews.com/drmn/spotlight_columnists/article/0,2777,DRMN_23962_3722278,00.html.

2 RECRUITING MEMBERS

OVERCOMING BOOK GROUP ANXIETY

Why would someone want to join a book group at your library? What emotional, physical, or geographical factors might encourage or prevent them from joining a group that meets at a public library, rather than the living room of a friend?

Book groups run and held at public libraries face particular challenges. For one thing, most of the people who come to your first meeting may not know each other very well. In addition, some may fear that if a professional librarian is leading the group, it will be more like an academic literature course than an informal gathering. Factor in the unfortunate, lingering stereotype of librarians as stern know-it-alls, and you might find that even the folks brave enough to show up at the first meeting won't say much because they are intimidated.

It's important to relieve "book group anxiety" right from the start by setting a reassuring, friendly tone. In conversations with staff and patrons and in your publicity materials, let people know that your book group is a way to get to know *neighbors* (a more positive word than *strangers*) and discuss ideas relevant to life in the community. (Robertson 2002) Emphasize that there are no right or wrong answers and no pop quizzes. Tell folks that the library book group is simply a chance to learn more from one another than would be possible by reading a book alone in a vacuum. Make sure to let prospective members know that the group is offered free of charge. In keeping with the informal tone, let people know that your group will welcome new members at any time and that, while you hope people will show up regularly, they can come as often as they are able to—even if it is just once or twice a year. Make it easy for folks to drop in on the spur of the moment; they should not have to R.S.V.P. or pre-register.

HOW TO POLL READERS AT YOUR LIBRARY

If you're lucky, readers will approach you clamoring for a book group. If you're observant, you probably already have a good sense of who might want to join. If there are a lot of seniors who use your library in the morning, perhaps you can approach them with the idea of a morning group. If you have a lot of high school students who study at the library regularly, you might ask if they would show up for an after-school book group. Moms of young children might want to meet after dropping the kids off at school or before picking them up. Parents of teenagers might want to talk about books with their kids, so perhaps a "mother-daughter" or family night discussion group would work.

You can study your circulation statistics to see the topics and the books that are popular with people in your community. Are people reading more fiction or nonfiction? Do you have a lot of mystery readers? Some book groups focus on one particular genre. For example, there are groups that just read mysteries, science fiction, or historical novels, while some groups just do poetry. Often libraries hold more than one book discussion group—one may cover a mix of fiction and/or nonfiction books for a general audience while other groups may meet for people with more focused interests. Many library leaders with a personal interest in a genre or a particular prolific writer, perhaps Shakespeare or Edith Wharton or Stephen King or Proust, have founded book groups after finding that they were already chatting about these authors with patrons seeking recommendations.

Keep in mind that audience development is not a onetime process. You will probably have a "core" group that regularly attends, but you might also get some new faces each month. Often people will show up for just one book or to talk about one author that they particularly love. If you feature the work of a hometown literary hero or heroine, such as Wallace Stegner in the Northern California area or Anne Rice in New Orleans, you may attract people who actually know or knew the author. And if you hold an author talk that draws a crowd at the library from time to time, make sure that you let the audience know about your book group, either in an announcement before the talk or by distributing flyers. The same holds true if your library hosts a book fair or other larger community event. You already know that the folks who show up at these events like to read, so why not promote your group.

Here are some more ideas to ensure and increase attendance.

> "Two ways to attract men: read more nonfiction and serve food!" (McCarthy 2004)

AUDIENCE DEVELOPMENT TIPS

If you work at the circulation or reference desks and have time between handling requests, ask users what they are reading or what they plan to read next. You can then ask if they would be interested in a group where they could share their ideas with others. If you can, make it a team effort so that you are not the only one at the library promoting the group. Share your ideas for the group with coworkers and once it is off the ground, invite them to attend the group and encourage them to recruit patrons.

If your library has a Friends group or a foundation, poll the members about their reading tastes and ask if they might be interested in attending your group or know others who might want to attend. It's a good idea to get the Friends and foundation involved early in the process because, along the way, these are the folks who might provide support—by baking cookies for a discussion, recruiting a local author to speak, or funding the purchase of paperback copies of a book so that book group members can have them for free.

If your library has a bulletin board, check it to see which community groups are posting flyers. You might find announcements from private book groups, local colleges, senior centers, the chamber of commerce, or groups like the local garden club. Make a note of who the group leaders are—they might be good people to turn to for advice on audience development. If you have more time, you could copy some of these announcements and file them in order to build a list of people to contact about a new book group.

Distribute a brief survey to library patrons that can be filled out on the spot. Put the survey, some pencils, and a slotted box at different library locations, including, for example, the new books section, a rental books section, or at the reference or circulation desk. (See Figure 2–1, a sample survey.)

"COMMUNITY OUTREACH"

Obviously, the more people that you reach, the more people you may attract, so it pays to get out into the community. If you are a public services librarian, you may likely already be meeting with community groups. If you work at the circulation desk or reference desk, however, community outreach is obviously going to be more of a challenge. If you can't get out of the library to do personal networking, perhaps you can send a representative. Book group members, student interns, or Friends of the Library may be able to help out in spreading the word. Who should you talk to and where should you go? Consider the following suggestions:

Visit a local bookstore—If you can, visit a local independent bookstore, rather than a chain. Independent bookstores will often give you a lot of personal attention because they have to, in order to stay in business. Even if the store itself sponsors a book group, you will not be viewed as competition. In fact, most independent stores and chains encourage libraries in their communities to form book groups and develop an audience, because a community that reads is a community that buys books. If you are a first-time leader, try attending a book discussion at a local bookstore to network and observe how the leader runs the group. You might even recruit some members this way, since many avid readers belong to more than one book group!

It pays to establish a relationship early on, because some stores offer discount cards to book group members or libraries who buy multiple copies. Still other chain and independent bookstores will host an event with representatives of publishers that run book group programs or provide book group materials. If the bookstore owner is involved in the day-to-day management of the store, ask if you can leave some book group surveys at the store. And if the store has a Web site, ask if you could post an announcement or survey online. Be forewarned that if you are like most people who enjoy leading book discussion groups, you probably won't be able to walk out of the store without a purchase!

Visit the local schools—If you live in a small town, you may already know the school principal(s) and the local teachers, so it may simply be a matter of making one or two telephone calls asking them if their students might be interested in a public library book group or book series. If the students can't come to you, and you have the staff and time to visit the school and run programs there, offer to do so. If you live in a large urban area, you might want to start by calling or visiting the school superintendent's office. Whether or not the schools are directly involved in planning your book group programs for children or teens, you'll need their permission to post or drop off flyers advertising your group. Some school leaders may even wish to approve the content of your flyers.

Get to know your local businesspeople—Real estate agents know who's new in town—and these newcomers might find that joining a book group is a great way to connect to a new community. Agents may already be touting your library as a great community/family resource, so they might be interested in receiving book group flyers or joining a mailing list. The agents may also be able to connect you to local newcomers clubs.

Books and food and coffee often go together, so ask local restaurants and coffeehouses if you can post announcements. If your community has a farmer's market, ask if you can set up a table promoting the book group and perhaps other library programs. And if you are lucky enough to have an independent movie theater in your town, you should get to know the owners and ask if you can post book group announcements there, too. This can also help you to tie in reading programs related to a local film showing.

Communicate in Cyberspace—If your library has its own Web site or is included in a larger county Web site, use the site to announce plans to form a book group. If there is room, you might even post a survey for prospective members to fill out and e-mail back.

You can also do audience development by posting to Chamber of Commerce and other community Web sites. If you live in a larger metropolitan area, you could announce your group in the community section of the free nationwide online community bulletin board called Craigslist (www.craigslist.org), founded in 1995 by San Francisco-based Java and Web programmer Craig Newmark.

POLLING BEFORE (OR JUST AFTER) THE FIRST MEETING

Your very first meeting might simply be an administrative one in which you choose one or more books for future meetings. Alternatively, you could pick a book, see who shows up for the discussion, and do the administrative housekeeping a few minutes before the meeting ends. Either way, you will most likely be passing around a sign-up sheet with contact information, including e-mail addresses.

Before your second meeting, you can use this list to telephone or e-mail people and ask what you can do together to ensure the group's success. Ask if they prefer that the librarian facilitate every discussion or that the group members themselves rotate that responsibility with the help of a library leader. This would also be a time to find out if the group members might be interested in participating in events outside the regularly scheduled meeting, such as an author talk or a film that ties in with a specific month's selection.

If you are still having doubts about getting started, you are not alone. In the sidebars, three librarians interviewed by telephone and e-mail in the fall of 2004 share their stories.

Sherry Evans, Head of Public Services and Programming and Head of Circulation at the Portsmouth (N.H.) Public Library

I was new on the job when I started our monthly evening adult fiction group. Portsmouth is a community of twenty thousand people, and ours is the biggest library here! We serve ten other towns in New Hampshire, Maine, and Massachusetts, so we are quite a nucleus. There hadn't been a book group at Portsmouth Public Library in quite some time, but I had led groups before and it was always one of my favorite parts of the job.

At our first meeting, eleven people showed up—ten women and one man. Some were library staff members who came to show their support, which I really appreciated as a new person. I selected the novel *Unless* by Carol Shields, mostly because I really loved it, but also because I thought that it would appeal to what I thought would be mostly seniors. Turns out that the people who came were all ages—some in their twenties all the way up to some people in their seventies.

So there I was with a mixed age group of people who didn't know each other and didn't know me. Many were shy about sharing opinions. I found that I did a lot of the talking that night. But almost a year later, people are comfortable enough to disagree. We are even getting into discussions about local politics. Best of all, these days, whether they are book group members or not, people come up to the circulation desk and tell us what books they think we should discuss.

How did we get started? We advertised the group in the local papers, including the *Portsmouth Herald* New Hampshire, which runs a *Reading and Signings* section every Friday. We also papered the library with book group posters. And I talked about the group at two local bookstores, the independent River Run in Portsmouth and Barnes & Noble. But what helped the most was getting the library staff people who serve the public to start talking it up. In my dual role as head of public services and head of circulation I talked to a lot of people about what they were reading, but coming here new I didn't have a lot of contacts. So the combined staff efforts helped a lot.

Alison Anson, Public Services Librarian at San Carlos Public Library, California

I wanted to start a book group at the library during my first year. But there was concern that it would compete with the existing Friends of the Library evening book group, which is run by patrons rather than library staff. As it turned out, the daytime group I eventually did start has not competed at all.

I decided to offer a group during the day, because our library serves many seniors who have an easier time getting around during the day. Some can no longer drive. In fact, the final impetus for starting the group was when a woman in her eighties, who had early on expressed an interest in a book group, came up to me at the reference desk three months later and said loudly, "Are you going to wait until I die before you start a group?" That was it. With the help of that woman, whom I now refer to as "the founding member," I contacted the San Carlos Senior Center and the Recreation Director of the Elms, a retirement complex across the street. I started the group the next Wednesday at 10 a.m. and five people showed up—from the Senior Center and the Elms. One lady needed to be wheeled over from the Elms, so I did that at 9:45 on Wednesday mornings. She is too ill now to come, but she was fabulous and had lots of experience as a teacher.

Another member of the library staff got involved and talked up the book club while she worked at the circulation desk. She recruited three people—two of whom were men—which enriched the group as we were initially all female. My book group is now entering its third year and we have twelve steady participants.

Robin Shader, Library County Coordinator, Live Oak Public Libraries, headquartered in Savannah, Georgia. She manages two branches in Liberty County, Georgia.

I personally like mysteries and I knew that kids liked them, which is why back in the fall of 2001, I started a monthly book club for fourth-, fifth-, and sixth-graders at the Brick Branch of the Ocean County (N.J.) Public Library. I was one of three children's librarians there, and I really enjoyed talking about mysteries with the kids and taking them to the juvenile mystery section and showing them all the different types of mysteries written for them.

At the time, most of our library's school-aged programming efforts focused on the younger kids in kindergarten through third grade. I wanted to try and reach out to older kids. Also I knew that boys in grades four through six enjoyed mysteries as much as the girls did and liked to talk about them. This was important, because boys at this age are often reluctant to read and share their feelings about books in a group setting.

Our first series of hour-long monthly meetings began in October. I scheduled it in the fall because in New Jersey, springtime is when the kids focus more on outdoor sports. I decided to hold just four meetings, so that the kids didn't feel that they had to commit themselves forever. And each meeting featured an activity as well as discussion of the book. We experimented with invisible ink, held scavenger hunts, and unraveled secret codes. All of our strategies worked—we had twenty-five kids sign up.

What really attracted the kids was a wonderful poster that our library graphics department created. The lettering with the heading "Mystery Book Club" was done in green on a black background and an illustration featured two green peering eyes. We hung the posters throughout the children's area and the juvenile mystery section and brought the posters to the local elementary schools and asked the librarians there to display them. The poster campaign was so successful that we had adults asking to join, who in turn encouraged their kids.

One club member, Jack, was encouraged to join by his grandmother. Jack only enjoyed reading horror stories, but he was ready to move beyond the *Goosebumps* series. Our eye-catching posters lured him into the group and got him reading outside the horror genre, since we featured ghost stories and detective stories, too. Jack's grandmother was pleased and he eventually became one of the club's most outspoken members.

One memorable moment came when we discussed the book *The Serial Sneak Thief* by E.W. Hildick, which features a detective who also happens to be a children's librarian. To provide some atmosphere, I created and placed a papier-mache body dressed in a shirt and jeans on the floor, surrounded by a chalk outline and yellow police tape. I didn't think it was all that scary, but as I was setting up, a library staff member walked in to the room, saw the figure on the floor and screamed. So, I guess I'd have to advise that it's important to let all your coworkers know what you are doing beforehand.

Figure 2–1   Sample Survey: Starting a Group for the First Time

Dear Reader:

`   Our library is planning to offer a free monthly book discussion group starting this fall. We plan to meet for between one to two hours here in the library for our book talks.

   Whether you are interested in attending our group, or have some advice for us, we hope that you will take a few minutes to fill out this brief survey. We are interested in your ideas.

1) I like to read: (check all that apply)
   Classic fiction
   Popular fiction
   Biographies/Memoirs
   History/Political books
   Science/Nature books
   Science fiction
   Other types of books (tell us which)_____

2) Is there a specific book or books that you would like to discuss? If so, tell us here:
   Title   Author
   _____

3) Do you personally know a local or nationally known author who might be willing to speak to our
   book group? Is there an author that you would like us to invite? If so, tell us here.
   _____
   _____
   _____

4) The best time(s) for me to come to a book group is: (check all that apply)
   Weekday morning
   Weekday afternoon
   Weekday evening
   Saturday afternoon
   Sunday afternoon

5) If you have a specific day and time that work best for you, tell us here_____

6) The discussion format that I prefer is: (check all that apply)
   Moderated group discussion in which a leader introduces the book and we all share ideas.
   Author talk followed by questions and answers.
   An online book group or discussion board that I can participate in from home
   Check below if you are interested in a group especially designed for:
   Teenagers/young adults_____
   Seniors _____
   Do you have any other ideas for our book group? If so, tell us here. If you would like to discuss
   the book group in greater detail, you can contact _____.
   _____
   _____

   Optional—Tell us your name, town, and e-mail and regular mailing address info for a future
book discussion mailing list.

REFERENCES

Evans, Sherry. "But I Only Want To Read Books With Happy Endings." *Public Libraries* (November/December 2003), pp. 347–349.

McCarthy, Sherri. "How to start a public library book discussion group." (2004) Penfield Public Library. www.penfieldlibrary.org

Roberston, Deb. "Oprah and Out: Keep book clubs flourishing; reading enthusiasts come and go, but book clubs party on at your library." *American Libraries* vol. 33, no. 8 (Sept. 2002), pp. 52–54.

Shader, Robin. "The butler did it; trouble attracting older readers? Consider starting a mystery book club." *School Library Journal* vol. 48, no. 6 (June 2002), pp. 37–39.

3 CHOOSING THE RIGHT BOOKS

A FEW GOOD RULES

When it comes to book selection, many library leaders report that they feel overwhelmed by the sheer number of print and online book reviews available. Others say that, whether choosing alone or by committee, they simply go for books that at least one person has already enjoyed and couldn't wait to talk about. Certainly, the enthusiasm of the leader goes a long way. Still, there are going to be readers who may be quite articulate in telling you why they hated *your* selection. When that happens (and it surely will), remember that great disagreements can lead to great discussions. The worst case scenario is when no one has anything at all to say about a book.

In this chapter we hope to simplify your book selection strategies with an overview of the most popular book group genres: classic fiction, nonfiction, current books and best-sellers, mysteries, science fiction and fantasy. Within each genre, you'll find tip sheets for book selection.

But before we even look at the resources that can help you to decide what to pick, here are some general rules for successful book selection:

> **Rule #1: Read what you can get.** Most people who attend book groups at public libraries expect to borrow the books for free. They expect the books to be on hand or be fairly easy to borrow from other libraries. Some libraries lucky enough to have generous patrons or sponsors can buy the books (usually paperbacks) and set them aside for their members. Sometimes members are allowed to keep the donated books. Other groups are asked to eventually return the books for general circulation or library book fair sales. If you have already chosen books for future discussions, you can hand these out in advance. For example, the March selection could be distributed at the end of the February meeting, with some copies kept on reserve for members who didn't show up. If you have a bookmobile, make sure that the staff has your book group selections on hand as well as promotional material. The physical access to books is espe-

cially important in rural areas where weather and travel distances might make it hard for people to make extra trips to the library. Some libraries borrow extra copies of book group selections in advance from other branches in their county. But if you live in a small county with few branches, this might be harder to do. So as you plan your list, determine how difficult it will be to get and distribute each book.

Rule #2: Choose what lots of other folks at your library and in your community are reading. As librarians, you most certainly notice what folks are reading and asking to read. You even set trends yourselves each time you recommend a book at work, at home, or in your community. If you are curious about what library patrons across the United States are reading, *Library Journal* now publishes a list of the most requested fiction and nonfiction books at public libraries across America—based on a representative survey of libraries large and small. You'll find the list on the back page of every issue.

Rule #3: Check your literary ego at the door. It's O.K. to love the books that you suggest. But, it's not O.K. to impose your tastes on everyone else. In 2003, the *San Francisco Chronicle* reported on some well-heeled private book groups that were paying a group leader with a Ph.D. in English literature upwards of a hundred dollars per book group meeting. (Lara 2003) In some cases, however, people felt intimidated by the leaders and their choices. Many of the books on the list were what I call "should books"—as in "I should read this book to be a well-rounded person, but I'm not sure that I really want to." If your public library readers suggest a work by Marcel Proust or James Joyce's epic *Ulysses* and you are comfortable leading the discussion, more power to you. But if you love Proust or Joyce and your audience does not ask to read their works, it's not O.K. to force-feed them. In the end, it's about sharing ideas, not imposing them.

HAVING FUN WITH CLASSIC FICTION

A classic is a book that has withstood the test of time, whether the time period is half a century or millennia. Public library book groups have enjoyed American classics such as F. Scott Fitzgerald's *The Great Gatsby* (1925) and Harper Lee's *To Kill a Mockingbird* (1960). They may take on an international classic like Russian author Vladimir Nabokov's *Lolita* (1955) or *The Little Prince* (1943) by French author Antoine de Saint-Exupéry. Going further back in time, works by William Shakespeare (1564–1616) and Victor Hugo (1802–1885) have been discussed. And then, of course, there are the ancient classics such as Homer's *The Iliad* and *The Odyssey* (8th century B.C.)

Regardless of the century in which they have been written, these books have lasted for many reasons—there might be a strong social message and/or unforgettable characters, an elegant writing style, or a powerful description of a particular time and place. Some of these books or authors may have won awards, such as a Pulitzer Prize. There are many reasons why members of your book group might want to read a classic. Some may even think that it will be fun to do! Here are a few more good reasons:

- They read the book in high school or college but want to go back and revisit it in a more relaxed setting.
- A movie or play featuring the author's work has just come out or come to town. For example, films such as *Pride and Prejudice, The Age of Innocence,* and even *Troy* have inspired book groups, as have regional theater productions of plays ranging from *Our Town* to *Romeo and Juliet.*
- The author is a "local hero" who once lived in the area— e.g., Thoreau in Massachusetts or Samuel Clemens (Mark Twain) in Hannibal, Missouri.
- The author's work is a holiday classic, such as Charles Dickens' *A Christmas Carol* or Arthur Conan Doyle's Sherlock Holmes mystery *The Hound of the Baskervilles* (at Halloween).
- Oprah or another celebrity has recommended the book.

Regardless of motive, a book discussion featuring a classic presents special challenges. Because these books have been around for a while, lots of people have commented on them, and they wind up on the reading lists of high schools and universities. That's both good news and bad news for book group leaders. On the plus side, there will be a lot of commentary and "ready-made" study questions available. On the other hand, you and your readers may be somewhat intimidated by the scholarship.

Beware of the book group selection that sounds good at the time but that few will actually take the time and effort to read. As Mark Twain once said, "A classic is something that everybody wants to *have read* and nobody wants to read."

If you put Herman Melville's long whaling saga *Moby-Dick* on your classic list, will people take the time to read it and show up for the talk? What about a work written in difficult language such as James Joyce's *Finnegans Wake*? If you and your book group are really honest with each other from the start, you can make better classic choices. Another idea is to split the discussion of a long and/or challenging book over two book group sessions.

CLASSIC FICTION SELECTION TIPS

1) **Ask an expert.** If you live in a university town or know a popular high school literature teacher, you may be lucky enough to get some advice from people who teach classics for a living. Sometimes they might even be willing to come and lead a session or a series of book discussions.

2) **Check out Gale's series of literary reference works.** Gale's *Contemporary Authors* has been published since 1962 and provides biographical and bibliographical data on modern fiction and nonfiction writers, including novelists, poets, playwrights, scriptwriters, journalists, biographers, essayists, and media people. Perhaps your library still has the softcover indexes and hardcover abstracts that high school and college students have used for years to do their term papers. Gale's now also has an online series of literary criticism resources which some libraries have made available to their patrons to search at the library or at home through the library Web site.

The hardcover Gale's *Nineteenth and Twentieth Century Contemporary Literary Criticism* volumes tell you about the author's life and works and give you a chance to see what the critics said when a book came out. There are also annotated bibliographies for further reading about authors and their work which can be used for comparative analysis. For example, if your group is trying to choose between two nineteenth-century classics like Dumas' *The Count of Monte Cristo* (1844–45) or Nathaniel Hawthorne's *The Scarlet Letter,* then the Gale's volumes can't be beat. To check out the most recent online literary criticism reference works from Gale's, go to www. Gale.com.

3) **Check out SparkNotes** (www.sparknotes.com). This is another popular online literary criticism source favored by high school and college students. Now owned by Barnes & Noble, SparkNotes was originally started by two Harvard students on their winter break. Some people compare the service to Cliffs Notes, but the SparkNotes content is more readable and contemporary. Many of the freelancers who write for the SparkNotes site are students themselves who are enthusiastic about their subjects. They also avoid academic jargon and write in an approachable style. In addition, the site is broader in scope than traditional Cliffs Notes. For example, SparkNotes offers plot and theme analysis of Shakespeare, but it also does J.R.R. Tolkien and J. K. Rowling. There's even an analysis of Mitch Albom's best-seller, *Tuesdays with Morrie.*

4) **Check out the Library of America Web site** The Library of America (www.loa.org), based in New York City, is a nonprofit publisher and cultural institution that publishes American clas-

sics. Started in 1979 with seed money from the National Endowment for the Humanities and the Ford Foundation, the series currently includes 140 volumes and constitutes a national library of nineteenth- and twentieth-century fiction, plays, poetry, nonfiction, and anthologies. The LOA catalog includes works by Louisa May Alcott, James Baldwin, Willa Cather, John Dos Passos, and Flannery O'Connor. The Library of America also offers grants to public libraries to run book programs on authors that the organization publishes. Using its Web site, you can order books from the organization, listen to audio sections of books, check out book reviews, and sign up for an e-newsletter of events and new releases. A subject index on the Web site leads you to classics in subjects including Southern writers, African-American writers, and science/nature writers.

5) **See what's playing at the movies or on Broadway or at your community theater.** *Vanity Fair, Pride and Prejudice,* even the remake of *The Manchurian Candidate*—all of these movies were once classic books. Is the community theater doing *Our Town* by Thornton Wilder? You might consider reading the play. The musical *South Pacific* comes from a collection of short stories called *Tales of the South Pacific* by James Michener. Tie-ins work well when it comes to classics, with dramatic revivals often reviving interest in the books they were based on.

THE NONFICTION CHALLENGE

These days, fiction selections appear to be more popular with book groups than nonfiction, in part because Oprah Winfrey often chooses fiction selections for her book group. However, earlier in the twentieth century, people did a lot of nonfiction reading in book groups in order to enhance or supplant university educations. Why the return to fiction today? Here are a few possible reasons:

- It's easier to debate religion, politics, and moral and ethical decisions when a fictional character is involved rather than, for instance, our current American president.
- Not all nonfiction books about science and technology are "layperson friendly." Unless everyone has the same educational background, these books can be harder to discuss.
- Readers report that it generally takes longer to read nonfiction, some comparing the task (and to them, it feels like a task) to reading a textbook.

- Many people come to book groups to escape from the pressures of daily life. They seek the grown-up equivalent to a child's asking, "Tell me a story."
- Many people are more confident speaking about fiction rather than nonfiction for fear of appearing uninformed about politics or science or cooking, or whatever the topic happens to be.

All of these factors come into play when you consider that many public librarians recently have been asked for fiction set in Afghanistan and other Muslim countries. In the wake of 9/11, readers truly want to understand these cultures. But an informal survey shows that far fewer librarian book group leaders are asked for nonfiction accounts. As a result, *The Kite Runner,* a novel by Khaled Hosseini, in which a young man leaves Afghanistan and adjusts to life in California, is a popular book group selection. So is *Brick Lane* by Monica Ali, a novel about a traditional woman from India adjusting to life in London. Less requested are *New York Times* journalist Thomas Friedman's books about the Middle East or Karen Armstrong's *A Short History of Islam*. Bridging the gap are memoirs such as Azar Nafisi's best-selling *Reading Lolita in Tehran*, in which the author relates how in 1995, after resigning from her job as a professor at a university in Tehran due to repressive policies, she invited seven of her best female students to attend a weekly study of great Western literature in her home.

Biographies and memoirs are great choices for understanding different cultures and learning about American and world history. To differentiate, biographies tend to be like photographs of a life with precise, factual information, while memoirs are more like Impressionist paintings in which events are recalled the way that the author remembers them, with less attention paid to chronological details. Former president Bill Clinton's *My Life* is an example of a biography while in the memoir genre is book group favorite *Angela's Ashes*, Frank McCourt's tale of growing up in poverty in Ireland and immigrating to America. Another popular memoir is *I Know Why the Caged Bird Sings*, African-American poet and writer Maya Angelou's account of her difficult childhood and teenage years.

Many book group readers have also been interested in nonfiction books that can help them to become smarter consumers. *Fast Food Nation* by journalist Eric Schlosser is an exposé about America's fast food industry that tells you what's really in a Big Mac and why your french fries taste so good. Although some people don't want to know, based on reading lists at public libraries around the country, there are a lot of book group readers who do.

Perhaps your readers are interested in new medical advances, ranging from stem cell research to gene therapy to treatment of neurological diseases. Book groups have enjoyed discussions of *The Double Helix* by James D. Watson, which covers the discovery of DNA, and neurologist Oliver Sacks' *The Man Who Mistook His Wife for a Hat,* in which he recounts the case histories of patients trapped by neurological disorders. These books can also provide opportunities for science and medical experts to be guest speakers at your library.

NONFICTION SELECTION TIPS

1. Pick shorter nonfiction books ranging from two hundred to three hundred pages. Presidential and "Founding Fathers" biographies may be fascinating, but you need time to read and absorb them, and you can't easily zip through them with yellow Post-it notes marking interesting passages for discussion.

2. Don't rely solely on reviews. Often nonfiction books are peer-reviewed—by another expert in the author's field. It may be a brilliant book, but it might be hard for the layperson to understand.

3. Try memoirs. A memoir in which the author takes more creative liberties and tells you what the air smelled like and the food tasted like can work better than a fact-by-fact autobiography. This is why Rick Bragg's memoir *All Over but the Shoutin'* and *Ava's Man* about growing up poor in the southern United States are mostly likely better book group picks than Bill Clinton's autobiography.

4. Try other kinds of narrative nonfiction in which telling a good story is as important as sharing the facts. Many book groups have enjoyed the fabulous storytelling and character development in Laura Hillenbrand's book about racehorse Seabiscuit. Another popular selection is Sebastian Junger's *The Perfect Storm,* a tale about a doomed fishing voyage off the coast of Gloucester, Massachusetts.

5. Choose nonfiction books that read like fiction. In the book *The Prize Winner of Defiance, Ohio* by Terry Ryan, our heroine is a midwestern mother of ten married to an alcoholic man with violent tendencies. She keeps her family afloat during the 1950s and 1960s by entering and winning contests for jingles and advertising slogans. One of the contests that she wins for Beech Nut lands her a Triumph TR3 sports car, a jukebox, a trip to New York, and an appearance on the Merv Griffin show. Sounds like fiction, but it's not. It's a real-life memoir and book groups love it. You'll find more examples of nonfiction that reads like fiction in Figure 3–1 taken from the Web site of Downer's Grove Public Library in Downer's Grove, Illinois.

Case Study: How one librarian meets the nonfiction challenge.

Our group, of mostly retired people, including two married couples, meets from 1–2:30 on the third Thursday of each month. We vary the topics from politics, history, biography, and health. Right now there is a lot of interest in the Middle East, and we are looking not just for current reporting but for histories that provide a broader overview.

Our best picks happen when someone in the group has already read the book and is excited about it and wants to discuss it. Readers suggested Katharine Graham's autobiography *Personal History* and Tracy Kidder's *Mountains Beyond Mountains*, a profile of a public health crusader in Haiti. We had great discussions of each of these books. But when we have gone with what we thought would be good choices based on reviews, we have often been disappointed. The book was *American Dynasty* by Kevin Phillips about the Bush family. It was well-researched but too academic and dry.

One thing that I personally prefer as a book group leader is that when it comes to nonfiction is to pick shorter books. That's because nonfiction often takes longer to read and absorb than fiction. So as much as we enjoyed Katharine Graham's autobiography, it took us a long time to read 688 pages. These days, we pick books that are less than five hundred pages.

Sherry Markrow, Library Assistant and Book Group Leader of the Portola (CA) Valley Public Library Nonfiction Book Discussion Group. (Telephone interview 10/14/2005)

Figure 3–1 Web Site: Downer's Grove Public Library Get Real – Nonfiction for Fiction Lovers, Downer's Grove, Ilinois.

Get Real – Nonfiction for Fiction Lovers
From the Web site of Downer's Grove (IL)Public Library
www.downersgrovelibrary.org/pages/getreal.html

1) Berendt, John. *Midnight in the Garden of Good and Evil: A Savannah Story.* 1999, 386 pages (available in paperback)

Set in one of the South's grandest cities, this true murder mystery tells of the 1981 shooting of young Danny Hansford by flamboyant antiques dealer and Savannah party-giver Jim Williams. A remarkable cast of characters appears in the telling of the tale. Masterfully written, it holds the record for the longest run on the *New York Times* best-seller list. An engrossing reading experience.

2) D'Orso, Michael. *Like Judgment Day: The Ruin and Redemption of a Town Called Rosewood.* 1996, 373 pages (hardcover only)

Until the 1997 release of the film *Rosewood*, most Americans had never heard of this Florida town. The black hamlet was destroyed by vigilantes in 1923 after a white woman in the neighboring town of Sumner falsely charged that a black man had assaulted and beaten her. At least eight people were murdered, Rosewood was leveled, and all of the residents were driven off. Yet authorities at the time found that there was "insufficient evidence" to bring any charges. D'Orso weaves this story with the events of six decades later when a descendant of one of the massacre's survivors sought justice and closure.

3) Goodwin, Doris Kearns, *Wait Till Next Year: A Memoir.* 1997, 272 pages (available in paperback)

If you remember a time when the corner store was a gathering spot, when the first television was delivered to your house, and when baseball was played on grass, you'll probably enjoy historian Goodwin's memoir of her 1950s Brooklyn childhood. If, like the author, you grew up in a household or neighborhood where baseball was an obsession, you'll find particular delight in recollections of her beloved Dodgers and of the local competition with Giant and Yankee fans. Beyond baseball, Goodwin shares vivid memories of the times that were not always idyllic (McCarthyism, the polio scare, Sputnik) and of her journey to adulthood in the comforting cocoon provided by her parents and her environment.

4) Harr, Jonathan. *A Civil Action.* 1995, 512 pages (available in paperback)

Readers who enjoy John Grisham might want to try this true-life legal thriller by journalist Jonathan Harr. In a courtroom clash of good and evil, we learn the plight of residents of Woburn, Massachusetts, where a high rate of leukemia and other illnesses resulted from cancer-causing industrial solvents being dumped into their water supply. Hotshot lawyer Jan Schlichtman (played in the film version by John Travolta) was hired to take on the mega corporations responsible. The narrative is exciting, tense, and well written.

5) Johnston, Tracy. *Shooting the Boh: A Woman's Voyage Down the Wildest River in Borneo.* 1992, 272 pages (available in paperback)

Although journalist Johnston was facing middle age, she decided to seek adventure on a rafting trip down Borneo's Boh River. The expedition was off to a shaky start, however, when she learned that all of her carefully packed gear was left behind at the L.A. airport, and that the travel company

Figure 3–1   *(Continued)*

failed to mention that no one had ever run this section of the Boh before. Still game, Johnston attempted to befriend an odd assortment of traveling companions and to brace for the mental and physical trials ahead (including aggressive bees, moldy clothes, and unrelenting heat). The narrative includes both gripping accounts of nerve-racking situations and reflective moments of self-discovery. If you'd rather visit Borneo while sitting in an armchair, let Tracy Johnston be your guide.

6) Junger, Sebastian. *The Perfect Storm: A True Story of Men Against the Sea.* 1997, 256 pages (available in paperback)

Written like a gripping drama of man against nature, *The Perfect Storm* retells the events of October 1991 when the fishing boat the *Andrea Gail* was caught in "the storm of the century." Readers who enjoy real-ife adventure will be mesmerized by Junger's account, gathered from published material, radio records, eyewitness interviews, and the experiences of people who have survived similar disasters. A suspenseful read.

7) Lamott, Anne. *Operating Instructions: A Journal of My Son's First Year.* 1993, 272 pages (available in paperback).

One doesn't have to be a single mother like the author to enjoy this honest, funny, and sometimes poignant account of the first year of motherhood. Lamott's less-than-perfect past does not prevent her from representing everywoman as she teeters between maternal bliss and postpartum depression. Her amusing journal entries introduce us to baby Sam, as well as to a crazy quilt of characters who form her unconventional family and support group. Readers of this book often react by wanting to share it with someone.

8) McCourt, Frank. *Angela's Ashes: A Memoir.* 1996, 368 pages (available in paperback)

"When I look back on my childhood I wonder how I survived it at all," writes McCourt on the opening page of this lyrical memoir. You'll wonder, too, how a boy's life in Limerick on and off the dole could result in such a moving and eloquent story. McCourt's storytelling skill, natural wit, and graceful prose provide the satisfaction you'd expect from a fine novel.

9) Reichl, Ruth. *Tender at the Bone: Growing Up at the Table.* 1998, 288 pges (available in paperback)

New York Times food critic Ruth Reichl has written a celebration of food as well as a candid and comical memoir. She serves up stories of her childhood in Greenwich Village with a cooking-impaired mother, and continues through a full menu of experiences with places and personalities that helped define her passion for food. A natural storyteller, Reichl shares anecdotes (and an occasional recipe) in an accessible style that leaves the reader with a feeling of kitchen-table intimacy.

10) Schomaker, Mary. *LifeLine: How One Night Changed Five Lives: A True Story.* 1996, 308 pages (hardcover only)

Donald Mills was declared brain-dead after he was struck by a van one evening as he bicycled across Minneapolis. The author skillfully blends the emotions and facts faced by Donald's family and the families of the patients awaiting his donated organs. As we learn of their desperation and their hope, we can feel the clock ticking. This is an interesting and informative chronicle, infused with the humanity and drama of the situation.

Prepared by Lori Sennebogen, November 1999

CHOOSING CURRENT BOOKS AND BEST-SELLERS

At any given time you'll have many library readers clamoring for the same two or three new fiction or nonfiction books. Your readers might have heard about these titles from a neighbor. Or perhaps the author has been interviewed on the Oprah or Charlie Rose television shows. Or perhaps the local bookstore is doing a big promotion. In 2004 it was *The Da Vinci Code*, the thriller by Dan Brown. In earlier years it was *Tuesdays with Morrie* by Mitch Albom. And who can forget the surprise 1992 hit, *The Bridges of Madison County* by Robert James Waller. This novel about a brief affair between an Iowa farm wife and a National Geographic photographer had a plot that some readers loved and others dismissed as trite, but it was a book that evoked much discussion.

There are really no hard-and-fast rules when it comes to choosing new best-sellers for your book group. Romance novelist Danielle Steel often makes the best-seller lists, as do mystery writers like Sue Grafton and Janet Evanovich. Some book groups take on these authors while others dismiss their books as "airport" or "beach" reading. Keep in mind, however, that self-help and diet books which often hit the best-seller list, usually are not good choices for book groups because they lead to the discussion of too many personal problems. On the other hand, if your readers really want to go this route, you might want to get a dietician or nutritionist to visit the library and compare diet books or a psychologist or social worker to add perspective to a self-help book. If there's a buzz about a book, whether it is fine literature or not, chances are it will generate a good discussion, so don't be afraid to try—especially if you are able to call in an outside expert to assist.

CURRENT BOOK AND BEST-SELLER SELECTION TIPS

1) Check out national and local newspaper and magazine reviews. Keep in mind that while the *New York Times* and *Los Angeles Times* and *Washington Post* all have great book review sections, your local paper might run a review about a book of more interest or importance to your readers.

2) Take a look at *Bookmarks Magazine*. This magazine is available in print and online (www.bookmarksmagazine.com), comes out every two months, and is independently published in both print and online versions. *Library Journal* named it as one of the best new magazines of 2002. The book reviews tend to be four hundred words or less, which means that they can be quickly scanned. The magazine also prints excerpts of multiple reviews of one particular book enabling readers to see what a variety of critics had to say.

3) **Scan some book review portals.** Simply speaking, a portal is a Web site that connects you to like-minded Web sites. One of the best is Bookspot.com (www.bookspot.com/reviews) which includes lists of literature prizewinners, best-seller lists, and author interviews. If you are looking for specific genres, such as Native American literature, Bookspot.com provides lists and reviews. Bookspot.com also offers you a chance to check out public library reading lists (www.bookspot.com/readinglists).

4) **Check out Booksense (www.booksense.com).** This is a free monthly print and online newsletter published by independent bookstores across the United States. In each issue there are minireviews of recommended trade fiction and nonfiction books. The reviews are all written by independent bookstore owners and employees, and most of the books on the list are ones that they are recommending to their customers every day. If you live or work near an independent bookstore, you may be able to pick up a bunch of copies to hand out to your book group members.

5) **Check out BookPage online (www.bookpage.com) or order print copies for you and your patrons.** This monthly general interest book review typically reviews up to one hundred of each month's new fiction, nonfiction, business, children's, spoken word audio, and how-to books. The editors, based in Nashville, Tennessee, say that BookPage was created to serve four groups at once: booksellers, libraries, readers, and publishers. BookPage contains author interviews, a section with advice for writers, and in-depth reviews. To get a sense of what a typical issue contains, the October 2005 online edition included the following: an interview with actor/comedian Billy Crystal, whose one-man-show *700 Sundays* had just been issued in print form; an interview with John Berendt, author of *The City of Falling Angels* and *Midnight in the Garden of Good and Evil*; a review of *The March*, a Civil War novel by E. L. Doctorow, and a review of two new nonfiction books about the 1906 San Francisco earthquake. Individual paid subscriptions to the BookPage print edition were $25 per year in 2005. You will have to contact the publishers to negotiate your library rate and the number of copies that you wish to receive. You can place your order through the Web site or by calling 800-726-4242 ext.34

6) **Check out the American Library Association's Booklist and Book Awards prepared by the Young Adult Library Services Association** (www.ala.org/ala/yalsa/booklistsawards/booklistsbook.htm).

The list includes "great graphic novels for teens" and "quick picks for reluctant young adult readers."

7) **See if any authors are coming to town.** Tie in your selection with an author appearance either at your library or at a local university or bookstore. If you plan your reading list a year in advance, this might be hard to do since tours are often announced only a few weeks or months in advance. But if you have more flexibility, this is worth a try.

CHOOSING MYSTERIES

Any mystery lover will tell you that there is more to the genre than simply finding out who did it. There's also the when, the where, the how, and the why in all their infinite variations. In mysteries known as "cozies," the characters tend to be genteel people who drink tea (a cozy is the quilted cover of a teapot), there's little or no violence, and never is heard a four-letter word. The language can get grittier in mysteries known as police procedurals, where detectives, cops, and other law enforcement types solve crimes using investigative and forensic techniques. Some public libraries have separate mystery book groups while others will include a mystery or two on their book group reading list. Readers can get very specific in their mystery preferences, requesting, for example, mysteries set in a particular country or featuring a detective of a particular nationality or ethnic group. The list of mystery reference books in Figure 3–2 can help you to sort out the choices.

Librarian Nancy Pearl, former director of the Washington Center for the Book, suggests that the best mystery books for book discussions are character- rather than plot-driven. In many mysteries, she warns, "all anyone can discuss is at what point each reader realized who the murderer was, or how this particular book compared with other titles by the same author—which may take all of ten minutes!!!" One classic mystery that she suggests as a good choice for book groups is *Gaudy Night* by Dorothy Sayers, written in 1936 and set in a women's college in 1930s Oxford. The heroine is Harriet Vane, an amateur sleuth and professional writer who is also a feminist ahead of her time. (Pearl 2004)

MYSTERY SELECTION TIPS

1) **Visit the nearest mystery bookstore either in person or online.** Many large cities and university towns have bookstores solely

devoted to mysteries. There's Something Wicked in Evanston, Illinois, Space-Crime Continuum in Northampton, Massachusetts, and the venerable Murder Ink I and Murder Ink II on the East and West Sides of New York City. You can get a good list of retail mystery bookstores in the United States at www.mysterynet.com/bookstores or check the Web site of the Independent Mystery Booksellers Association www.mystery booksellers.com/membersh.html

2) **Check out the Edgar winners.** The Edgar Allan Poe Awards® (the "Edgars®"), established in 1946 by the Mystery Writers of America, are awarded to authors of distinguished work in various mystery categories. In case you have not already guessed, they are named for a patron saint of mystery writers. All the usual suspects are here, including writers like Ken Follett, Dick Francis, and Tony Hillerman. But there are some surprises, too. For example, in 1966, Truman Capote won for *In Cold Blood* under a historic new category called "best fact crime." You can find an online archive of Edgar award winners at the Mystery Writers of America Web site, www.mysterywriters.org.

3) **Try to attend a mystery conference, or check in with someone else who has, or stay home and check out the Web site.** The address changes yearly—in 2004 it was: www.bouchercon2004. com. The Anthony Boucher Memorial World Mystery Convention, more commonly called "BoucherCon," is an annual celebration of the mystery and crime writing genre gathering together writers, fans, readers, collectors, booksellers, publishers, agents, and interested media. It is named after mystery writer and editor Anthony Boucher (1911–1968). In 2004, the convention met in Toronto, Canada.

4) **Get to know Sisters in Crime.** This organization of authors, readers, publishers, agents, booksellers, and librarians was founded by Sara Paretsky and a group of women at the 1986 BoucherCon in Baltimore as a support group of sorts for women mystery writers. Today there are forty-eight chapters worldwide, offering networking, advice, and support to mystery authors. *Books in Print* is the organization's annual listing of books by member authors. It is distributed to bookstores, libraries, and readers. Check out their Web site (www.sistersincrime.org) to see if there is a local chapter near your library. If so, the chapter could be a great resource for organizing author talks and special programs.

5) **Subscribe to or order individual copies of the quarterly *Mystery Readers Journal*.** The journal is published by Mystery Readers International, an organization made up of readers, fans, critics, editors, publishers, and writers. Founded in Berkeley, California, it now has members in all fifty of the United States and eighteen

foreign countries. In 2004 it cost $28 to join the organization, with the journal subscription included with membership. In many areas, there are local chapters which hold "at homes"—intimate evenings with mystery writers—as well as classes and discussion groups. If you don't want to commit to joining the organization, you might want to get one of the back issues of the journal. Each issue has its own theme, including culinary mysteries, murder in the garden, senior sleuths, suburban mysteries, political mysteries, and mysteries set in different parts of the United States. Back issues are $9.00 each, and you can find a listing at the Web site (www.mysteryreaders.org.)

The organization also presents mystery writers with an annual award, the Macavity Award, named after the "mystery cat" of T. S. Eliot's *Old Possum's Book of Practical Cats*.

Figure 3–2   An Annotated Bibliography: Mystery Reference Sources

---

The Oxford Companion to Crime and Mystery Writing (Oxford University. 1999. ISBN 0 19 507239 1. $65) was put together by Rosemary Herbert, a former librarian and the mystery book review columnist for the *Boston Herald*. Herbert compiled and edited entries from over two hundred experts, including librarians, mystery writers, and literature professors. Recommendations for mysteries abound. There are lists of types of detectives (e.g., under the letter "B" there's an entry for British lawyers—sleuths, while "medical sleuths" are found under "M"); methodologies (e.g., "sleight of hand"); and settings (e.g., "country house milieu" and "nautical mysteries"). Entries are presented alphabetically with the added benefit of extensive cross-references. There is also a useful index and a glossary. Some authors supply their own bibliographies at the end of their entry and the history of each genre is provided where applicable. Readers beware: the entry on "least likely suspects" reveals who they are.

The Encyclopedia of Murder and Mystery (Palgrave Macmillan. 2002. ISBN 0 312 29414 X. pap. $24.95) reflects the literary likes and dislikes of its author, Bruce F. Murphy, who is also editor of the fourth edition of *Benet's Reader's Encyclopedia*. (For the record, cat mysteries are one of Murphy's pet peeves.) Alphabetically arranged entries cover authors, series characters, book titles, themes and subgenres, and famous criminal cases and murder techniques.

Places for Dead Bodies (University of Texas. 2000. ISBN 0 292 73130 2. pap. $18.95) is for mystery buffs who put locale first—as well as readers who are planning a trip and want a mystery set at their destination. The author, geography professor and mystery fan Gary J. Hausladen, presents scholarly but highly readable chapters are that are organized by place. The most coverage is given to police procedurals set in the United States, Europe, and Asia (thirty-three authors are profiled in-depth here with many more mentioned in passing). There is also a chapter entitled "Murder in Historical Context," which covers mysteries set in locales including ancient Rome and turn-of-the-century Cairo. Hausladen offers some literary criticism along the way, comparing and contrasting, for example, the Venetian mysteries of Donna Leon and Michael Dibdin. Alphabetical author and geography indexes round out the text.

For readers who choose mysteries based upon the detectives, there are two companion volumes by Willetta L. Heising: *Detecting Women: A Reader's Guide and Checklist for Mystery Series Written by Women,* 3rd ed. (Purple Moon. 1999. ISBN 0 9644593 5 3. $44.95), and *Detecting Men: A Reader's Guide for Mystery Series Written by Men* (Purple Moon. 1998. ISBN 0 9644593 3 7. pap. $29.95). Serving as a "Who's Who" of mystery writers and their characters, each volume covers some six hundred authors and contains an alphabetical master list of authors, an alphabetical title list, a chronology of books from the 1930s through the late 1990s, and a breakdown of books in four subgenres: police procedurals, private investigators, amateur detectives, and espionage. Award winners are listed, too.

The Mystery Readers' Advisory: Librarian's Clues to Murder and Mayhem (American Library Association 2002. ISBN 0 8389 0811 X. pap. $30) is edited by Scottsdale, AZ, public librarians John Charles, Joanna Morrison, and Candace Clark. The book is aimed at librarians charged with buying and recommending good mysteries but it will appeal to general readers, too. Besides an annotated list of twenty-two additional mystery reference sources, there are lists of mystery books organized by theme and genre, recommendations for book discussion groups, and tips on how to start and run a mystery book group.

CHOOSING SCIENCE FICTION AND FANTASY

"Don't believe that only computer geeks read science fiction," Texas librarian Kim G. Kofmel wrote in *Library Journal* in 2004. "Despite the stereotype of the average reader as a young, probably white male engineer, sci-fi readers are male and female, straight, gay, trans, young, and old. They span the racial spectrum and have various education and employment backgrounds," she continued. Though libraries often shelve their science fiction and fantasy books in the same section, there are some key differences, says Kofmel. While science fiction and fantasy are both fantastic, speculative genres, the speculation in sci-fi is based on science and technology, (e.g., *Fahrenheit 451* and *2001: A Space Odyssey*), while the speculation in fantasy is based on myth, magic, and the supernatural. (e.g., *Harry Potter* and *The Lord of the Rings* trilogy). In fact, some groups that discuss both sci-fi and fantasy refer to themselves as "speculative fiction" groups.

SCIENCE FICTION AND FANTASY SELECTION TIPS

1) **Consider award winners.** There are two major awards that can help you to decide what's "classic" or "best"—the Hugo Awards and the Nebula Awards. The Hugos, which began in 1946, are awarded by the members of the World Science Fiction Society, organizers of an annual science fiction convention called Worldcon. This organization is open to everyone, so there is a wide range of people voting, including writers and fans. For its award list go to worldcon.org/hy.html. The Nebula, which began in 1965, is an award of peers—the only folks who can vote are authors who belong to the Science Fiction and Fantasy Writers of America, Inc. For its award list go to www.sfwa.org/awards/archive/pastwin.htm.

2) **Check out the Reader's Robot,** produced as an online outreach project by the Thompson Nicola Regional District Library System, in Kamloops, British Columbia, Canada. The Web site (www.tnrdlib.bc.ca/rr.html) has a search engine that enables a reader to search science fiction listings by category and author. There is a user questionnaire that you can fill out to get customized reading recommendations. And reader's weigh in on a discussion board with their own reviews.

3) **Take a look at the print or online versions of *Locus Magazine*** (www.locusmag.com). This monthly publication, based in Oakland, California, has been covering the fields of science fic-

tion and fantasy since 1968. Each issue has interviews with well-known and/or up-and-coming authors and there are full-length book reviews of new books. There's also publishing news, convention news, industry gossip, and suggested reading lists. Think of it as the *Publishers Weekly* of the sci-fi fantasy world, except, of course, that it is monthly. The book reviews and author interviews are indexed back to 1987.

4) **Visit or check out the Web site of Seattle's brand-new Science Fiction Museum and Hall of Fame** (www.sciencefiction experience.com). The museum opened in the summer of 2004 with an advisory board including Ray Bradbury, Arthur C. Clarke, Steven Spielberg, and Octavia Butler. The educational outreach department of the museum offers reading lists and book club suggestions for kids, young adults, and adults.

5) **Check out scifi.com,** a Web site established in 1995 by USA Networks Interactive. The site, aimed at the young adult market, covers all kinds of science fiction media, including movies and television shows as well as books.

CHOOSING PRIZEWINNERS

The Pulitzer (pronounced Pull-It-Sir) Prize and the Nobel Prize in Literature are considered the most prestigious awards that an author can receive. The Pulitzer honors works by American authors, while the Nobel Prize honors writers from all over the world. If you choose one of these prizewinning books or authors for your group, you can be assured of finding lots of commentary and reviews. If you pick a Nobel Prize-winning author, for example, your book talk can be enhanced by reading part or all of the text of the author's acceptance speech.

The Pulitzer Prize was established in 1917 in the will of *New York Globe* newspaper publisher Joseph Pulitzer. Writers and their publishers enter the annual competition and their works are judged by juries of their peers—in other words, other writers, editors, professors, and academics. The competition itself is administered by Columbia University in New York City. There are a variety of Pulitzer Prizes for journalism, literature, and drama. The ones that you will want to pay particular attention to are the awards in the following four categories, referred to as *letters:*

- Fiction by an American author
- American history

- Biography or autobiography by an American author
- Nonfiction by an American author

Keep in mind that because these books are peer-reviewed, not all of them will have mass appeal. In fact, while some of the honored letters books have made the best-seller lists, most have not. If you are interested in what American writers and readers were thinking at a particular time in the twentieth century, however, check out the entire list of award winners at the Web site (www.pulitzer.org).

The Nobel Prize in Literature can be awarded to writers of works including poetry, novels, short stories, plays, essays, and speeches. It is a lifetime achievement award granted in recognition of a writer's body of work rather than one particular work. The award was established through inventor and industrialist Alfred Nobel's will, and it has been administered by the Swedish Academy in Stockholm since 1901. Starting off with the first prize in 1901 to the poet and philosopher Sully Prudhomme, author of *Stances et Poèmes* (1865), the Nobel Prize in Literature has distinguished the works of well known and unknown authors from different languages and cultural backgrounds. A complete list can be found at nobelprize.org/literature. Writers cannot apply for the award—instead they are nominated by people including professors of literature and linguistics, previous Nobel Prize Laureates in Literature, presidents of international societies of authors, and members of the Swedish Academy in Stockholm, which administers the award.

Keeping Records

Try and keep an annotated list of what you have read, if only so that you can put it in a time capsule in the cornerstone of your new library building some day. More practically speaking, group members come and go, and it is sometimes helpful to be able to refer to your records. However, I think it's perfectly fine to repeat a popular book every couple of years. I bring a book group notebook divided into four sections to each meeting. The first section consists of our mailing list so that I can easily add new members to it. The second section contains notes on the current book. The third section has notes on past selections, and the fourth section of my notebook contains loose-leaf paper and manila pockets for new reading suggestions. Book reviews clipped from newspapers and book recommendations written on restaurant napkins and menus (I kid you not) go in the pockets. And I write down book suggestions that come up during the meeting on the loose-leaf sheets in the fourth section. I imagine you could do this all on a Palm Pilot, too, but I like the pockets for all the slips of paper that members hand me.

REFERENCES

Kofmel, Kim G. "Sci-fi 101: A focused study gives insight into what draws patrons to this flexible genre and what drives them away." *Library Journal* (9/1/2004). Available: www.libraryjournal.com/article/CA447055.html

Lara, Adair. "Queen of Clubs: Paid facilitators introduce once-informal reading groups to more sophisticated literature." *San Francisco Chronicle* (5/10/2003), p. D1.

Pearl, Nancy, editor, and Lauren John (guest columnist). "Get a Clue: Book Club Mysteries, The Reader's Shelf." *Library Journal* (10/15/2004), p. 100.

4 PLANNING WHEN AND WHERE TO MEET

CHOOSING THE PLACE: MYTH VS. REALITY

In the best of all worlds, public library leaders would have a meeting space with all the comforts of home and/or the ambience of a local coffeehouse. There would be attractive plush chairs and couches for readers to sink into, natural lighting from a picture window, the aroma of fresh brewed coffee and baked goods, and maybe even a cozy fire. The reality is that book groups at public libraries usually have to make do with what's available. Your space might be a cramped windowless staff lounge, a corner in the back of the library, or a library table partitioned off by a room divider. For a host of reasons ranging from limited space to limited staff hours, you might not be able to meet in the library at all.

"Ideally, you want a private space where the sole focus of the gathering is on the book," suggests Kay Sodowsky, Library Manager at the Metropolitan Community College Library in Independence, Missouri. "It's a challenge to maintain ambience if you're in a high-traffic space," she acknowledges, but then adds, "I've also had groups meet in private homes and in crowded noisy restaurants, with varying degrees of success. Any space is better than no space, so I'm all for experimentation, even if it's a picnic table out behind the library." Kay suggests using whimsical little touches (music, maps, travel brochures, costumes, photographs, foreign coins, etc.) to create a mood. She also suggests that wherever you hold your group, you aim for privacy and few external distractions. She says that she tells her readers, "Turn off your cell phones and let's have one hour to escape the outside world and celebrate this particular book!"*

Some public library book groups are unable to actually meet at the library for reasons including library renovation, budget cuts, or even roads blocked by bad weather. Instead, they meet for convenience at restaurants, coffee shops, local senior centers, and even online, as will be discussed in Chapter 8. Other book groups have the entire library to themselves because (sigh!) their library has reduced its hours of public service and no other patrons are around.

Carolyn Singh, a former employee and current volunteer at the Shasta County Library in Redding, California, has led the library's book group in a variety of settings. At first, she says, the Friends

*All quotes obtained via e-mail and telephone interviews conducted in 2004.

of Shasta County Libraries book group met for about three years in a quiet area on the mezzanine of the Main Library. But then, in compliance with an Americans with Disabilities Act (ADA) ruling, the library learned that it was required to hold all library programming on the main floor for wheelchair accessibility. The book group then attempted one meeting in a rear corner of the library, but the noise level of the bustling library detracted from the discussion and there was concern that the group itself was disturbing other library patrons. Here's Carolyn's report on what happened next:

A nearby pizza restaurant, with free parking and wheelchair access, offered a party room, free of charge, for our monthly meetings. While the restaurant did not require a minimum purchase, about two-thirds of the folks came a little early for lunch. While we were grateful for the temporary home (we met there for over a year), it was far from an ideal venue. Parking was free but limited, the party room could get stuffy, restaurant noise distracted from discussion, and the room only seated ten people comfortably, although our discussions sometimes attracted up to twenty readers. What's more, I think that the commercial setting intimidated some potential members.

Eventually the book group was able to move back to the ground floor of the library, but it was a bittersweet opportunity. The area was now quieter because the Shasta County Library suffered a major reduction in hours and employees so that most days, the library would not open until noon or 1:00 p.m. In an e-mail posted in December 2004 on the Infopeople class bulletin board for the author's distance learning class, *How to Start, Run, and Maintain a Book Discussion,* Carolyn reports, "We now begin our meeting one hour before the library opens to the public—a staffer lets us in through the exit door. We are close to wrapping up by the time that the library gets hopping. Members can then make use of the library after our discussion."

SETTING A TIME

There are a lot of commonsense and external factors that you will have to take into account when planning the day and time for your book group, but most public library book group leaders report that Mondays and Fridays are bad days to meet. "Both librarians and their patrons are involved with the duties of starting and ending the work- and schoolweeks and don't have time to relax with book talk," says Cynthia Creedon, book group coordinator at the Shrewsbury Public Library in Massachusetts. Some readers (especially seniors and empty nesters) may have the time to meet on Saturday afternoons, but Saturdays may be your library's busiest time, and it may be hard for staff to step away from their posts to lead the group, Creedon adds. On the other hand, with so many people already coming to the library, perhaps a volunteer could lead the group on a Saturday, assisted by a staff member who prepares discussion questions and background earlier in the week.

If you have the luxury of picking and choosing your day, an informal poll of librarians who lead book discussions indicates that Tuesdays, Wednesdays, and Thursdays are the most popular meeting days for both book group leaders and book group members. Group demographics and preferences will help you to decide whether to hold a morning, afternoon, or evening group. Seniors may prefer to meet in the morning, teens will have to meet after school, young mothers might want to meet in the afternoon before picking their kids up from school, and adults with nine-to-five jobs will want to meet in the evening. If you have the staff and resources to do it, you may want to give people a choice of times to discuss a particular book.

Here's how the Shrewsbury Public Library in Massachusetts organized its Fall 2004 meetings:

Figure 4–1   The Shrewsbury Public Library Book Group Schedule for Fall 2004

Thursday, September 16, 3 pm Thursday, September 30, 10:30 am	*The Inn at Lake Devine* by Elinor Lipman
Thursday, October 14, 3 pm Thursday, October 29, 10:30 am	*The Haunting of Hill House* by Shirley Jackson
Thursday, November 4, 3 pm Thursday, November 18, 10:30 am	*A Heartbreaking Work of Staggering Genius* by Dave Eggers
Thursday, December 2, 3 pm Thursday, December 16, 10:30 am	*A Christmas Carol* by Charles Dickens
January Date and time to be announced	*Fast Food Nation* by Eric Schlosser

There will be two opportunities each month to discuss each book; each discussion will feature the same format but is being offered twice to accommodate your schedule. We'll provide the snacks but please bring your own beverage. We hope that you can find a time to join us. Books will be available at the Front Desk of the Library after the 15th day of the month prior to discussion. All meetings will be held in the large meeting room at the Shrewsbury Public Library.

ARRANGING THE SPACE

Try to meet at the library if you can. First of all, it gives you a chance to expose your readers to new library books and services. Second, "a same time/same place" policy will make it easy for readers to find you and make it easier for new people to show up on a whim. Finally, it saves wear and tear on book group leaders, who won't have to traipse across town to get to meetings and set things up. Your library may have a wonderful meeting room or you may simply have a back table next to the periodicals. Either way, people have to be able to hear and see each other and each should feel that they have an equal place at the table—if, that is, you have a large circular or rectangular table available.

Before her library was remodeled, Linda Chiochios, a public services librarian at the Belmont Public Library in Northern California, had no private meeting room. Instead, her group met out in the open reading area. "I've noticed that seating works best if participants are grouped around a table or tables," she says. "You might have to put two or three together. We let go of the idea that our library was not big enough. We just organized our programs at times when less impact was the pattern, and just went for it."

If you schedule an author appearance or other special event that may draw more than twenty people to your book group and don't have room in the library, you may want to consider an alternate space just outside the library, such as a library patio or lawn, or choose nearby space partnering with a local bookstore or using a community meeting room.

FIVE EASY PROPS

What other equipment might you need when setting up your space? Here are some props that work well with groups of five to twenty people:

- **Name tags**—Ask your group members if they are willing to use name tags. These can be pin or paste-on "Hello My Name Is" tags or, if you are seated around a table, you might want to try using larger triangular paper signs or insert slips of paper with members 'names on them into small Lucite picture frames that stand on their own. These are great because people can write on them using larger letters, enabling people seated across from them to easily see their names.

- **Whiteboards**—You can use whiteboards to post the names of the characters in the book, define unfamiliar words or places, or even list your discussion questions. Whiteboards can also serve as room dividers if you are meeting in a section of your reading area.
- **VCRS, DVD Players, and Tape Recorders**—If you have a room to yourself, consider using a VCR or DVD player to show filmed author interviews or excerpts of a film based on the book. If the book is available on tape, you might also want to bring in a tape recorder and play out loud a particular section.
- **Water Pitcher and Glasses**—Some groups have a coffee-maker and serve coffee, some keep an electric teakettle on hand to heat up water, and some leaders bring pre-made coffee or other beverages in a carafe. Fancier groups can serve the beverages in Friends of the Library mugs, but its fine to have paper or Styrofoam cups. At minimum, it's pretty easy for most groups to have water on hand.
- **Rolling Book Cart**—Once again, a book cart can act as a space divider, if you need one. You can put the books for upcoming groups on the cart, or use it to "show and tell" the group about other library books and resources related to your current reading. For example, if you are reading John Steinbeck's *East of Eden*, you might have his other books on hand, as well as any biographies of the author or film versions of his books. If you are reading Tolstoy's *Anna Karenina*, it could be an opportunity to display other books by or about Tolstoy, as well as books about Russian culture.

SERVING SNACKS

Some groups serve elaborate snacks related to the theme of the book that they are reading, some simply have a pitcher of water or bottled water on hand, and some brew coffee or tea. If you hold a book group meeting at lunchtime, people may bring sack lunches that you can supplement with a beverage and/or dessert. Some groups serve the same type of cookie or favorite finger snack at each meeting, in order to establish a tradition of sorts. Some groups get a local bakery or coffeehouse to sponsor the snacks. If there is someone in your book group who bakes great cookies, by all means encourage them to share with the group. On the other hand, some libraries actually have rules discouraging people from bringing in homemade goods and require store-bought snacks because of liability issues (e.g., someone allergic to peanuts might get sick because they didn't know that peanut butter was mixed into the cookie batter).

Here are some ideas from some public library book group leaders in California who posted their ideas on the Infopeople class bulletin board in December 2004:

- When we started, the snacks were brought by a different person each discussion.
- Now we just provide bottled water and an occasional treat.
- One of the best we had was fresh-cut fruit that I bought at that evening's Farmer's Market: cantaloupe, watermelon, honeydew, pineapple, mango, and cucumber spears. The shape made it easy to eat or cut into smaller pieces, didn't have to worry about pre-peeling, and had very refreshing taste.
- I find snacks also help by allowing the members get socializing out of their system before the discussion, plus it doesn't make them feel awkward if they are late.

Sandy Smith, Reference Librarian, Lodi (CA) Public Library.

Why not pair the book discussion with a finger food based on the setting of the book? There's a hand-held small pie in every culture: empandas (Mexico and Spain), sfiha (Syria), pirozhki (Russia). And there's a multitude of cookies. Every group has a cook, or a couple could get together before the meeting. I'm not talking about a cooking club here, or making the snack more important than the discussion, but it might add an extra level.

Deborah Dean, Librarian, Burney Branch of the Shasta County (CA) Library.

Every month I serve punch and the same cookie. Dark chocolate cover LITTLE SCHOOL BOY cookies. My daughter loved them and I first bought them because I missed buying them for her. Some members of the group loved them. Now they are a standard and people ask where they are if I do not put them out immediately. I think serving food to go with the book is great. A tradition is good too. It is also cheaper and less complicated and perhaps better for every meeting.

Pat Koskinen, Book Group Leader, Oroville (CA) Public Library.

5 GENERATING PUBLICITY

There are three important places to promote your library book group: at the library, in your community, and in cyberspace via e-mail and the Internet. In this chapter we will talk about ways to get the word out in all of these places. But before we look at what to do where, let's take a look at your overall message. What do you want people to know about your group? Why should they join? And why should sponsors support you?

CRAFTING A MESSAGE

In 2005, a wonderful article about programs at local libraries appeared in the education section of the *Kentucky Post,* a newspaper serving several counties in the northern part of the state. Entitled "Libraries Step Out of Their Traditional Bounds," the article quoted two library community/public relations specialists talking about the wide range of programs at their libraries. These programs included book discussion groups and play readings as well as music trivia singles gatherings, quilting and crafts classes, and free tax preparation help for seniors. "All Boone County residents will find materials, programs and services that fuel the imagination, explore popular topics and trends, and provide a variety of recreational experiences," asserted Boone County Library Public Relations Coordinator Becky Kempf (Storer 2005), adding that the programs fit in with the library mission statement that stated, "working to connect you with the books you love, the information you need, and the world you live in."

More than likely, these are the goals of your book discussion group, although you might not have thought to say it in the same way as Boone County Library. You may not have a public relations coordinator at your library, and your library may not even have a formal mission statement, but spend some time brainstorming with book group members and library staff to come up with a few key phrases on your own, either for the book group itself or for library programming as a whole. If you are talking to or writing for the press, you'll sound articulate if, like the Boone County librarians, you have some positive statements in mind. Public library book groups *can* fuel the imagination and connect readers to the world that they live in. When talking to patrons or potential sponsors, consistently emphasize that library-sponsored book groups are fun and usually free, while the books chosen are readily available through the public library system. Don't forget to mention the free snacks, if your book group offers them.

THE STAFF AS STAKEHOLDERS

You will certainly be spending a lot of time communicating with potential book group members. But make sure that the staff knows what you are doing, too. "A big problem in organizations (this is not limited to libraries) is inadequate internal communications," says Daniel Stuhlman, library science professor at San Jose State University and chair of Stuhlman Management Consultants in Chicago. "Seek the opinion of all levels of staff when creating a philosophy of operation, priorities, policies and rules. When staff members have a stake in the decision making, they will be better able to follow the policy . . . [and, when] the public sees a well informed staff, they have a positive view of the library," he adds. (Stuhlman 2003). Here are some ways to reach out to staff:

- Place book group flyers in staff areas (e.g., whether a lounge, work area, or staff mailboxes). Make sure that staff members know that they are invited to participate in your group or simply "audit" whenever they want to whether they have read the book or not.
- Announce book group activities at staff meetings and Friends of the Library meetings and invite everyone to attend.
- On the day of your book group meeting, let staff know that people will be coming and tell them where the meeting will be held.
- Poll staff either formally or through informal chats about reading recommendations.
- Make sure that everyone knows that you are leading the group and that they know how to reach you.

These suggestions should be easy enough to implement if you work regular shifts in one place. But if you work at several libraries, have retired but are staying on as group leader, or lead the group as a volunteer, be sure to introduce yourself to library staff and make sure your contact information is readily available. If the library has issued you a business card, add the words "Book Group Leader" to it, and pass it around.

SHOWING YOUR STUFF

Aside from word of mouth, it helps to have some attractive in-house displays, known in the bookstore world as "point-of-sale" displays. If you have enough discussion group books on hand, you'll want to make sure that they can be easily seen and checked out. If you don't have enough books on hand or will have to go through interlibrary loan to get them, then at the least you should have book group schedules and flyers that patrons can take home with them. Here a few promotional ideas:

- Give patrons an accessible, consistent place to find book group information. Perhaps you can allocate a specific section of your library's bulletin board for book group news, or can set up a book group table near the circulation desk with copies of the month's reading selection and information about the author. Flyers can be posted or placed on library tables in clear Lucite frames or even attractive picture frames. Some flyers might feature the reading selection for the month while others might have the list for the year. If your copier machine has a feature for two-sided copies, you can even fold one sheet of paper in four, and create reading list booklets that can be kept at the reference and circulation desks.
- Place additional posters and materials for individual reading selections in the corresponding section of the library. If you are reading a mystery at Halloween, add a display or post flyers in the mystery section. If your book covers the Middle East, add some flyers in the corresponding nonfiction section of the library.
- Ask other public libraries in your community for permission to post your book group materials.
- Decide how and if you will promote the group on the day of the program. Librarians differ about how and what to communicate on the actual day of the program. Some libraries issue invitations on the public address system a few minutes before the meeting. Others prefer not to announce book group discussions at the last minute, lest they attract people who have not read the book but who may come only for the snacks. If you do not have a separate meeting room for your book group and need to partition off part of the general reading room, it helps as a courtesy to have a sign posted, letting patrons know that a group is in progress. It's up to you whether you want the sign to also have an invitation to the general public to join in.

FLYERS FOR DUMMIES

You don't have to be a great artist and you don't have to have sophisticated printing equipment in order to create promotional flyers. Large black-and-white type on a single-sided sheet of paper will do. I have purchased packs of decorative printer paper at copy shops and stationery stores that have colorful drawings of books around the borders. The border creates the interest, and then I simply type in my announcement using black and white ink and my Microsoft Word program. If you have the time, staff, or interest, experiment with fonts, images, or colored or specialty papers. Attractive graphic images can be downloaded for free at: www.abcteach.com/directory/teaching_extras. If you really don't have time to make flyers and can't find volunteer help, you might be able to get some ready-made ones. For example, Barnes & Noble bookstores offer posters of classic book covers and authors starting at $19.95 for a standard paper poster (twenty by twenty-nine inches). You might not want to buy one for just one book discussion, but if your library is running a program or festival on a classic author like Shakespeare or Virginia Woolf, it might be worth a purchase.

If you decide to make the flyers yourself, here are a few basic rules:

- Use large print for easy reading.
- If you experiment with color, use high contrast combinations, such as black type on yellow paper or green on white. Yellow type on black paper also shows up well and looks great on Halloween displays.
- Take advantage of clip art for simple illustrations and shapes. For example, a love story can be illustrated with a few hearts, suspense with a skull and crossbones, and science fiction with a sun, moon, or stars.
- Don't limit yourself to one size. You can make one large poster for a display board, letter-size flyers for handouts, and smaller bookmarks announcing book group programs and events.
- If your program is free, emphasize this in the body of your message.
- If you have sponsors, thank them in large type.

You can see a sample flyer that I made for a book discussion of Thornton Wilder's *The Bridge of San Luis Rey* in Figure 5–1.

Figure 5–1   Poster: Promoting *The Bridge of San Luis Rey*

Menlo Park Public Library Book Group invites you to discuss the Pulitzer Prize winning novel:

THE BRIDGE OF SAN LUIS REY
By Thornton Wilder
Tuesday, November 9, 2004 at 7 p.m.
Lower Level Meeting Room of the Menlo Park Library
800 Alma Street at Ravenswood

Thornton Wilder (1897- 1975) is best known for his 1938 play, *Our Town,* set in New Hampshire and performed more often than any other American play But it was his novel *The Bridge of San Luis Rey* that Prime Minister Tony Blair brought to a memorial service for British citizens killed in the September 11th attacks.

The novel (our reading selection for November) is a parable about the struggle to find meaning in chance and inexplicable tragedy after a bridge collapses in 18th century Peru, killing five people. Blair read aloud from its ending:

"But soon we will die, and all memories of those five will have left Earth, and
we ourselves shall be loved for a while and forgotten. But the love will have been enough; all those impulses of love return to the love that made them. Even memory is not necessary for love. There is a land of the living and a land of the dead, and the bridge is love. The only survival, the only meaning."

The Bridge of San Luis Rey won a Pulitzer Prize in 1928. There were two movies made about it, and a third was filmed in Spain last year starring Robert De Niro, Harvey Keitel and Kathy Bates.

Meanwhile, contemporary writer Mitch Albom's bestseller, *The Five People You Meet In Heaven,* draws more than a little inspiration from Wilder's work. Please join us for what may be one of our more philosophical discussions. (Or come for the chocolate chip cookies and film clips)

This free program is sponsored by the generous Friends of the Menlo Park Public Library.
Peruvian snacks will be served!

For more information contact book group leader Lauren John
john@plsinfo.org   650 533-4088

A WORD ABOUT COPYRIGHT

Many public library book group flyers and promotional book group materials feature copies of the book covers. Some librarians scan in the covers from books that the library already owns. Others cut and paste the book covers from online bookstore, publisher, and author Web sites. Is this legal to do or does it violate copyright law? To date, the jury is still out. "The reality is that no librarians have been taken to court for copyright infringement for book-related activities," says Carrie Russell, Copyright Specialist for the American Library Association Office for Information Technology Policy in Washington, D.C., via e-mail in 2005.

Figure 5–2 shows a sample flyer for an Author Program. Note that I did not reproduce the book covers, opting for clip art instead. In one case, however, I did use an authorized photo of the author.

Figure 5–2   Sample Flyer: Author Program

Shanghai, China in the 1930s and 1940s...
Los Angeles in the 1940s and 1950s...

A father who puts career before family and loses
everything...
A daughter who struggles to understand...

Join the Menlo Park Library Book Club in a conversation with a local writer who
has won national and international acclaim:

BO CALDWELL
Author of the historic novel:

The Distant Land of My Father
Tuesday, June 8, 2004 at 7p.m.
Lower Level Meeting Room at Menlo Park Library:
 800 Alma Street at Ravenswood

The *Distant Land of my Father* is Bo Caldwell's first novel. It is based on the life of her American uncle who
was raised in a Nazarene mission in China. Ms. Caldwell, who lives in the South Bay, was educated at Stanford
where she majored in English with a concentration in creative writing. At Stanford, she held a Wallace Stegner
Fellowship in Creative Writing and a Jones Lectureship in Creative Writing. She has written both fiction and
non fiction essays for the *Washington Post,* and has collaborated on several business and finance books.

'Rich in imaginative possibilities... steady and impressive...
the story of a remarkable place and a remarkable time'
Times Literary Supplement

'I was crazy about this book, couldn't put it down, was occasionally
moved to tears... It's beautiful'
Washington Post

Refreshments will be served.   Ms. Caldwell will be signing books after her talk

This free program is brought to you by the Friends of the Menlo
Park Public Library. For more info contact Lauren John 650 xxx-
xxxx or john@plsinfo.org

Depending upon how much time you have to do legwork and how many volunteers you have, there are lots of places in your community where you can physically place flyers. Potential locations include coffeehouses, bookstores, community kiosks, bulletin boards at universities and schools, senior centers, community centers, and houses of worship. Better yet, depending on time and staffing constraints, show up yourself to promote the group, setting up a book group table at a local book fair or even at a bookstore or shopping mall. Inspired by University of Washington Information School professor Joe Janes, librarians in the Multnomah County Library System created the "Knowmobile," a rolling reference cart that enabled staff to answer reference questions, make library cards, and promote library services at events ranging from baseball games to farmer's markets. (Sass 2002:39) The most effective way to reach the most people with the least effort may be to send press releases to the local media. Although writing your very first press release may be difficult, once you have established a template, the next ones should be far easier to do. Here are some tips:

FIVE TIPS FOR EFFECTIVE PRESS RELEASES

1) **Know your outlets.** Learn all that you can about the newspaper, radio, or television programs that may carry your announcements. If you take the time to read the local paper every day for a week, it will help you to determine which section editor to address your announcements or press releases to. Check each section or make a call to find out how the editors prefer to receive submissions: by mail, fax, or e-mail. If you live in a smaller town with a smaller paper, you may simply get a regular listing on a community bulletin board/local events section of the newspaper. But it helps to know what day and how often that bulletin board is published. Larger newspapers or college or local public broadcasting stations may have a book editor or book reviewer. Don't pitch *every* book group selection or event to them, but tailor your press releases to their interests. If you know that the local book review editor enjoys Civil War fiction and your group is going to read *Gone With the Wind* moderated by a local history professor who grew up in Atlanta, drop the editor a line and invite her to come. This restraint ensures that you will be paid more attention when you *do* call.

2) **Let the media know what you can do for** *them*! If you get the chance to meet your local arts and entertainment reporters, try to find out what kinds of stories they cover and let them know how you can help. "Remember the old saying, one hand washes the other," say University of Albany (N.Y.) reference librarians Jane Kessler and Carol Anne Germain. (Kessler and Germain 2003) If a local or nationally prominent author speaks at your library, it is most likely newsworthy, so invite the local press to come. Or if you have time and staff, offer to do a write-up of the event or at least supply photos.

3) **All announcements and press releases should include the 5 Ws: who, what, when, where, and why.** Editors will pay more attention to announcements that are limited to one page so include these essential elements first. You don't even have to write things up in paragraph form; just list the facts. Most book groups are free, but be sure to say so anyway. And if there are any costs for the event, indicate that, too. If your book group is sponsored by the Friends of the Library or a local bookstore, acknowledge the sponsor. Finally, with your book group leader's permission, try to have a name, phone number, and e-mail listing for the actual person running the group rather than just mentioning the general library phone number. That way, interested people don't get transferred from person to person or get endlessly placed on hold until you track down the book group leader.

4) **Have your library director and/or other key decision makers approve of your press release** *before* **you send it out.** Not only does this policy ensure accuracy, it also ensures that there are no surprises, like a group showing up for an author event that the director did not know about in advance. Additionally, it lets people in charge know in advance what you are planning so that they can "talk up" the group with patrons.

5) **Proof your submission and proof again.** If you cite a Web page, make sure it is still available. Double-check to ensure that you have included the correct date and time for the event. Also make sure that you spelled the author's name correctly, especially if you are featuring an international author.

Figure 5-3 is an example of a press release that I sent via e-mail to the editor in chief and the photography editor of my weekly community newspaper, the *Menlo Park Almanac*. A staff writer followed up by interviewing me for five minutes over the phone and they ran a three-hundred-word story with a photo the week before the group met. Forty people showed up for the talk.

Figure 5–3   E-mail Press Release: The Menlo Park Almanac Weekly Community Newspaper, Menlo Park, California

Dear Mr. Hines and Ms. Ivey,

I am writing to tell you and your readers about an upcoming author event on Tuesday, June 8, 2004, at 7 p.m. at the Menlo Park Library. On that night our book group will host Bo Caldwell, a local author from Cupertino who has been recognized nationally and internationally. Ms. Caldwell is the author of the historic novel *The Distant Land of My Father,* which is about a father/daughter relationship. The story is set in Shanghai, China, and Pasadena, California, both before and after World War II. This month, the author won a 2004 National Endowment for the Arts Literature Fellowship to work on future books.

This free event is open to all in the community and will take place in the lower level meeting room of the library at 800 Alma Street at Ravenswood in Menlo Park. Ms. Caldwell will be reading from the book, taking questions from the audience, and signing and selling books afterwards. We will be serving free almond cookies and sweets from the Hong Kong bakery in Mountain View.

I have included two attachments. One is of a book talk flyer that I am distributing around town and the other contains a digital JPEG photo of the author that was supplied by her publisher.

Here is a quote from me, Lauren John, the Book Group Leader: "This book appeals to people of all generations and is included in the young adult collections of many public libraries. We hope that family members will attend the discussion together."

Roberta Roth, our library's outreach coordinator who suggested that we read the books explains: "Because this is a story about a daughter's search for the truth about her father, I thought it would be a good pick for Father's Day. Although the story is set in an exotic locale, the same father/daughter and family issues occur today in Silicon Valley."

If you would like to speak with me, I can be reached at 650 xxx-xxxx. You can use this phone number as a contact number in your program announcement.

Sincerely,
Lauren John

ONLINE PUBLICITY

Once upon a time, public library book groups kept in touch between meetings via postcards, phone calls, and even letters. Today e-mail lists are a great time-saver that can be used both to answer patron queries about the group and to promote your meeting and book selections. Your book group sign-up sheets should record e-mail addresses and your library Web site should offer prospective book group members the ability to sign up for an e-mail list. Today, more people are using e-mail and checking library Web sites for book group announcements. If there are people in your group such as seniors who do not own computers or are not comfortable with e-mail, make sure that you make arrangements to phone them or send postcards. And make sure that you proactively ask all members how they prefer to communicate—because some folks may be reluctant to admit that they don't own a computer or don't know how to use e-mail. If you can find postcards with a literary or library theme at your local stationery store or at a book fair, so much the better, because it will get readers' attention. Or perhaps you or a talented volunteer could even create your own postcards using thicker pre-cut paper from an office supply store.

ANSWERING BOOK GROUP QUERIES/FAQS

As librarians, many of us are drawn to the Frequently Asked Questions (FAQ) sections of reference and vendor Web sites. Prospective book group members will also ask the same questions over and over, so it can help to create a "boilerplate" or "template" document containing basic facts about your group. The material can appear in a FAQ section on the library Web site, or it can be incorporated into more personal e-mail responses to patron inquiries. Figure 5–4 shows an e-mail query that I received, followed by my answer. Keep in mind that your response can be much briefer and less detailed. If you keep the basic information on "when we meet," "who we are," and "what we read" on file, you can cut and paste it into an e-mail when asked.

Depending on how much time you have to devote to the group, here are a few more things you can do when responding to an individual query via e-mail:

- Provide your patrons with an opportunity to follow up with you more personally, either on their next library visit or over the telephone.

- Let patrons know how and where they can access additional materials about the group, such as current reading lists and/or news clippings about your group.
- Let people know that they can sign up for the e-mail list, even if they have no immediate plans to attend the group. While postage can get expensive for mailings to folks who don't show up, it costs nothing to add a few extra names to an e-mail list except your time. Some people rely on the mailings for advice on book selection even if they don't show up at the discussions.
- If your group is free of charge, make sure you say so.
- If your group has sponsors, mention them and thank them prominently. You can even use larger fonts or bold type for emphasis.

Figure 5–4   Sample Correspondence: Writing to an Interested Patron

---

Here is an inquiry that came to me from a woman in the community via e-mail:

Hello Lauren:

   I am writing to find out more about joining the Menlo Park Library Book Discussion Group. I am an avid reader who lives about ten miles away from the library in San Carlos. What are the demographics of the group? Is there a structure or format for discussing the selections? How large is the group? Is there anything else I should know? Thanks in advance for your help. Regards: H.E.

Dear H. E.:

   Thanks for your interest in our book group. The best way to learn about us is to simply show up. Though most people who join us have read the book we choose, everyone is welcome whether or not they have read the book. **Our next meeting is on Tuesday, Sept 14th when we will read** *Disgrace* **by J.M. Coetzee. Hope you will join us.** I have tried to answer your questions below. But feel free to stop by the library and speak to me or give me a call if you want to know more. There have been two recent articles in the *Menlo Park Almanac* about the book group. I'll be glad to send them to you via e-mail or snail mail, if you'd like. Or if you drop by the reference desk on my Saturday afternoon shift (1–5) I will give you copies.

   When we meet: We get together in the lower level meeting room of the library (800 Alma Street at Ravenswood in Menlo Park, 94025) on the second Tuesday of each month for an hour to an hour and a half. We do not meet in July and August. For the past two years our December meeting has been a holiday party at which a local theater professor reads short stories, poems, and excerpts of classic novels out loud.

   Who we are: Most of us are women ranging in age from our forties to our eighties. I am 46 and our student volunteer, Dana, from Menlo-Atherton High School is 15. At any given meeting we usually have one or two men, although many more attend when we host author events. We also attract some international students and faculty spouses from Stanford University.

   What we read: We read fiction and nonfiction including biographies—and try to do several books by international authors. Right now our group favors historical fiction—as well as fiction by regional California writers including John Steinbeck and Wallace Stegner. You can check out our current reading list on the Menlo Park Library Web site (*www.menloparklibrary.org*) or if you answer back with your address, I'll mail one to you. We tend to choose books that are widely available through the Peninsula Library System, of which San Carlos is a part. So you generally can borrow the books for free.

   What to expect: Meetings are fairly structured. I keep a master list of questions based on ready-made reading group guides and the interests of the group. But we don't always get to all the questions and readers are encouraged to bring in questions of their own. We don't chat about personal stuff during the meeting. I introduce the book, tell a bit about the author, and sometimes show a video interview of the author or a clip from a movie based on the book. Members are encouraged to bring in their own materials related to the book. At the meeting, everyone gets handouts with background on the authors and their other works. The library also provides snacks. **All of this is provided free by the Friends of the Menlo Park Public Library.**

   If you can't do this right now: Even if you are unable to join us right away, let me know if you want to be on our e-mail list. Some people read the books we suggest and never come to the meetings at all—simply commenting from time to time via e-mail. I look forward to hearing from you and/or meeting with you.

   Regards Lauren John Book Group Leader Phone: 650 xxx-xxxx

MANAGING E-MAIL ANNOUNCEMENTS

Once you have created an online mailing list how often should you communicate with book group members? Many library leaders send out one announcement a month issuing it about two to three weeks before a meeting. Other leaders communicate with their groups more frequently, for example, if an event related to the book will take place in your community. If you are lucky, perhaps the author will be in town reading at a local bookstore. Or maybe you'll want to tell members about a new movie or a television documentary that relates to the theme of the book.

The subject line of your e-mail should contain the date and time of the next meeting and the book title. For example, "Library book group discusses *To Kill a Mockingbird* on Feb 23rd at 7 p.m." The text of your announcement may simply reinforce the subject line, saying, simply, "*To Kill a Mockingbird* by Harper Lee is the book we will discuss in the library community room on Tuesday, February 23 at 7 p.m." You can use longer e-mail announcements to promote special programs or get readers thinking in advance about some themes that the group might want to explore. Some leaders use their e-mail communication opportunities to show book group members how the themes of the books can be applied directly to their own lives or communities. Others mention related library news of interest such as new library purchases of other books by the same author or links to online library information sources such as *Contemporary Authors*. Some libraries alternate the responsibility for preparing and sending out the group e-mails. Once you have sent a few, ask for feedback from your group. Do they enjoy longer e-mails or do they find them annoying? You'll find out soon enough.

Figure 5–5 shows an e-mail that I sent to my book group in late January 2004 to promote a Steinbeck program at Menlo Park Library that was presented in mid-February. Although, this e-mail is long, my book group members liked it—at least they said that they did. If you are pressed for time, an e-mail of just a few sentences can be equally effective. Figure 5–6 contains a briefer announcement for a book group meeting.

Figure 5–5   Book Group E-mail: Slide Talk Based on John Steinbeck's *East of Eden*

Dear Book Group Members:

Imagine sitting down right now, on Super Bowl Sunday weekend, and writing a few words for posterity—telling your kids, your grandkids, your nieces and nephews about the world *outside* your window, rather than the one you see on the TV screen or in your living room. If you've lived here all of your life, imagine telling them what the geography of Menlo Park or Silicon Valley looked like when *you* were a kid. If you grew up somewhere else, what would you say about your child-hood home?

Would you describe the hills of the Stanford campus, the fruit orchards in San Jose, or the creation of Highway 280? Maybe, like me, you grew up back East and you'd be describing a January ice storm. Here's what John Steinbeck had to say to his kids about the place he grew up:

It was a deluge of a winter in the Salinas Valley, wet and wonderful. The rains fell gently and soaked in and did not freshen. The feed was deep in January, and in February the hills were fat with grass and the coats of the cattle looked tight and sleek. In March the soft rains continued, and each storm waited courteously until its predecessor sank beneath the ground. The warmth flooded the valley and the earth burst into bloom—yellow and blue and gold.

The passage appears in this month's reading selection *East of Eden.* It is a long family saga—a tale of two families, actually, set in the years between the Civil War and World War II. Though most of the action takes place in the Salinas Valley and King City, California, Steinbeck wrote it from New York City, with his third wife, Elaine, by his side. The Hamilton family, including Steinbeck's mother, Olive, were pillars of the Salinas community. The Trask family was completely fictional.

Steinbeck says that he wrote *East of Eden,* in part, for his children so that they would know their family history and understand their father's philosophy of life. One thing that he wanted them to learn about and to respect was the land settled by their ancestors.

On Tuesday, February 10th, we'll be talking about the land and seeing magnificent slides, in a presentation by Steinbeck scholar and local historian David Laws of Windy Hill Press in Portola Valley. He'll show you what Steinbeck Country looked like in Steinbeck's time and what remains today. Best of all, he'll tell you how you can see much of it for yourselves within a one- to two-hour drive from Menlo Park.

I hope you will take the time to read *East of Eden*, but you will get a lot out of this program even if you don't. Hope to see you at the Menlo Park Library on February 10th at 7pm. (800 Alma at Ravenswood) in the lower level meeting room. This free program is open to everyone in the com-munity and refreshments will be served.

Figure 5–6   Book Group E-mail: Book Discussion of Thornton Wilder's _The Bridge of San Luis Rey_

Dear Book Group Members:

Thornton Wilder (1897–1975) is best known for his 1938 play, **_Our Town_,** set in New Hampshire and performed more often than any other American play. But it was his novel **_The Bridge of San Luis Rey_** that Prime Minister Tony Blair brought to a memorial service for British citizens killed in the September 11th attacks.

The novel (our reading selection for November) is a parable about the struggle to find meaning in chance and inexplicable tragedy after a bridge collapses in 18th-century Peru, killing five people. Blair read aloud from its ending:

"But soon we will die, and all memories of those five will have left Earth, and we ourselves shall be loved for a while and forgotten. But the love will have been enough; all those impulses of love return to the love that made them. Even memory is not necessary for love. There is a land of the living and a land of the dead, and the bridge is love. The only survival, the only meaning."

The Bridge of San Luis Rey won a Pulitzer Prize in 1928. There were several films based upon it, the most recent one filmed in Spain, starring Harvey Keitel and Kathy Bates. Meanwhile, contemporary writer Mitch Albom's best-seller _The Five People You Meet in Heaven_ draws more than a little inspiration from Wilder's work.

Please join us for what I hope becomes one of our more philosophical discussions.

Or come for the chocolate chip cookies and film clips!

Regards
Lauren John, Book Group Leader

WEB SITE PROMOTIONS

At a minimum, your library Web site can be used to post your book group announcements. At many libraries, however, the Web site also enable readers to order book group selections, communicate with library book group leaders, and gather online reference materials about the books. Some library Web sites even enable readers to share their thoughts with each other via discussion boards. We'll talk more about online book discussions in Chapter 8.

The "Book Groups Page" from the Boone County Public Library Web site (www.bcpl.org/bookgroups.html) is displayed in Figure 5–7 and shows the wide variety of library-sponsored reading groups available in the county, with author recommendations from groups at each of the branches. Note that the groups have given themselves names including "Best of the Best" and "Chick Picks" for what appear to be combined mystery and fiction groups and "Real Men Read" for a combination of fiction, nonfiction, and mystery books that appeal to the men in the group. The links in the shaded column to the left enable patrons to conduct a variety of book group–related activities that include ordering books through interlibrary loan, recommending books, checking out staff picks, joining an online book group, and ordering book discussion kits.

Figure 5-7   Web Site Page: Book Groups of Boone County Public Library, Kentucky,

www.bcpl.org/bookgroups.html

Book Links

Book Discussion Kits
eBooks
Hot Authors
Hot Titles
Interlibrary Loan Request
New Books in February
Nonfiction Reads
N. Ky. Talking Books
Online Book Clubs
Read-a-likes
Recommend a Book
Staff Picks
This Week's Online Titles
What to Read & More

Bestseller Lists

New York Times
Publishers Weekly
USA Today

Literary Awards

Pulitzer Prize
National Book
RITA (Romance)
Christy (Inspirational)
Hugo (Science Fiction)
Spur (Western)
Bram Stoker (Horror)
Edgar (Mystery)
Agatha (Mystery)
Alex (Teen books)
Caldecott (Picture books)
New

Are you looking for a good book to read? Book groups are a fun way to discover new authors, meet people, and share your thoughts. Pick a book group that fits your time schedule, read the book, and then come and discuss it with others. Please call the participating library to register, so enough books and refreshments will be available.

Florence

"Best of the Best" meets at 3 p.m. on the 1st Thursday of each month. *The Pilot's Wife* by Anita Shreve will be discussed in March. For more information, call 859-371-6222.

Directions to the Florence Branch.

> *"Best of the Best"* recommends these authors:

Marion Babson	Anne George
Maeve Binchy	Elizabeth George
Jill Churchill	J. A. Jance
Robin Cook	Rosamund Pilcher
E. X. Ferrars	Sidney Sheldon

Lents

"Chick Picks" meets at 10 a.m. on the 3rd Thursday of each month. *Angels and Demons* by Dan Brown will be discussed in February. For more information, call 859-586-8163.

Directions to the Lents Branch.

> *"Chick Picks"* recommends these authors:

David Baldacci	Luanne Rice
Pat Conroy	Karen Robards
Catherine Coulter	Nora Roberts
Janet Evanovich	Joanna Trollope
Julie Garwood	Penelope Williamson
Jodi Picoult	

Scheben

"Chapter & Verse" meets at 7 p.m. on the 2nd Tuesday of each month. *Second Glance* by Jodi Picoult will be discussed in March. For more information, call 859-384-5550.

Directions to the Scheben Branch.

> *"Chapter & Verse"* recommends these authors:

Maeve Binchy	Frances Mayes
Nicholas Evans	J. K. Rowling
Sue Grafton	Susan Sloan
Jan Karon	Nicholas Sparks
Belva Plain	

Figure 5-7 (Continued)

"Real Men Read" meets at 10:30 a.m. on the 3rd Wednesday of each month. This group reads a variety of books each month and the members give book reviews. *Legends, Lies, and Cherished Myths of World History* by Richard Shenkman will be one of the books discussed in February. For more information, call 859-384-5550.

Directions to the **Scheben Branch**.

"Real Men Read" recommends these authors:

Stephen Ambrose	Patricia Cornwell
Jean Auel	John Grisham
Nevada Barr	Jack Higgins
Sandra Brown	William Manchester
Tom Clancy	Jesse Stuart
Stephen Coonts	Margaret Truman

Between the Covers...

Calling all romance readers! Romance readers are invited to join us for a discussion of *For the Roses* by Barbara Delinsky. This group will meet the first Saturday of each month at 2:00 p.m. at the Florence Branch. 859-371-6222

Directions to the Florence Branch.

Monday 4 Mystery

Do you like to read mysteries? Join us for a discussion about mystery books written by featured authors/topics.

Raymond Chandler - Monday, February 28 at 7:00 p.m. at the Scheben Branch. Come for a discussion of the works written this wonderful mystery author.

Directions to the Scheben Branch.

Dear Readers Online Book Clubs

Join up to four free online book clubs: Nonfiction Books, Fiction Books, Teen Books, and/or Mystery Books. Monday through Friday you will receive an e-mail with a 5-minute selection from each book club you join.

The links included in the book discussion section of Iowa's Bettendorf Public Library Web site (www.bettendorflibrary.org/services/bkdisclists.htm), as displayed in Figure 5–8, offer book group members opportunities to conduct more general library activities such as checking the library catalog and learning about volunteer activities.

The library offers patrons four different discussion groups: two based on contemporary fiction and nonfiction and two mystery discussion groups. Note the detailed description of how each group is run. What's more, in honor of the ninetieth anniversary of the local Quad Cities Symphony, the library has created a musical theme to tie in the selections of all of the groups.

Figure 5–8   Web Site Page: Book Group of Bettendorf Public Library, Bettendorf, Iowa

www.bettendorflibrary.org/services/bkdisclists.htm

Book Discussion Groups Reading Lists

Contemporary Books Discussion | Mystery Book Discussion

Contemporary Books Discussion Group
The contemporary group reads both classic and current popular fiction and nonfiction titles which are chosen by a vote of the entire group at the end of each discussion year. The leaders are volunteers from the group who are given supplemental material (author biographies, book reviews, etc.) by the Library liaison. The Library provides the books, which are loaned to the participants. This group offers both afternoon and evening sessions.
CONTEMPORARY BOOKS DISCUSSIONS 2004-2005
Meeting the 2nd Wednesday of the month Sept.-May
1-2:30 p.m. and 7-8:30 p.m. Malmros Conference Room**8 September**
Afternoon: *The Color of Water* by James McBride
Evening: *Atonement* by Ian McEwan

12 October
Afternoon: *Niagara Falls All Over Again* by Elizabeth McCracken
Evening: *The Color of Water* by James McBride

Theme Nov-May:
Music -- In honor of the 90th anniversary season of the QC Symphony

10 November
Afternoon: *Cry to Heaven* by Anne Rice
Evening: *Niagara Falls All Over Again* by Elizabeth McCracken

8 December
Afternoon: *The Piano Tuner* by Daniel Mason
Evening: *Cry to Heaven* by Anne Rice

Figure 5–8 (*Continued*)

---

12 January
Afternoon: *Music & Silence* by Rose Tremain
Evening: *The Piano Tuner* by Daniel Mason

9 February
Afternoon: *Body & Soul* by Frank Conroy
Evening: *Music & Silence* by Rose Tremain

9 March
Afternoon: *1929* by Frederick Turner
Evening: *Body & Soul* by Frank Conroy

13 April
Afternoon: *Bel Canto* by Ann Patchett
Evening: *1929* by Frederick Turner

11 May
Afternoon: *Atonement* by Ian McEwan
Evening: *Bel Canto* by Ann Patchett

A good book is the precious lifeblood of a master spirit, embalmed and treasured up on purpose to a life beyond life.
--John Milton, Areopagitica

Mystery Book Discussion Group
The mystery group is lead by the Library liaison. The mysteries to be discussed are chosen for the year based on a theme upon which the group votes. The books may be literary criticism, biographies, or true crime as well as fictional mysteries. The Library provides the books, which are loaned to the participants.

MYSTERY BOOKS DISCUSSION
September 2004 to May 2005
Sponsored by the Friends of the Bettendorf Public Library
Saturdays from 9:30-11 A.M.
Malmros Conference Room

25 September
I, Richard by Elizabeth George

Musical Mysteries in honor of the QC Symphony's 90th Season:
October
Evanly Choirs by Rhys Bowen

27 November
Black Cherry Blues by James Lee Burke

REFERENCES

Davis, Ronnie. "The Bay Area's Best Value: A Tight Collaboration Leverages Company Support and Ad Dollars To Get The Word Out About Libraries." *Library Journal* (September 15, 2004), pp. 32–34.

Kessler, Jane, and Carol Anne Germain. "Extra! Extra! Extra! Read All About It Fundamentals of Good Press Releases." *Public Libraries* (September/October 2003), pp. 300–302.

Rippel. Chris. "What Public Libraries Can Learn From Superbookstores." *Australasian Public Libraries and Information Services* (December 1, 2003).

Russell, Carrie. "Is It A Crime to Copy? Libraries often use scans of book covers to promote reading" (Carrie on Copyright). *School Library Journal* (January 1, 2002).

Sass, Rivkah K. "Marketing the worth of your library: for the cost of a latte a week, your library brings you the world." *Library Journal* (June 15, 2002), pp. 37–39.

Storer, Amy. "Libraries Step Out of Their Traditional Bounds." (Kentucky Life: Education. *The Kentucky Post* (1/18/2005).

Stuhlman, Dan. "Think Like A Business, Act Like A Library." *Information Outlook* (9/1/2003),

Part II

How to Run a Successful
Book Discussion Group

6 TALKING THE TALK

Imagine that you are about to lead your very first book group at your library. You know some of the folks who will be there because they are frequent library patrons, but you don't know them well. You expect one husband and wife to attend, as well as two women who know each other from their volunteer work with the Friends of the Library. But you are meeting the rest of the folks for the very first time. As an icebreaker, you plan to ask each member to introduce themselves briefly and tell the group what kinds of books and films they enjoy. You have even provided optional nameplates, the tented paper kind that members can place on the table in front of them. Still, insecurities remain. How do you open the conversation? How do you keep it moving? And how do you get people to feel comfortable with each other and with you?

This chapter will offer some ideas, inspirations, and encouragement. Keep in mind that book group leadership is a skill that generally improves as you go along. If you are a first-time leader in a community where there are several book groups that are either publicly or privately run, it might help to watch a few of these groups in action. If you are lucky, you'll find a leader whose style you admire and who is willing to mentor you.

BREAKING THE ICE

You are at your very first meeting and everyone has introduced themselves. Ideally, you are seated in a circle, either around a large conference table or on chairs and couches placed near each other. You, the leader, are seated in the center and everyone is either wearing name tags or has homemade tented nameplates in front of them. Your group has agreed in advance that people will not bring small children, although young adults who have read the book are always welcome. Nevertheless, one woman who could not find a babysitter has brought her six-month-old baby, who is sleeping peacefully in a carriage. She knows that if the child starts to fuss, she can wheel him out to the lobby, as she would if she were visiting the children's section of the library.

Before you start, you announce that if anyone in the group has trouble hearing, it is perfectly fine to ask participants to speak up. Everyone should be able to hear everyone else and not feel shy about asking to have comments repeated. You also tell folks who have not read or finished the book that they are welcome to attend and ask questions, but that in the course of the conversation they should be prepared to hear how the book turns out. Those who don't want to know the ending will proceed at their own risk. Some library book groups agree in advance that members must read the book in order to participate, while other book group leaders, in the interest of community outreach, welcome everyone whether they have read the book or not. Be sure to mention your rules on meeting flyers and notices.

Now members are ready to introduce themselves. As part of their introduction, you might ask them to tell the group what kinds of books they enjoy or to name a favorite author. If you have a more fanciful group, you might ask them one by one, which author, living or dead, they would like to sit next to on an airplane or invite to dinner.

Now it's time to talk about the book. How do you begin the conversation? Here are a few time-tested icebreakers for first meetings suggested both by library leaders and private book group leaders across the United States and Canada.

- Ask the participants to rate the book on a scale of one to five. (One = "How on earth did this book get published?" Five = Highly recommended.) At the end of the discussion, some group leaders ask participants to rate the book again. Often, based on the discussion, readers discover something new about the book that alters their opinion favorably or unfavorably.
- Read aloud part or all of a book review written by a local or national critic and ask readers if they agree or disagree with the comments. This works especially well in a group where people don't know each other very well yet and are reluctant to disagree with each other. Sometimes it is safer to disagree with an outside critic.
- Let them know if something momentous was going on in the author's life while the book was being written. Was the author going through a divorce or illness or military service? Were they having an affair? Were they recently elected to or impeached from public office?
- Tell your readers a bit about the author's life or hand out a one-page biography at the start of the session. Ask if knowing about the author's life gives them more or less insight into the book and why.
- If it is not completely obvious why the author chose the title of the book, ask about it. Why did Anne Lamott call her novel *Blue Shoe*? And why did Steinbeck call his book

The Grapes of Wrath? What was Harper Lee trying to tell us with the title *To Kill a Mockingbird*? If you can track down an author interview in which the author explains why he or she chose a title, so much the better, but its not absolutely necessary. It's the conversation that counts.

- Ask readers if they think that the book would make a good movie. If yes, who would they cast? If the book has already been made into a movie that people have seen, compare and contrast the book and the film.

KEEPING THE CONVERSATION GOING

Once you have opened the conversation, what kinds of questions will keep it flowing? Here are a few ground rules:

- **Be prepared . . . but be flexible.** While it helps to have a list of questions prepared in advance, you should not feel compelled to stick to it, no matter what. If the conversation takes a different direction and people want to spend more time talking about the author's life than they do about the plot or setting, that's OK. Unlike a formal literature class in which a professor may wish to cover all aspects of a book, the goal here is to share ideas and have fun. You may wish to break in with a question to keep the conversation focused on the book, rather than a tangential subject. But it's fine to spend more time on some questions because you don't have to finish the list. Some book group leaders actively participate in the discussion, adding their own thoughts and opinions, while others act as facilitators. The role that you pick is really up to you, but if you choose to participate, do so as a peer, not as an expert. On the other hand, if there is someone in your group who is an expert on the subject of your book, be sure to draw them out. An art historian might add a lot to a discussion of Dan Brown's *The Da Vinci Code,* while someone who personally knows former President Bill Clinton might have a lot to say about his autobiography.
- **Personal anecdotes are fine; group therapy is not.** If one of your goals is to create a sense of community, you may want to invite readers to share personal information. Many librarians ask their readers questions such as whether or not a fictional character reminded them of someone in

their own family—or whether a reader was faced with a decision similar to that of a character in a novel or biography. You might not want to do this at the first meeting, especially if members don't know each other very well. If someone volunteers the information, however, it could be interesting to hear them out, provided that they don't dominate the discussion with personal observations or reminiscences. When my group read Jimmy Carter's autobiography *An Hour Before Daylight*, which began with a depiction of his childhood on a Georgia farm, one of our readers read excerpts of her childhood diary written on a farm in the Midwest. Because the group found many similarities between her experiences and Carter's, this contribution was enriching to the discussion. On the other hand, I recall what happened during a discussion of a nonfiction book about the creation of the Sistine Chapel, *Michelangelo and the Pope's Ceiling* by Ross King. When a reader began a lengthy discussion of problems that she faced remodeling the ceiling of her suburban home, I strategically interjected a question about whether anyone had visited the Sistine Chapel.

- **Ask members to back up their opinions.** If someone gushes that they just loved the book, or crosses their arms in front of them and says that it was the worst thing they ever read, ask why. For example, did the use of language, the strong or weak characters, or the marvelous suspense influence their opinions? If two people disagree strongly, encourage others to join in the disagreement. In the novel *The Lovely Bones* by Alice Sebold, a young girl looks down on her friends and family from heaven after she is brutally murdered. One mother in my book discussion said that she found the book difficult to read because it was too depressing and kept her imagining how she would react if something like that happened to her teenage daughter. On the other hand, there was a young woman in her early twenties at that book meeting who found the book to be inspiring. "So we have the mother of a teenager who finds this book too depressing . . . and a woman just a few years out of her teen years who was inspired . . . can we have some grandparents weigh in on this?" I asked. "Do you think that different generations might react differently? Do you think that people who don't have kids might react differently from people who do?"

- **Base a question on an opening or closing paragraph or both.** If the book has a particularly moving and/or well-written first paragraph, open the discussion by reading it out loud or have a group member to read it. Then ask how it set the tone for what followed. If the book has a moving or thought-provoking closing paragraph, end your group by reading it and ask what kind of mood was established.

- **Socialize either before the meeting or after, not during.** If any of your readers remark at the end of a meeting, "Gee, we hardly talked about the book," then you have failed in your mission. People certainly join book groups to make new friends and to catch up on local gossip. Such gossip may be less of an issue at a public library meeting which attracts a wide range of folks who may not know each other well. But when the discussion turns personal for a lengthy amount of time, do what book group leader and author Mickey Pearlman of New Jersey does. She cuts off the gossip, telling members, "You can continue as a friendship club or you can continue as a book club." (Meier 2003) Another idea is to set aside a separate date for an outing or social event.

- **Set clear policies about the book selection process and stick to them.** Hold a separate meeting to discuss book selections for the coming year, poll readers online and post their suggestions, or tell people to drop notes in your library mailbox or stop by the reference or circulation desk with ideas. If you have been leading the same group for a while, and your readers trust you, you can prepare a reading list for them based on their interests and demographics—much the way Oprah's team does. Or prepare a list and give your members veto power. Another option is to linger for five or ten minutes after your meeting to hear what other books people are reading and what they would like to discuss in the future. But above all, don't let discussions about *future* selections dominate book talks about your *current* selection.

READY-MADE QUESTIONS

There are a number of sources for ready-made questions that can be used in book discussions. Commercial and academic book publishers, bookstores, libraries, online book clubs, and even fee-based discussion group consultants are now posting free lists of discussion questions on the Internet. Some publishers, especially paperback publishers, insert discussion questions at the back of their books. Literature professors often post their class questions and syllabi on the Internet.

Although you'll find more material on current best-sellers and well-studied classics, the Web can yield plentiful material on more obscure books too. Here are some resources for finding good book group questions online, starting with the easiest (and cheapest) places to find ready-made questions and ending with a fee-based resource.

- **Google (www.google.com).** A Google search is a "quick and dirty" way to find book group questions. Simply combine the title of your book with the phrase "book group" or "book discussion." A Google search for "*The Diary of Anne Frank*" and "book discussion" (conducted in March 2005) yielded questions from sites including the Random House Reader's Guide, The Multnomah County Library Homework Center, and the State of Vermont Department of Libraries, which also offered a book discussion kit.
- **Amazon (www.amazon.com).** Some of the publishers that sell books on Amazon provide reader's guides and questions. To find discussion questions when they are included, search, for the book by title and click on the title to get more information. At this point, a book information box will appear in the left-hand column. Generally, the box includes links to customer and editorial reviews, but if the publisher has also provided reading group guides and questions, you'll find them here.
- **The Book Report Network (www.tbrnetwork.com).** This site is a portal that links to a growing number of Web sites that provide author interviews, reviews, and commentary—along with interactive elements such as polls, message boards, questions, and contests. The Book Report Network was founded in 1996 and is physically based in New York City. One of the sites that it links to, ReadingGroupGuides.com, enables readers to search for guides that include discussion questions. Another Web site, AuthorYellowPages.com, is a searchable directory of author Web sites. Many of these author Web sites also provide links to discussion questions.
- **The Internet Public Library Online Literary Criticism Collection (www.ipl.org).** The Internet Public Library was an online reference service founded in 1995 as part of a gradu-

ate seminar at the School of Library and Information Science at the University of Michigan at Ann Arbor. Today the University of Michigan continues to support this site with funding from Sun Microsystems and Intel. The FAQ for the site describes it as "the first public library of and for the Internet community." Among the many wonderful reference services offered here, you will find many resources for group leaders. The full text of many literary works is available here, including the complete works of Shakespeare, Aesop's Fables, classic mythology, and American short stories and novels by writers including Mark Twain, Louisa May Alcott, and Willa Cather. The Online Literary Criticism Collection (www.ipl.org/div/litcrit) contains critical and biographical Web sites about authors and their works that can be browsed by author, title, nationality, and literary period. The collection links readers to criticism of American, Canadian, European, Latin American, and Asian literature, in some cases going as far back as medieval and ancient times. Because this section is not updated regularly, it is a better source for classics and well-reviewed books that are at least ten years old rather than best sellers. I have personally used the site to find comprehensive information on writers including Truman Capote, Kurt Vonnegut, Toni Morrison, and Alice Munro. This is also a good place to find links to published interviews with contemporary authors. Figure 6–1 shows the portal pages for the Online Literary Criticism Collection.

Figure 6–1   Web Site: The Internet Public Library Literary Criticism Collection

www.ipl.org/div/litcrit

Home > Special Collections > Literary Criticism

	Search	This Collection

The IPL Literary Criticism Collection contains critical and biographical websites about authors and their works that can be browsed by author, by title, or by nationality and literary period.

The collection is not inclusive of all the work on the web, nor does it plan to be. The sites are selected with some thought to their overall usefulness.

Browse for criticism by author's last name:
A-B | C-D | E-F | G-H | I-J | K-L | M-N | O-P | Q-R | S-T | U-W | X-Z | All

Browse Works by Title Beginning with:
A-B | C-D | E-F | G-H | I-J | K-L | M-N | O-P | Q-R | S-T | U-W | X-Z | All

Browse for criticism and Authors by Literary period:

American Literature
    1600-1783
    1783-1865
    1865-1900
    20th Century

British Literature
    Pre-1500
    1500-1700
    18th Century
    19th Century
    20th Century

Canadian Literature
    Pre-1900
    20th Century

French Literature
    Pre-1500
    1500-1600
    1600-1789
    1789-1900
    20th Century

Italian Literature
    Pre-1375
    1375-1585
    1585-1748
    1748-1814
    1814-1900
    20th Century

German Literature
    Pre-1517
    1750-1900
    20th Century

Russian Literature
    1700-1917
    1917-

Spanish Literature
    Pre-1516
    1516-1700
    1700-1900
    20th Century

Latin American Literature
    1519-1826
    20th Century

Japanese Literature
    Pre-1185
    1770-1945
    1945-

Chinese Literature
    Pre-221 BCE
    221 BCE - 618
    1912-

Other Literatures
    Greek (Classical) | Latin
    Polish | Czech | Romanian | Scandinavian
    Middle Eastern | Indian | South East Asian
    Caribbean | African
    Australian & New Zealandic

Need further sources of criticism? Find help from our **Online Literary Criticism Guide** for lit crit links. **Need some criticism search help?** See our **Literary Criticism Pathfinder**, which has strategy suggestions for finding criticism in your library and on the Web.

- **SparkNotes** (www.sparknotes.com). The "Literature Study Guides" section of this Web site, which includes guides with study questions to both contemporary and classic literature, is prepared by literature students but appreciated by a far wider audience. A question from the SparkNotes guide to J. K. Rowling's *Harry Potter and the Chamber of Secrets* asks, "What do the origins and parts of the names reveal about their characters? Consider the names of Lucius Malfoy, Albus Dumbledore, and Voldemort?" Here's a question from the SparkNotes guide to Vladimir Nabokov's *Lolita:* "How does Humbert change over the course of the novel? How does his attitude towards Lolita change (if it changes), and what is Humbert's attitude about Lolita and the whole affair when he writes this manuscript in his jail cell?"

PUBLISHER-SPONSORED READER'S GUIDES

Many publishers have discovered that it is good business to provide reader's guides for book groups. Sometimes the questions are included at the back of the book itself, especially if there is a new paperback edition. If you plan to read a popular or classic book that continues to sell well in bookstores, check the publisher's Web site and see if they provide questions in a reader's advisory and/or book group section of their Web site. If you are pressed for time, you can download and print the questions making copies for everyone in your group. If you have more time, mix and match, using some of the publisher's questions and developing questions of your own. The following Web sites provide discussion guides compiled by well-known publishers of book group paperbacks.

- **Random House Reader Resources** (www.randomhouse.com/ reader_resources/browsetitle). Questions can be searched by title, author, and subject.
- **HarperCollins Reader Resources** (**www.harpercollins. com/hc/readers**).
- **Time Warner Books Reading Guides** (**www.twbookmark. com/books/reading_guides_bytitle.html#tz**). There's also a link for upcoming books by the publisher.
- **Beacon Press** (**www.beacon.org/readguide/index.html**). A Boston-based independent publisher of serious nonfiction

and fiction, the current focus of Beacon Press is in on African-American studies, anthropology, essays, gay/lesbian/gender studies, education, children and family issues, nature and the environment, religion, science and society, and women's studies. Beacon Press books are published under the auspices of the Unitarian Universalist Association of Congregations. Many of the books are published to promote the ideas of diversity and tolerance. however there is no attempt to promote the religion. There are a lot of good discussion guides here for books that you might not find otherwise, including *Kindred* by Octavia Butler, which is about a twenty-six-year-old black woman who is abruptly snatched from her home in present-day California and transported back to the antebellum South. In *Fist, Stick, Knife, Gun*, author Geoffrey Canada presents memories of his youth in the streets of the South Bronx.

- **Farrar, Straus and Giroux (www.fsgbooks.com/readers-guides/index.htm).** This publisher offers an international list of literary fiction, nonfiction, poetry, and children's books. Fiction authors include Tom Wolfe, Susan Sontag, Marilynne Robinson, and Jamaica Kincaid, with a translation of Homer's *Odyssey* thrown in for good measure.

NOVELIST (WWW.EPNET.COM/PUBLIC/NOVELIST)

A fee-based fiction reader's advisory database, NoveList is offered by subscription through EBSCO Information Services. Quite often, a group of libraries or your state library organization will cover or share subscription costs. NoveList contains full-text reviews for adult, young adult, children's, and easy fiction titles. Readers can search for books by title, author, or by simply describing a book they would like to read. This database includes more than thirty-six thousand individual subject headings for fiction and more than seventy-five thousand full-text reviews and descriptions from sources including *Booklist, Library Journal, Publishers Weekly,* and *School Library Journal.* Other features include over one thousand pre-constructed booklists on popular themes and topics, read-alikes for popular authors and book discussion guides, book talks, and resources for teachers.

ASKING IN ADVANCE—BOOK GROUP HOMEWORK ASSIGNMENTS

Some book group members like to consider a question or two as they read the book. That way, they can take some notes and have some time to think about their answers before joining the group. Advance questions work particularly well for public library groups in which people may drop in and out, attending just one or two meetings a year. If you announce your book meetings via post-card or e-mail, include questions to help members focus their reading, whether they ultimately attend the discussion or not. The questions don't have to be complicated. For example, if the book has won a literature prize, the question might be something as simple as whether or not your readers thought the book deserved it. If the dialogue is written in a regional dialect, they might consider whether this enhanced or took away from their enjoyment.

You can present your advance questions via a group e-mail or at the end of the meeting held the month before you read the book. If you bring up your "homework" questions at a meeting, you can present them on a handout, write them on a whiteboard, or simply mention them to the class. Then you can follow up with an e-mail to your readers as a whole. Here are some examples:

- At our next meeting we are going to discuss the novel *A Thousand Acres* by Jane Smiley. Critics have called the story, which is about the relationship between three sisters and their father on an Iowa farm, a modern-day re-telling of Shakespeare's *King Lear*. If you are familiar with the Shakespeare play, think about that as you read the novel and note where the parallels occur.
- Our next meeting takes place on June 16, just before Father's Day weekend. In honor of Father's Day, we have chosen the memoir *Big Russ and Me*, by *Meet the Press* television moderator Tim Russert. Russert, who grew up in the 1950s in a blue-collar Irish Catholic family living in Buffalo, New York, talks about the many life lessons he learned from his dad. As a young man, he lived through the Kennedy assassinations and the unrest of the 1960s, a time when many young people were rebelling against their parents. As you read through this book, think about some of the reasons why he and his dad remained close. If you grew up in the 1960s, compare his childhood experience with your own.

PLAYING DEVIL'S ADVOCATE

Let's say that you've picked a book that everyone in your group absolutely loves. That's a good thing—right? Not always. Often when everybody agrees, the resulting discussion is boring. This might be the time for the library leader to play devil's advocate and bring up a controversial opinion even if you do not personally share it. One fall, for example, I led a book discussion of John Steinbeck's travel memoir *Travels With Charley* which is about a road trip that Steinbeck took across the United States in 1962 accompanied by his poodle, Charley. The book has been praised, in part, because of the wonderful descriptions of the people Steinbeck meets along the way. But while leafing through a "tell-all" memoir called *The Other Side of Eden,* cowritten by Steinbeck's embittered son, the late John Steinbeck IV, I read some controversial allegations. According to the son, his dad really didn't like most people, drank too much, and most likely sat in the trailer camp in his recreational vehicle, writing and drinking alone.

Although I hoped that Steinbeck's son was wrong, I wondered what would happen if I raised the issue with my group members, who universally adore Steinbeck. I waited until halfway through the discussion when one of the women praised the descriptions of a crowd demonstrating against school integration in New Orleans. "Do you think Steinbeck was there at all?" I asked, taking my cues from his son. "Do you think that maybe he sat on a lawn chair back in a trailer park and read the newspaper reports and made up his account?" Although the crowd turned against me, a fascinating conversation followed including a look at the differing characteristics of newspaper travel accounts, political accounts, and personal memoirs.

> "Every group has its Ruth. She's not particularly confrontational. She's not playing devil's advocate, but in each meeting, she opens the others' eyes to another reality. She's the single woman in a group of married mothers; she's the working mom in a group of retired professors; she sees the world from a whole different height . . . I come for Ruth."
> —Book Group Leader Fran Cohen

READERS WHO TALK TOO MUCH

If you're lucky, the person who talks the most at your book group will have intelligent things to say. If you're unlucky, the primary talker will be insensitive and clueless. Either way, you can count on having at least one person in your group who will talk a whole lot more than the others.

Before you decide that this person is monopolizing your group, make sure that you are not the only one who thinks so. Often a book group leader will spend hours preparing commentary and questions, only to be upstaged by someone else in the group. Are your other members enjoying what your competitor has to say and listening raptly? Or do you notice negative body language including sighs, eye rolling, and fidgeting?

Sometimes all it takes to break the flow of a domineering person is a compliment or a distraction. For example, if Mary, the outspoken member in your group, is talking endlessly about why *Moby-Dick* would be a more interesting book if the setting were in New Zealand where she vacationed last year rather than in New England, you might interrupt with, "Mary raises a very interesting point here. Would anyone else like to discuss their reactions to the setting?" If you happen to have lots of props on hand you might interrupt in the interest of edification and say, "Lets take a look at a map of the ocean where Captain Ahab did his fishing." Or, better yet, send Mary out to the reference area to get a map. If Mary still does not get the message, take her aside before or after a meeting and tell her that she is so intelligent and astute that some people feel intimidated by her. Make her a partner in running your group and ask for her cooperation in encouraging others to speak. If that still doesn't work, try partnering with someone else in the group and ask for their help in managing Mary. In we were in the high school cafeteria, we might refer to this as ganging up on someone, but in the library world we prefer to say that this is a way of applying gentle peer pressure.

This strategy works especially well if you talk to other members outside of meetings and they have complained. If Linda runs into you at the supermarket and says that Mary is getting on her nerves, get Linda on your team. Your strategy might work as follows. You are discussing William Faulkner's descriptions of the Mississippi heat in his novel *Absalom, Absalom*! and Mary begins a long anecdote about the time her car air conditioner broke down. Break in and say, "You know, I need to buy a new air conditioner for *my* car and maybe you could help me out after the meeting. But right now I'd like Linda to share with us what she told me earlier this week about Faulkner's descriptions of summer heat. It just so happens that we ran into each other in the supermarket."

In a worst case scenario, you can be passive-aggressive by skipping a monthly meeting or changing the day and time, hoping that it will be inconvenient for Mary to come. You could also break Mary's dominant pattern by planning a meeting where everyone gets to talk a bit about a book that they enjoyed. This often works well if your group meets in September after a summer break. But usually, if you can cause a distraction or break the flow of a person who dominates, you'll do just fine.

"If you work in the library where the group is held, most likely you will have opportunities to chat with your readers outside of the group setting. My readers do not have my personal e-mail address, but they do have my work e-mail address and phone. They do not hesitate to contact me about things that they do and don't like about the group. I try my best to be approachable and non-judgmental—much like a good reference librarian."
—Lauren John

READERS WHO TALK TOO LITTLE

I think that it's important to enable as many people as possible to voice their opinions about a book. However, in every group that I have ever run there are people who say very little or nothing at all. "Why do they bother to show up if they aren't going to participate?" one more vocal member of the group asked me after a meeting. I replied that people come to public library book groups for various reasons. Perhaps they happen to be at the library at the same time that the group is meeting and they are curious about a book they haven't had a chance to read. Others may wander in looking for a comfortable place to promptly fall asleep while many will come if the author is going to appear. Hopefully, enough members will have read the book to keep the conversation flowing. As a group leader, make sure that people who haven't read the book don't disrupt the conversation of those who have.

While there are lots of professional seminars in how to deal with "problem patrons" and even with difficult staff members, there is little in the library literature that addresses book group dynamics in public libraries. I suggest that you pick up some cues by watching other leaders at work.

I did find one particularly useful article on running book groups in public settings, however, written by Monica Edinger, a fourth-grade elementary school teacher whose ideas can certainly be applied to grown-up groups.

> I begin the year by establishing an environment in which children can talk honestly and comfortably about books with me and their peers. The best activities and questions will be useless unless your students feel that their comments are valued and that no one will laugh at them or belittle them in the group. It is my job to make every child feel safe and be willing to take risks, and to say something unusual about a book. To help establish such a tone, I make it clear that I am genuinely interested in what each child has to say. I sprinkle my feedback with comments like, "That is something I never thought of!" or "Boy, that is really fascinating, what else can you tell me about that idea?" Don't worry about going overboard with your encouragement—even the most confident children in your classroom need to hear assuring words. (Edinger 1990)

Here is an actual scripted conversation from a book group that

Eidinger led. Although the participants were fourth-graders, some of her techniques can be applied to book groups for readers of all ages:

> It is last period and I am leading a book talk with half of my fourth grade class.
>
> "George hasn't said much so I'll let him have a turn," I say. (We are engrossed in a discussion comparing *The Wizard of Oz* to *Alice in Wonderland.)*
>
> "I think that Alice, in Wonderland, she wanders around and wonders in her head," George says. "Wandering and wondering."
>
> "Wandering and wondering," I repeat, enjoying the sound of the words. "And Dorothy doesn't wander and wonder in Oz?"
>
> "She knows where she is going. She has a goal," George replies.
>
> "She has a goal and is very determined," I say, as Meredith practically falls off her chair in her efforts to be recognized. "Quick, this really has to be the last thing."
>
> "There is really a big difference in how they get to the land!" exclaims Meredith. "Alice kind of falls into the rabbit hole while Dorothy goes to Oz in a tornado!"
>
> "Hey, that's right! One goes up and one goes down!"
>
> "Yeah!" is the group's response.
>
> That's a good point. Okay, we'll continue this tomorrow." (Edinger 1990)

BOOK DISCUSSION KITS

Some public libraries and/or public library systems or cooperatives have begun assembling free book discussion kits that contain multiple paperback copies of a book, discussion guides and questions, and background materials such as author biographies and lists of the author's other works. Sometimes the kits are used only by book groups run by the library. Sometimes they are also loaned to outside groups. Often, private book discussion groups will donate their books to the library when they are done with them, especially if they are low-cost paperbacks. At that point, the librarians can enhance the donation with reader's guides and supplemental material. Or the library leader can pass on the materials that they used for the groups to other librarians at other local branches.

The Greater Cincinnati Library Consortium has taken things a bit further, posting available book discussion kits on its Web site (www.gclc-lib.org/resources/bookkits/index.html.) The postings enable patrons, fellow librarians, and other book discussion leaders to see the titles available for circulation. Each of over one hundred titles has been made into a kit that contains a bag with at least twelve paperback copies of the title, author information, discussion questions, book reviews, and recommendations for further reading (a.k.a. "If you liked this book and author, then you might like . . . "). The books chosen for the book kits include fiction, nonfiction, and biography selections, and there are two separate kits for including Barbara Kingsolver's novel *The Bean Trees,* Anne Patchett's novel *Bel Canto,* and Sue Monk Kidd's *The Secret Life of Bees*. The book kit database also indicates which library has the kit and how to get it via interlibrary loan. Each kit may be checked out for six weeks and may not be renewed.

Carrie A. Herrmann, the Circulation Services Coordinator for Boone County Public Library in Kentucky, is a Cincinnati Consortium member who creates the book group kits for her branch. When asked how she comes up with the questions, she replied, "I think of some of them on my own, some are from publishers' Web sites, and some are from EBSCO's subscription service NoveList." Figure 6–2 contains excerpts of the Reader's Guide material that she prepared, including her list of discussion questions for the mystery *The Church of Dead Girls* by Stephen Dobyns.

Figure 6–2   Book Discussion Kit: Stephen Dobyns' *The Church of Dead Girls*

SUMMARY

For decades, the faded, rural upstate New York village has lain dormant-—until it is startlingly stirred to life when one by one, three young girls vanish. Nightmares are turned into horrifying reality when their corpses are found, brutally murdered, each missing their left hand. Now, as the search for a madman gets under way, suspicion shrouds the quiet streets of Aurelius when its residents soon realize that a monster lives amongst them. But not even prayers can save their loved ones from the rage of a twisted mind who has only just begun his slaughter . . .

AUTHOR INFORMATION

Stephen Dobyns was born in Orange, New Jersey, on February 19, 1941. He graduated from Wayne State University in 1964 and received his M.F.A. from the University of Iowa in 1967.

Dobyns taught English at State University of New York College at Brockport 1968–1969. He was a reporter for the *Detroit News* 1969–1971. Dobyns was a visiting lecturer in creative writing at the University of New Hampshire 1973–1975, at the University of Iowa 1977–1978, and at Boston University 1978–1979. He was a member of the staff at Goddard College 1978–1980 and at Wilson College 1981.

Dobyns has won numerous awards. *Cemetery Nights* won a Melville Cane Award. *Black Dog, Red Dog* was a winner in the National Poetry Series. *Concurring Beasts* was the 1972 Lamont Selection of the Academy of American Poets. He has received fellowships from the National Endowment for the Arts and the Guggenheim Foundation. His novels have been translated into more than ten languages.

In an interview Stephen Dobyns said, "Although I sometimes write fiction, I do it only as a diversion. I consider myself entirely a poet, am concerned with it twenty-four hours a day . . . " He is one of a select few modern writers who has enjoyed critical success for his poetry as well as popular success with his fiction. Dobyns lives in Boston with his wife and three children.

Figure 6–2 (*Continued*)

IF YOU LIKE THIS BOOK YOU MAY LIKE . . .
Sunflower by Martha Powers
Darkness Peering by Alice Blanchard
Bleeding Heart by Martha Powers
Blue Diary by Alice Hoffman
Bloodstream by P. M. Carlson
Biting the Moon by Martha Grimes
Other novels by Stephen Dobyns:
   A Man of Little Evils (1973)
   Dancer with One Leg (1983)
   Cold Soup Dog (1985)
   A Boat Off the Coast (1987)
   The Two Deaths of Señora Puccini (1988)
   The House on Alexandrine (1990)
   After Shocks/Near Escapes (1991)
   The Wrestler's Cruel Study (1993)
   Boy in the Water (1999)
   Eating Naked (2000)
   Porcupine's Kisses (2002)

QUESTIONS
When did you discover who the serial killer was?
Who was your favorite character?
Will the town ever return to normal after what happened?
Is this novel a good psychological thriller?
Does it bother you that the narrator is never named?
Are all of the characters treated equally?
Did you like the author's writing style?
What are the book's strengths?
What are the book's weaknesses?
How did you feel about the ending?
Would this novel make a good movie?
Who should star in the movie?

Figure 6–3 shows Boone County Public Library's Instructions for patrons interested in obtaining a book discussion kit (www.bcpl.org/bookdiscussionkits.html).

Figure 6–3   Book Discussion Kit: Instructions for Patrons, Boone County Public Library, Kentucky

   Boone County Public Library Book Discussion Kits

What is a Book Discussion Kit?
A Book Discussion Kit is a set of 12–15 paperback copies of a book, discussion questions, author information, book reviews, and information on how to run a successful book discussion group.

How do I get a Book Discussion Kit?
Print out and fill out the Book Discussion Kit Request Form and speak to Carrie Herrmann at the Scheben Branch. In order to view the Request Form file, you must have or download Adobe Acrobat Reader software.

How long can I keep a kit?
They check out for 6 weeks and may not be renewed. The kits can be booked in advance.

What titles do you have in the Boone County Book Discussion Kits?
Ahab's Wife or, The Stargazer by Sena Jeter Naslund
Autobiography of a Face by Lucy Grealy
The Beekeeper's Apprentice by Laurie R. King
The Bonesetter's Daughter by Amy Tan
The Church of Dead Girls by Stephen Dobyns
Clay's Quilt by Silas House
A Cup of Comfort by Colleen Sell
The Day the World Came to Town: 911 in Gander, Newfoundland by Jim DeFede
The Diary of an American Au Pair by Marjorie Ford
The Dive from Clausen's Pier by Ann Packer
Double Indemnity by James M. Cain
Driving Over Lemons: an Optimist in Spain by Chris Stewart
Evening Class by Maeve Binchy
Follow the River by James Alexander Thom
Fortune's Rocks by Anita Shreve
The Fresco by Sheri Tepper
Galileo's Daughter: Historical Memoir of Science, Faith, and Love by Dava Sobel
Guilt by Association by Susan Sloan
Hangman's Beautiful Daughter by Sharyn McCrumb
Hidden in Plain View: A Secret Story of Quilts and the Underground Railroad by Jacqueline L. Tobin
I Don't Know How She Does It by Allison Pearson
In Pursuit of the Proper Sinner by Elizabeth George
A Lesson Before Dying by Ernest J. Gaines
Letter of the Law by Tim Green
Life of Pi by Yann Martell
Map of Love by Ahdaf Soueif

Figure 6–3 (*Continued*)

Mariner's Compass by Earlene Fowler
Money for Nothing by Donald Westlake
The Nazi Officer's Wife: How One Jewish Woman Survived the Holocaust by Edith Hahn-Beer
Night Ride Home by Barbara Esstman
Not Without My Daughter by Betty Mahmoody
A Parchment of Leaves by Silas House
Personal History by Katharine Graham
Protect and Defend by Richard North Patterson
Range of Motion by Elizabeth Berg
Roses are Red by James Patterson
Sculptress by Minette Walters
She Walks These Hills by Sharyn McCrumb
The Sparrow by Mary Doria Russell
Storming Heaven by Denise Giardina
Transfer of Power by Vince Flynn
A Walk in the Woods by Bill Bryson
Welcome to the World, Baby Girl! by Fanny Flagg
When the Emperor was Divine by Julie Otsuka
When You Look Like Your Passport Photo, It's Time to Go Home by Erma Bombeck
Wide Sargasso Sea by Jean Rhys

What other libraries in the area have them? Greater Cincinnati Consortium Libraries (GCLC) list their kits at this page on the GCLC Web site.
Are there any book discussion groups meeting currently? Yes, there are currently four monthly Book Groups meeting at Boone County branches.
What if I don't have time to attend or lead a book discussion group? Check out the Online Book Clubs to receive weekday e-mails from one or more of the chosen titles of the four Book Clubs.

Note: Patrons can click on any of the titles for a plot summary and information on how to get the book kit.
Here is what the entry looks like for Amy Tan's *The Bonesetter's Daughter:*
This novel tells the stories of three generations of women, beginning at the turn of the twentieth century in a small Chinese village, where the bonesetter, a skilled healer, defies tradition and teaches his daughter everything he knows. Intelligent and willful, she vehemently rejects the marriage proposal of the vulgar coffinmaker, who curses her, thus setting in motion a tragic sequence of events that continues to unfold a century later in San Francisco, where a Chinese American woman finally reads the memoir her mother wrote for her. For more information about this book kit or to request it from Boone County Public Library,
    contact: Carrie Herrmann Phone:_____ E-mail:_____

REFERENCES

Cohen, Fran. "The Ties That Bind: What Brings Readers Together? A Book Group Leader Tells All." *Book* (November 1, 2001).

Edinger, Monica. "How to Lead Better Book Talks: My Classroom Strategies for Insightful Book Discussions." *Instructor* (May 1, 1995).

Meier, Peg. "Rx for Book Clubs." *Minneapolis/St Paul Star Tribune* (August 2, 2003), p. 40.

7 BOOKING AN AUTHOR AND PLANNING AN EVENT

Author events at public libraries are often presented in the following three ways:

1) The author is invited to participate in a reading or roundtable discussion with members of your book group who have read the book in advance.

2) The author is invited to do a reading, book signing, and question-and-answer session at the library at which all members of the public will be welcome.

3) The author is asked to participate in a panel discussion with other authors or community leaders, centered on a particular theme. For example, you might host a mystery writers' panel at Halloween or an environmental/science writers' panel for Earth Day. Perhaps, a group of writers and community religious leaders might be interested in tackling the spiritual issues raised by the popular mystery *The Da Vinci Code* by Dan Brown. The panel format is also a good way to explore other literary genres, including poetry, short stories, and plays.

Of course, before you can plan any of these events, you have to invite the authors. But, fear not, many authors are standing by, waiting to take your call.

WHAT'S IN IT FOR THEM?

Most authors don't charge for their appearances and you may be surprised at how many will be interested in accepting your invitation. Why should an author show up at your library and talk for free? "Authors want to bring books to sell on the spot because that's unfortunately how many books get sold if you are not in the Tom Clancy category," says Manhattan-based author and travel writer Alan Behr, who wrote *Once Around the Fountain*, published in 2001. "All a librarian has to do is find out which well-reviewed books were written by authors one tank of gas away and call the publisher or, even better, drop an e-mail on the author's personal Web site," Behr suggests. How much lead time should you give? "Six or eight weeks in advance is best," advises Behr. "This gives the author enough time to make sure his mom will be there from Pompano Beach."

A book talk can also be a networking opportunity for authors, especially those who lead writing workshops or do freelance work on the side. If a writer has written a book promoting a political mission or social cause, this is also a way to spread the word. What's more, writing can be a lonely profession, and sociable authors will welcome the chance to communicate with readers, especially the thoughtful readers who can often be found in book groups.

THE BEST AUTHOR EVENT—EVER.

Still shy about asking an author to speak? Perhaps you will be inspired by the following true best case scenario.

You send an e-mail invitation to a local San Francisco author with a national following. Would he show up on a Thursday morning at 10:30 a.m. a month or two from now and for a half-hour to an hour to talk about his new best-seller? Would he stay on to take questions from the audience and sign books? And will he do this for free? No problem, says the author, responding by e-mail the same day. He adds that he has a fifteen-minute film associated with the book—a mystery set at the time of the 1906 San Francisco earthquake. He asks if he can show it.

Encouraged by his positive response, you agree to the screening and ask whether he will bring his own audiovisual equipment or if he wants the library to arrange the screening for him. Since the writer has replied so quickly and enthusiastically, and since the *San Francisco Chronicle* has just done an author profile of him, you also ask, "Would you be willing to stay on for lunch—our treat, of course—at a local restaurant with a few of our Friends of the Library who have been particularly generous to us this year?" The author replies the following morning and says he would be delighted. He asks if his wife can come, too. You say you'd love to have her dine with your group.

The day of the book talk arrives. The author and his wife show up a half-hour early, charm the entire library staff and the president of the Friends Group. Husband and wife work together to set up a film projector and screen to show a film clip of a forthcoming documentary based on the book. They are both gregarious, patient with your older patrons who do not hear so well, and have all the time in the world to mingle. What's more, before he begins to speak, the author makes a point of publicly thanking you by name for arranging the event.

Sixty people attend the talk. Twenty people go on to the local restaurant for the luncheon. You are concerned that they won't get as much personal contact with the author as a smaller group might. But this author is a pro. He table-hops, having salad at one table, the main course at another, and dessert at the third. Everyone talks about the event for days afterwards and asks you who is coming next month. One Friend of the Library who was thrilled by the talk and the lunch writes a check for $500 to the library, which more than covers the cost of treating the author and his wife to lunch.

I won't tell you the author's name because I don't want him to be besieged by requests. But I will say that I decided to contact him because he is based in the San Francisco·Bay area, as is my library. Perhaps we got particularly lucky because this was his first book. I know that he appreciated being able to meet people at the talk who were descendants of victims who had survived the 1906 quake. One woman even gave him a detailed account of the earthquake written by her great-grandfather, who had been a San Francisco fireman on duty at that time.

WHAT CAN GO WRONG

With a little advance work, your author talk should work out fine, but I have attended some that did not go so well. Most of these took place on author tour appearances at local bookstores. Here's what I have learned from the bookstore mishaps. While you want wonderful writers to accept your invitations, there are some really talented writers who should *never* meet their readers. Some authors really don't like people too much. Although it may be fun to read their character descriptions, it can be much less enjoyable to meet the misanthropic creators of these characters in person. Other authors may be genuinely nice people who are simply worn down by the end of a book tour. Some may have drug or alcohol problems that get worse before public appearances, while some are simply shy.

It helps to check authors out in advance, if you can. For example, a local literature teacher whom I admired a lot had written her first book, a memoir, at the age of seventy. I loved her book, which included some racy descriptions of sex after sixty, and I thought she would inspire (or outrage) the many women over the age of sixty in my book group. But first I wanted to see what kind of tone she would set at a book talk. Could she be a bit risqué without going overboard? And what passages would she select to read to the audience? I did some reconnaissance work by going to hear her speak at a writer's panel hosted by a local chapter of the Association of University Women. Unfortunately, the author was nothing like the bold, sassy woman who appeared in her memoir. Shy, ill at ease, and apparently exhausted, she was uncomfortable using the microphone and spoke very softly. What's more, she rushed off the stage, while the other two authors on the panel spent up to twenty minutes talking.

Wondering if she was simply having a bad day or was afraid of being judged by the many seniors in the audience, I went up and spoke to her after the talk, complimenting her on the book. She seemed distracted and a bit disoriented and had trouble making eye contact. I am not sure why this was the case. Perhaps she was ill and simply driving to the book talk from her home an hour away in the summer heat was too much for her. Ultimately, I decided *not* to invite her to speak.

GETTING GOOD AUTHORS—TEN KEY STRATEGIES

Here are some tips for getting the *right* people to say yes.

1) Do some advance work. If at all possible, try to see or meet authors in person before you issue an invitation. This, of course, will be easier if you plan to invite local authors who live or work within an hour's drive of your library. These folks are more likely to appear at local bookstores, schools and universities, and places of worship. If you can see them do a reading in advance, and have the chance to watch them interact with the audience, you will have a better idea of how your own library program might go. If you are planning to invite a well-known author on his or her only swing through your town, you might want to get in touch with librarians and/or bookstore owners in places that the author has already visited. Ask how things went. Was the author engaging? Or did a brawl break out during the Q&A? You can often find out where the author has previously appeared from the book publisher or book promotions staff. Before you issue an invitation, read the author's latest book—or at least a few long reviews. While flattery will get you far (e.g., I love your work), targeted flattery will get you further. What did you personally like or admire about the author's work. Did it change your life or personal outlook in any way? Who could say no to an invitation that begins, "I just loved your description in your book of the Napa Valley vineyards at harvest time—in fact, after reading your book I planned a trip to wine country with my boyfriend and it was there that he proposed."

2) Get as close as you can to the source—but not too close. You can often cut through a lot of red tape if you can get the author's personal e-mail or address. You'll also do better if you send an e-mail to an author's Web site, rather than the publisher's Web site. That's because many authors monitor their Web sites themselves. Many authors also teach literature or creative writing, and you might be able to get in touch with them through their university. Even if you have an author's home phone number, you probably won't want to use it unless the author or a person very close to the author gave it to you. Phone calls (even when they jump to voicemail) are an interruption, whereas e-mails can be scanned or ignored at will. And the more famous authors (as well as some highly cautious lesser ones) may be worried about being stalked. What's more, many authors are already seated at their desktops and laptops and may be right there when your e-mail message comes in. Many writers answer their e-mail surprisingly quickly, if only to tell you how busy they are.

3) Be direct. Whether phoning or e-mailing or writing, a few lines of the targeted flattery may work, but don't gush or ramble. Simply begin by telling authors your name, your role in the book group, the name and location of your library, and let them know that you want to invite them to a book talk (see the sample e-mail invitation in Figure 7–1).

4) Set financial expectations. If you want authors to do the talk for free (and most will) say so up front. If your Friends of the Library can offer an honorarium, let them know that, too.

5) Tell authors what else you can do for them. In most cases, when you issue your invitation, you will politely ask authors to work for free. But are there other benefits you can offer? Can you draw a crowd? Can you set up a table and help the author to sell books at the event? Could you take them to lunch? If they are coming from a distance, could you pick them up at the train, or even the airport? Is there someone local that the author might like to meet who will also be attending the talk? Let authors know what you can do for them *when* you issue the invitation, not after they accept.

6) If you have some flexibility in formatting and scheduling, ask the author for input. Maybe your book group meets at night and the author is only available during the day. Perhaps the author has a prepared talk or reading that he orshe would like to present or would like to talk about a new work in progress. Maybe the author would like to share the stage with a fellow author or collaborator. If you have some flexibility, let it be known.

7) **Give no more than one to two months lead time.** Successful authors are busy people who, in addition to writing, travel, attend retreats and workshops. Their plans can change at the drop of a muse. You don't want to leave things to the last minute because you need time to plan publicity, but the greater the lead time, the greater the chance of a cancellation.

8) **Make sure that you plan your event at a time when readers have fewer competing entertainment options.** Don't hold it on the night that Stephen King or Bill Clinton or Barbara Bush is speaking at the local bookstore. Unless you are featuring an author as part of a holiday celebration, avoid holidays or Super Bowl Sunday. Laments food and travel writer Laura Fraser, author of *An Italian Affair*, "I had a reading in L.A. on the night of the Lakers playoffs, and two people showed up."

9) **Give authors or their publicists a consistent contact person.** If that person is you, give the author or the publicist several easy ways to reach you. You don't want your author calling the library and getting put into the automated messaging system or transferred to a part-time person who may not know anything about your book discussion program.

10) **If the event is a success, share the good news.** Most authors will appreciate it if you build "buzz." Tell your colleagues at other libraries what great presentations they did, mention the event in your library's newsletter, and write up the event for the local newspaper. If anyone took flattering photos, post them on the library bulletin board, and send copies to the author.

WHAT AUTHORS WANT—IN THEIR OWN WORDS

If you really want to know why authors show up at book group meetings, ask an author. Here are some comments from three authors who have done library talks. They share what works, what doesn't work, and why.

Debbie Gisonni is the author of *Vita's Will: Real Life Lessons About Life, Death and Moving On* and *The Goddess of Happiness: A Down-to-Earth Guide for Heavenly Balance and Bliss*. To learn more about Ms. Gisonni, check out her Web site (www.goddessofhappiness.com).

The only negative I've seen in doing talks at libraries is if the library doesn't have a good following and less than 15 people show up. It's a bit disappointing from an author's point of view to spend the time to prepare a talk and show up when a very small group of people are there. At least that's how I feel. Also remember that libraries don't pay speakers, so if only a handful of people show up, the author isn't even able to get their word-of-mouth advertising out there for the book.

As for things that are positives for authors doing talks at libraries:

1. Ability to sell their books there.
2. The library offers to "feature" their book on a display for a month prior to and after the event.
3. A good crowd—15 or more.
4. Refreshment and chatting time afterward.
5. Close to home—a short drive.
6. A two-month advance notice or invitation.
7. Advance promotion in the local papers for the event, the book, and the author.
8. TV filming of the talk for local public TV—that way authors are guaranteed more people will see them and hear their talk.

Ron Hansen is the author, most recently, of the novel *Isn't It Romantic?* and a book of essays called *A Stay Against Confusion: Essays on Faith and Fiction.* Among his other books are *Desperadoes, The Assassination of Jesse James by the Coward Robert Ford, Nebraska, Mariette in Ecstasy, Atticus,* and a children's book, *The Shadowmaker.* You can learn more about Ron Hansen at the Nebraska Center for Writers Web site (mockingbird.creighton.edu/NCW/hansen.htm.)

Local (authors) in the community or teachers at nearby schools and colleges . . . seem the most likely to approach. Writers early on in their careers or still underappreciated would find these groups more attractive than others who are more established and have a host of invitations. A key to a successful invitation is some kind of guarantee in the number attending. Nothing kills off interest in such events than just a handful of readers showing up. Usually the invitation should be made at least a month in advance. There should be refreshments of some sort, possibly supplied by volunteers. The area should be closed off so browsers are not wandering in and out. Though a library is hosting the affair, books should still be for sale there. Nothing is so bruising to an author as realizing he's spent several hours (and more in terms of psychic energy) on an event and not sold a single book. A gift or honorarium should be provided that is equivalent to the price of the hardback book. Most writers I know are not prickly about invitations to speak that come by phone, but they should be followed up by a more formal letter of invitation.

Some writers will be unfamiliar with such events. Supply them with the format ahead of time, indicating a ten- to fifteen-minute reading followed by fifteen to thirty minutes of Q & A. Apprise them of what questions are likely to be asked. If the group is not an intimate one, often it works well to have the questions written out on three-by-five cards, permitting the introverts access and diminishing the fear of sounding stupid. Any introduction should be accurate, no more than five minutes long and no less than two, specific as to bibliography, and include sampling of book reviews or blurbs.

Laura Fraser is the author of *An Italian Affair* and *Losing It: False Hopes and Fat Profits In the Diet Industry*. To learn more about her, check out her Web site at www.laurafraser.com.

I always appreciate some kind of gift. It's always wonderful when a bookstore gives the author the opportunity to choose a book, for instance, or gives a pen or something. It seems little, but it makes a difference to writers, particularly if they aren't promoting their books. Also, of course it's great to have books to sell.

Figure 7–1 Sample E-Mail: Author Invitation

To: Laura Fraser
From: Lauren John
Sent: Wednesday, November 20, 2002 2:21 p.m.
Subject: Are you interested in doing a Valentine's Author Event at Menlo Park Public Library

Dear Ms. Fraser:

I am a librarian at the Menlo Park Public Library and am writing to ask if you would be interested in speaking to our book group about *An Italian Affair,* which is our Valentine's month reading selection. The group meets at the library at 7 p.m.—the day would be Tuesday, February 11, 2003. Our book club typically draws between eight to sixteen people—but if you were there, I think we could draw fifty to one hundred people and promote it as an author event. (The book has been circulating well at our library—I read it all in one sitting!)

We could also sell your books and have an author signing at the event, if you wanted to. We are right across the street from Kepler's independent bookstore and often arrange this through them, or you could bring copies of the book, yourself.

As for the format of the book talk—you could do a reading and then take questions from the audience. Or I could interview you about the book and about any current projects that you are working on. Although we could not pay you for your appearance, one of the women on our library commission is an accomplished Italian pastry chef and she promises to prepare cookies for you and the audience. Let me know if the date and time work for you. If not, perhaps we could arrange another date around that time.

Please respond via e-mail or call me at the library at 650 xxx-xxxx.

Regards
Lauren John
Book Group Leader and Librarian
Menlo Park Public Library 800 Alma Street, Menlo Park CA 94025
www.menloparklibrary.org

Figure 7–2   Sample: Thank-You Note to the Author

(I sent this as an e-mail, but you could also prepare a hand-written note)

From: Lauren John
Date: Tuesday, Feb 17, 2004
To: David Laws
Subject: Menlo Park Library appearance

Dear David:

I am still hearing from people who enjoyed your presentation last week on your book *Steinbeck Country: Exploring the Settings for the Stories.* The photos in your slide show were magnificent and your enthusiasm about Steinbeck and his landscapes came through loud and clear!

We had folks come from as far away as Saratoga and San Jose. I know that the article that we had in the *Menlo Park Almanac* helped to create interest. But I also think that we got a good crowd because *you* helped so much with the publicity.

Based on the detailed questions that folks asked you, it was clear that there were lots of Steinbeck fans in the audience. I even saw folks taking notes during your talk—I imagine that some are planning their own trips down to Steinbeck country right now.

I was excited to hear that you also have a book out about the history of Silicon Valley. Perhaps we can arrange another speaking engagement next year.

I hope that our paths cross again!

Regards
Lauren John
Book Group Leader
Menlo Park Public Library

3 ORGANIZING AN ONLINE LIBRARY-SPONSORED BOOK DISCUSSION GROUP

Online book discussion groups are a work in progress, evolving as fast as the new technologies that support them. Ideally a Web-based book club would make the entire book available online, supplemented by real time and bulletin board discussions. There could be multimedia links to author interviews, film clips, maps, and illustrations, like the ones now available on CD-ROM products and DVDs. Additionally, readers would have the chance to share their ideas in real time, twenty-four hours a day. For now, however, online book groups offered by public libraries have some, but not all, of these features.

Most librarians need at least some technical assistance in the beginning. Before initiating an online group, make sure that you have a lot of time to respond personally and quickly to messages until other readers begin to contribute to the online discussion. Rachel Jaffe, creator of "Rachel's Compendium of Online Book Discussions" (see: www.book-clubs-resource.com/online/rachel.php), points out:

> When you're just starting out, you need to be constantly providing new information, even if you don't see much traffic. It might seem like a waste of time—after all, why put out the effort if you don't have people reading? But you need to keep the site updated and current because you never know when that one great participant will be surfing by . . . Active discussion tends to entice participants, and stagnant discussions don't. You want your site to look active. And as opposed to a face-to-face book club, you never know when someone is checking out your club.

A TALE OF TWO ONLINE BOOK GROUP LEADERS

Denise Somers, an adult services librarian, runs an online book discussion group at the Alderney Gate Public Library in Halifax, Nova Scotia. Her members communicate by group e-mail messages posted to a password-protected bulletin board. (www. halifaxpubliclibraries.ca). She has a whopping 213-person membership list. She reports, however, that discussion is infrequent. Somers laments, "I had hoped to encourage discussion by having the members pick the upcoming titles. They did so, but no discussion! Every once in a while there will be a small flurry of discussion, but not consistently . . . Most of my moderating is rejecting spam."

Sharon Hilts McGlinn, a librarian with a reference background who works in Web services at Hennepin County Library in Minnetonka, Minnesota, manages its Readers Online Book Group. Members here communicate via group e-mail messages that they send to the group as a whole.

"I think it's very difficult to have a true book discussion with this format—at least here, people really like getting the reading suggestions but aren't very interested in contributing comments," she observes, adding, "Generally, I've noticed that many people who comment about the book had read it previously; others comment that they've been inspired to read it based on the e-mail comments, but not as many are commenting based on having read the book specifically for the discussion." McGlinn notes that between March 2002, when the group started, and August 2005, the mailing list grew to four hundred people. She mentions, "It's hard to say how many we had at the beginning—we started with zero and the number has gradually increased."

The Hennepin County Library Web site describes its program as follows (see www.helib.org/pub/books/OnlineBookDisc.cfm):

> Every month we will feature a new title or titles. The interests of the group will determine the type of books selected. Library staff will choose the books, but please send us your suggestions for future discussions. You will need to subscribe in order to participate. At the beginning of the month, you will receive an e-mail message that will announce upcoming selections and start the discussion about the current title. You can reply to the message and your comments will be sent to the group, or

you can send a message to the group at any time at ReadersOnline@lists.hclib.org.

Given the difficulties, why might you want to host an online book discussion group in the first place? Most public librarians who start online discussion groups do so to connect to readers who can't always show up at library meetings. These folks represent a quite large pool of potential readers and library patrons, including seniors, new parents, folks in rural areas, and everyone who lives in places with lots of snow! It is hardly surprising that not one, but two, online book discussions are offered by the Hennepin County Public Library based in Minnesota.

In addition to the library-run book group, the library offers a second program available by subscribing to a private service called DearReader.com, which will be discussed later in this chapter.

Online book groups are also a good way to reach middle and high school kids, many of whom would rather not have their parents drive them to the library. But they love using any kind of computer technology if it helps them talk to their friends. While many students don't like to talk in front of their peers, most have no problem posting to a blog. Some libraries offer online discussion groups targeted to these audiences. For example, the Roselle Public Library in Illinois has introduced a Blogger Book Club (www.roselle.lib.il.us/YouthServices/BookClub/BookClub _FAQ.htm) with selections aimed at young adults. The Bloggers FAQ is displayed in Figure 8–1.

Figure 8–1   Roselle Public Library Book Bloggers FAQ, Roselle, Illinois

---

www.roselle.lib.il.us/YouthServices/BookClub/BookClub_FAQ.htm

What is a blog?

A blog, or Web log, is a password-protected site on the Internet where a person can write their thoughts and have them appear on a Web page that anyone can read. It can belong to one person or to a group (a team, a family, a club, etc.).

There are two parts to a blog:

1. The Web site or form where you write and edit your thoughts or "posts." Only people who have been invited to participate can get to this site. This is the part that is password-protected.

2. The Web site where you can read the "posts." Anyone in the world can get to this site to read the posts.

Blogger Book Club members can get to both Web sites. They can both write and read the blog. People who are not members can only get to the site where they can read the blog.

What is a "Blogger Book Club?"

The Blogger Book Club is an "invitation only," online, book discussion group. It is an opportunity for kids to share their thoughts and ideas about books, anonymously, at their convenience and from wherever they happen to be (at home, on vacation, in the library . . . wherever!).

Most of the books we will be talking about are nominees for the Rebecca Caudill Young Readers Book Award.

Who can join?

The book club is open to kids in grades 4–6 who have a valid library card at any library.

If you are not a Roselle Library patron, the Blogger Book Club Team will contact your home library to verify that you are a registered user.

How do I get started?

Joining the Blogger Book Club is easy:

1. Fill out a registration form. Forms are available in the library at the Ask Me desk and online here.

2. After we receive your registration, the Blogger Book Club Team will send you a "Welcome to the Blogger Book Club" e-mail with instructions for reading the book club discussion and posting your comments to the discussion.

Who selects the books?

For this first experiment, the Youth Services librarians have selected books that are nominated for the 2004 Rebecca Caudill Young Readers Award.

I don't want to read all of the books. Can I still be part of the group?

Yes, absolutely. You are not required to read any of the books or participate in any of the discussions. There are no tests, papers, or grades. Some club members will want to read every book, while some will read none. You are free to choose only those books you are interested in and have the time to read.

I have a question that was not answered here. Who can help?

If you have a question about the Blogger Book Club, e-mail Amy.

TO BLOG OR NOT TO BLOG

Most librarians, by now, have heard the term "blog." Some love blogs, some hate blogs, and some are not sure what they are. The disagreement over the usefulness of blogs can be considered generational, since blogs tend to be a tool of the young.

What exactly is a blog? A blog, or Web log, is a site on the Internet where people can write their thoughts and have them appear on a Web page that anyone can read. It can belong to one person or to a group (a team, a family, a club, a library, etc.). Some blogs are password-protected while others are open to everyone. Blogs consist of the form where you write and edit your thoughts or "posts," and the Web page where you can read the "posts." Anyone in the world can access this page to read the posts. Many blogs provide links to other blogs and related resources. Whether or not you use a blog format is up to you. Some online groups do just fine distributing group e-mail messages. In the first mailing, for example, a library leader might offer some background information on the book and throw out some discussion questions. Then, in subsequent mailings, individual readers share their insights with the group. Other groups post their comments in online bulletin boards.

> Blogs, as librarians have been quick to discover, are great tools for communicating information, citing sources (through URLs), comparing facts (like differing versions of the same news story), and giving it all context—through links to previous stories, for example. But unlike a transaction at the reference desk, blogs needn't be neutral. In fact, many librarian-authored blogs are personal, opinionated, humorous, and scathing. Although typically written by one person, blogs—especially those by librarians—cross-reference each other, creating what Karen Schneider, the Free Range Librarian, has dubbed the "biblioblogosphere." Diving into this sometimes raucous online conversation is often more invigorating, rewarding, timely, and fun than any panel discussion at a conference." (Kenney & Stephens, 2005)

CHOOSING A FORMAT

If you decide to try an online book discussion at your library, the way in which you should set it up depends on whether or not you want to start from scratch and how many people will be needed to work on both the technical aspects of the Web site as well as the content. Does your staff have the time and energy to take this on? Is there a library volunteer who could do it?

At some public libraries, talented bloggers have created Web-based book group pages with links to discussion boards and background materials, including links to book reviews, author interviews, or even excerpts from the text. The readers order and read their books offline, but check in to the Web site for background and to add their opinions. Other libraries simply send out group e-mail messages that enable readers to share opinions.

If this sounds like too much work, you could chose to outsource your online book groups to a subscription service called DearReader.com (www.dearreader.com). This service enables readers to get best-seller chapters e-mailed to them a few times a week, and to post their reactions on an online discussion board. Other librarians with fewer online resources may refer patrons to long-standing online book groups run by other companies and non-profit groups, or even a group run by a library in another state or town.

DO-IT-YOURSELF DISCUSSIONS

Some libraries have created their own online book clubs where members read hard copies of the book and discuss them online. The librarians at the Tippecanoe County Public Library in Lafayette, Indiana, have worked together to design and manage this kind of club, which they call the Book Clique. A committee of librarians chooses one title per month based on suggestions from subscribers. They then announce their choices on the library Web site and also communicate with readers via e-mail. One librarian volunteers each month to lead the discussion and reader responses are posted on an online bulletin board. Readers even take a vote and evaluate each book on a scale of one to five, one being not worth the trouble and five being a "must read." The results are then posted on the book group's archive (see www.tcpl.lib.in.us/ref/bookgroup.html). The group's rules are shown in Figure 8–2.

Figure 8–2 Rules for Participating in the Tippecanoe Public Library's Online Book Group, Lafayette, Indiana

The Book Clique FAQ

Q: What is The Book Clique?

A: It is a group of people who read and discuss a book selection each month. It is much like traditional book groups with the exception that instead of having to meet somewhere, the discussion goes on over the Internet. Participants can read other people's opinions on the book selection and then reply to those opinions through their e-mail account.

Q: What exactly happens when I join an e-mail discussion group?

A: You will receive e-mails each time that someone posts a comment or question about the book. You can reply to these e-mails just like you would regular e-mails and your message will be sent to the entire group.

Q: How do I send a message to the group?

A: You can send a reply like the one above, or just send an original message to bookclique@tcpl.lib.in.us.

Q: OK, how do I sign up?

A: E-mail bookclique@tcpl.lib.in.us and put "subscribe" in the subject line of a blank message. Within a day or two you should get a welcome message with information about the group. After that you should begin to receive e-mails relating to the discussion as they are posted.

Q: How do I unsubscribe?

A: Same as you subscribe, just e-mail bookclique@tcpl.lib.in.us and put "unsubscribe" in the subject line of a blank message.

Q: How can I see old discussions?

A: Click on Archive, which will take you to a page where you can read old messages. Note: Please put the title of the book in the subject line of new messages to help keep the archives easy to browse.

Q: What kind of books do you discuss?

A: All kinds. Click on previous selections in order to see some of the ones which we have discussed in the past.

Q: What books are you discussing in the future?

A: The Book Clique homepage has a list of the upcoming selections.

Q: How can I get a copy of the book to read?

A: You can click on any of the current or upcoming titles to see if the library has any copies available or go directly to TIPCAT to find out if the book is checked in or to place a hold on it.

Q: Who chooses the books?

A: A group of librarians choose the selections. Feel free to make suggestions for future discussions by clicking on "Suggest a book for us to discuss,"

Q: How do I protect my privacy?

A: We at TCPL are very concerned with the safety and privacy of our customers; however, in a public forum such as this, privacy cannot be guaranteed. We recommend that you do not put personally identifiable information, such as your real name, address, or phone number in your e-mail messages. Please report to us any harassing or suspicious behavior. We ask that you respect others' privacy and only respond to their comments through the group unless they ask you to e-mail them directly.

Q: What if I have more questions?

A: Feel free to e-mail us.

Last updated 3/02/05 by Neal Starkey

"We use some simple LISTSERV software to moderate the list and the messages which are sent out strictly through e-mail," says Neal Starkey, the reference librarian and book group Webmaster at Tippecanoe County Public Library. Starkey reports that the library started the online book group in 1999, with about twenty subscribers. By 2005, the group was holding steady with around sixty subscribers. "Over the years we have found that the group serves more like a reader's advisory service and less like a traditional book group. The time delay between messages really limits the depth of the discussions. Most months we average about ten to fifteen messages," Starkey says.

Sharon McGlinn at Hennepin County Library manages their Readers Online Book Group (www.hclib.org/pub/books/Online BookDisc.cfm). with technical assistance from the library's IT staff but reports that "technical problems have been relatively few." McGlinn recalls that at first she spent a lot of time creating the online group, but these days more of the work is shared. "Either I or another librarian—I've recruited four or five now—chooses the title for the month and then the 'host' for the month sends one to three messages," McGlinn reports. A sample message that she sent to her group in August 2005 is shown in Figure 8–3. She also monitors the messages and maintains the mailing list. "We've automated that part more now using Web forms and that seems to work fine," adds McGlinn. "Now people can unsubscribe more easily, so we're not getting the irate messages from people who don't know why they're on the list and can't get off."

Figure 8–3   Hennepin County Readers Online Book Group Message

Thanks to everyone who commented on the July book! It's August and time to talk about summer reading. There's no featured title this month, so please take a moment to tell us about what you've been reading this summer and recommend some good books!

If you're looking for reading ideas, there's a new feature on HCL's website called "What We're Reading." Library staff recommend books that they've enjoyed; go to Find a Good Book-> http://www.hclib.org/pub/books/FindABook.cfm. Look for new titles every week!

To get us started this month, here's what I've just read:

A Changed Man by Francine Prose

Vincent, a homeless neo-Nazi, walks into the Manhattan office of a human rights foundation run by a famous Holocaust survivor, claiming to have undergone a life change and wanting to help keep "guys like him from turning into guys like him." Bonnie, the foundation's fund-raiser, agrees to let him stay with her and her two teenage sons out in the suburbs. The novel explores transformations of all kinds in the lives of Vincent, Bonnie, and her son, Danny.

There are dark moments but the story is lighter than it sounds; the premise seems strange but the characters are engaging.

Sharon Hilts McGlinn
Adult Services Librarian, Web Services
Hennepin County Library

GETTING TECHNICAL ASSISTANCE

For technical support with your online book groups contact your Internet Service Provider (ISP), particularly if you decide to do an e-mail-based discussion group. Some county library systems also have a centralized department for technical support.

Sharon McGlinn at Hennepin County Library uses a listserv mailing list for her group. When she started her book discussion, the list was not moderated so members could send messages directly to the entire group. After some annoying messages appeared as well as a few instances of inappropriate language, the library switched to a moderated format. McGlinn, explains, "All messages go first to the list owner and a couple of backup staff, and we have to approve them before they go to the group." She concludes, "So far it's working fine. We've avoided a lot of spam messages that way and a few questions about the group that could be dealt with privately."

The Online Book Discussion Group at the Alderney Gate Public Library in Nova Scotia was launched in April 2001, at the same time as the Halifax Public Library put up its Web site, also known as the "e-branch." The goal of both the Web site and the book group is to increase access points to library collections, services, and programs, according to librarian Denise Somers. "The online book discussion is part of the e-branch known as Reader's Cafe, an area of reading-related databases, Web sites, and resource lists to aid readers in making their reading choices," she says. The software package that keeps the online book group running is a LISTSERV built by Halifax Public Library's Systems Department. Readers sign up on the e-branch with their e-mail address. Each e-mail posted to the book discussion e-mail address is sent to each of the members as they are composed, or in a digest form. The titles for discussion for the upcoming four months (one title per month) are placed on the e-branch by the Webmaster.

David King is the IT and Web Project Manager of the Kansas City Public Library in Kansas City Missouri. He has not, to date, been asked to design an online book group. But here's what he suggests to those faced with the task:

1. Set up a Yahoo groups discussion group. Easy, free, and it works.
2. Set up your own online bulletin board with software like UBB (www.ubbcentral.com or www.yabbforum.com).
3. Go for something more bloglike. Drupal (www.drupal.org) is a content management system that includes blogs, forums, picture galleries, etc.—a technology-savvy library could set something like this up as a value-added online book discussion group, complete with pictures of events, discussions, etc.

MAKING THE RULES

As has been mentioned, some online book group leaders report that readers use inappropriate language on the discussion boards. Others must deal with spam or readers who have tried to use the boards to sell goods or services, as if using eBay. You can't control everyone's online behavior—all you can do is hope for the best. But you can let readers know right up front how you *hope* they'll behave.

Usually, it's easier for adults to set limits for kids than for each other. With this in mind, here are the rules for the middle schoolers who participate in the Roselle Public Library Blogger Book Club. This is a good set of rules for *all* book group members, whether they share ideas online or in person.

- We expect you to keep your posts civil and respectful.
- Remember that everyone has a right to his or her own opinion about the book being discussed; it is not necessary to agree on all points but let all people have their say.
- Remember this is a book discussion; we need to stay on-topic.
- Accept other members' ideas and respond in a manner that does not degrade or make anyone feel bad.
- Watch your language; do not use inappropriate or bad language.
- Members who violate these rules will be removed from the group.

Here are the online book club guidelines from the Halifax Public Library System:

- Messages that are for one person should not be posted to the list. Please use private e-mail to contact these individuals.
- Always include a subject line when posting to the list. The subject line should briefly summarize your topic.
- Stay within the guidelines for discussion. Although you are not limited to the suggested topics for discussion, we do ask that you post messages that are book- and reading-related only.
- Advertisements for products or services are not permitted. Halifax Public Libraries is not responsible for the content of any messages posted to the list. Book club members are solely responsible for the content of their messages
- In addition to our Online Book Club, several Halifax Public Library branches offer in-house monthly book discussion groups. For more information check out our program information online. Pick up one of our Library Guides or phone your local branch.

You can see a Halifax Library System Online Book Group announcement for prospective members in Figure 8–4.

Figure 8–4   Recruitment Ad: Halifax Public Libraries Online Book Club, Halifax, Nova Scotia, Canada

---

Join our Online Book Club

Join the Halifax Public Libraries Online Book Club. It's a great place to "get together" with other readers and share opinions about your favourite books, authors, and genres without ever leaving the comfort of your home!

The only requirements for this online discussion group are that you love to read and you have a valid e-mail address. Once you join, you can choose to participate in the discussion as little or as much as you like. You will receive a copy of every e-mail message posted to the group in your e-mail box for as long as you wish to subscribe.

Our list is librarian-moderated, and although we will post discussion titles and suggestions for topics from time to time, you may feel free to join in only when a title you are interested in is being discussed, or you want to recommend to others a book that you are reading.

How the Online Book Club works: A monthly topic or titles for discussion with a brief description of all titles recommended will be posted. Postings will occur several months in advance, so you will have plenty of time to place a hold on the books through the library's online catalog and read them in time for the discussion. You can read the titles we suggest or recommend others that you would like to share with other book club members. Discussion on the recommended titles will begin at the first of every month. Once in a while our moderator will post messages about book-related library events and activities. That's all there is to it!! So start reading and have fun!!

OUTSOURCING YOUR ONLINE BOOK GROUP

Many public libraries in the United States and Canada who wish to outsource their online book groups and readers advisory services are using a resource called DearReader.com (http://www.dearreader.com). The service works like this. Each day, Monday through Friday, readers are e-mailed chapters from a popular book, starting with the first chapter. Each chapter is broken into segments that take about five minutes to read. By Friday, after the readers have had a chance to read two to three chapters, they learn the name of the *next* book that will be featured the following Monday. In the meantime, if readers want to read the entire book that has just been sampled, they have the option of clicking on a link that reserves a hard copy of the book to be picked up at the local library. Readers can choose to receive books in up to eleven different genres including fiction, nonfiction, mysteries, science fiction, romance, teen reading, audio books, and business. They can even check out the first two or three chapters of books about to be released—a genre known as "pre-pub." There is also a category known as "good news," a book club of optimistic books that can be shared with the whole family, from children to seniors.

One advantage of DearReader.com is that it is a "turnkey" system. In other words, the company supplies all content, updates, book permission rights, mailing lists, and e-mail communications with readers. Libraries are informed eight weeks in advance of the books that are going to be featured, and as mentioned before, they can choose books in up to eleven different genres. In addition, each chapter is preceded by a brief daily column written by company founder Suzanne Beecher, and readers can communicate directly with Beecher and her staff about current and future selections. Currently Beecher says that her company receives about five hundred reader e-mails per day. All messages are answered the same day, and libraries can request copies of e-mail comments and inquiries sent by their patrons. DearReader.com also offers a Book Forum discussion board section where readers can post and share their opinions with others across the country.

Finally, DearReader.com has recently introduced services to help libraries with the online promotion and discussion component of their One Book One City programs. All of the content is provided and developed by the DearReader company. But your readers may not make that distinction, since they can register for the free service directly from your own library's Web site. Membership in the club is free, and participants do not have to be library card holders. Patrons can also participate using the free Internet and e-mail access at the library. According to DearReader.com founder Suzanne Beecher, over three thousand public libraries across the United States participate.

While the service is generally offered free to library users, the libraries themselves do have to pay for it. Library subscription fees are set according to the size of the library system, the number of branches, and the number of potential users. But libraries should be prepared to pay a minimum of $350 per year, with rates of several thousand dollars per year for larger branches or library systems. Often library foundations and local businesses pay for the subscription.

Sharon McGlinn, the adult and Web services librarian of Hennepin County, reports that the library has two thousand members participating in the various DearReader clubs, quite a contrast from the four hundred who have signed up with the library's in-house online club. However, McGlinn states, "We've never considered DearReader and our Readers Online groups to be comparable. We don't promote DearReader as a book club—instead we call it Books In Your E-mail."

OTHER GOOD ONLINE BOOK DISCUSSION GROUP SITES

As online book discussion groups become more popular, chances are your readers will turn to you for advice about the best groups for them. Most online discussion groups, to date, are not run by libraries, and they vary widely in quality. I have yet to find a comprehensive directory of them all, and compiling one would be tough because groups are constantly starting up and shutting down. Here are two relatively long-standing book discussion "portals" that are worth checking out and recommending:

- **Seniornet (discussions.seniornet.org).** The Seniornet group began in September 1996, with one book discussion and a small but enthusiastic corps of readers. Today the group, which is geared to seniors but welcomes people of all ages, has participants from all over the world, who join in more than thirty-five different book discussions. Some discussions of individual books continue for months or more. In addition, there are ongoing general discussions of books of particular interest, such as "Mysteries" and "Nonfiction." The site has a corps of volunteers who work together to make discussions run smoothly, either by leading discussions or providing technical support. Chatting is free, but there are also options for different levels of membership.
- **Readerville (www.readerville.com).** It costs eight dollars per month to subscribe to the readers forum section of this Web site which contains author interviews, book publishing news, gossip, random thoughts, and a soon-to-come link to author tours and appearances. The site is administered by a group of private investors in Napa Valley, California, but it is very loosely managed.
- **The Online Book Page.** Last but not least, your readers may ask where they can get the full text of books online. The Online Books Page (onlinebooks.library.upenn.edu), maintained at the University of Pennsylvania, is essentially a directory of online books that are freely available on the Internet. It includes more than fourteen thousand listings that can be searched by author or title, or browsed by Library of Congress call number category. Special online exhibits include "Banned Books Online" and "A Celebration of Women Writers." There is an archive of

foreign language sites and titles by subject category; there are more than twenty-five thousand songs and some online serials as well.

REFERENCES

Balas, Janet L. "Reading Is 'In.'" *Computers in Libraries* (September 1, 2001) p. 64.

Hoffert, Barbara. "Taking Back Reader's Advisory: Online Book Talk, From Simple Lists to 24/7 Live Chat Gives Librarians A New Way To Promote Reading." *Library Journal* vol. 128, no. 14 (September 2003) p. 44.

Kenney, Brian, and Michael Stephens. "Talkin' Blogs—LJ Round Table." *Library Journal* (October 1, 2005) p. 40.

McDermott, Irene E. "The Passion of the Blog." *Searcher Internet Express Column* (April 1, 2005) p. 8.

Minkel, Walter. "Time To Join the Club: Where Are All the Electronic Book Discussion Groups?" *School Library Journal* (July 1, 2003). Available at www.schoollibraryjournal.com/article/CA306223.html.

Reilly, Rob. "Building an Online Readers Advisory and Getting Good Reads (The Networks)." *Multimedia Schools* (September 1, 2003) p. 61.

Smokler, Kevin, ed. *Bookmark Now: Writing in Unreaderly Times.* New York: Basic Books, 2005.

Part III

Ten Guaranteed Crowd-Pleasing Book Discussions

OVERVIEW

SO MANY BOOKS . . . SO LITTLE TIME

Let's start with the obvious but often overlooked: In order to lead a book group, you have to take some time to read the book. That's why some group leaders only choose books that they have *already* read. But that doesn't work for the new best-sellers, and you'll want to refresh your memory if you are covering a classic. So when you start to allocate time to lead a discussion, save time for the reading, as well as for publicizing the meeting, developing the questions, and holding the group itself.

What follows is a year of ready-made book talks especially suited for public libraries. Our goal is to save you some time so that you can spend more of your time actually reading the books! We've included reader questions and suggestions for supporting materials, including props, tapes and videos, as well as follow-up activities. We offer ten books instead of twelve, since many groups do not meet in the summer months or over the winter holidays. But if you want to do a holiday program, we have some suggestions for that, too. In fact, overall, we have tried to select different themes to match different seasons. Even if you decide not to use any of these books, take a look at how the questions and materials are organized. They may inspire you when you create your own.

SEPTEMBER

Travels with Charley: In Search of America

BY JOHN STEINBECK

SUMMARY

On September 23, 1960, author John Steinbeck, then fifty-eight years old, began a road trip across America, accompanied by his large black poodle, Charley. They traveled in a camper truck that Steinbeck named Rosinante, after Don Quixote's horse. John and Charley left from Maine and traveled west across the northern border states, and then south down the California coast to Steinbeck's hometown of Salinas. They then went to Amarillo, Texas, to join Steinbeck's wife, Elaine, and her relatives for Thanksgiving. After the Thanksgiving feast, Steinbeck started his trip back home to Sag Harbor, New York. But first, he stopped in a racially tense New Orleans to witness the city's first attempts at school desegregation. As he traveled America's superhighways and back roads, Steinbeck commented on the weather, the geography, the food, the customs, beliefs, and dialects of the people he met, offering a portrait of America and Americans in the early sixties.

AUTHOR BIOGRAPHY

John Steinbeck (1902–1968) was born in the agricultural valley of Salinas, California, a town which is featured in many of his works, most notably *East of Eden* (1952), a fictional, semiauto-biographical family history. In 1919, he went to Stanford University, where he took some literature and writing courses, but he dropped out without getting a degree. He returned to his hometown of Salinas and began spending more time in the Pacific coast town of Monterey just twenty-five miles away. There he developed a lifelong interest in the natural environment and the ocean which are both reflected in his novels and nonfiction work including the novel *Cannery Row* (1945*)* and his nonfiction, *The Sea of Cortez* (1941), a journal that he kept with his friend, marine biologist Ed Ricketts.

Steinbeck first rose to national prominence with his novel *The Grapes of Wrath (1939)*, inspired by his magazine reporting about the struggles of 1930s migrant farmworkers in the California Central Valley. He won a Pulitzer Prize for *The Grapes of Wrath* and won the Nobel Prize for Literature in 1962, the same year that *Travels with Charley* was published. By that time, he was spending most of his time in New York City and Sag Harbor, Long Island. When he began his cross-country trip, he was recovering from a stroke and considering his own mortality. At first his wife tried to talk him out of taking the trip, but fortunately, they reached a compromise and Steinbeck commissioned the camper that he traveled in. *Travels with Charley* received positive reviews and sold well. Steinbeck died six years after the book was published. For more information see the Steinbeck entry in Gale's *Contemporary Authors*.

WHY THIS BOOK IS A GOOD CHOICE FOR A BOOK DISCUSSION GROUP

Travels with Charley is an American travel memoir that different generations can enjoy together. In 2005, it was the selection for a program called "Long Island Reads" organized by libraries in New York State's Nassau and Suffolk counties. There, librarians planned a series of dramatizations, book discussions, and field trips centered on *Travels with Charley*. The Long Island Reads committee announced their choice on their Web site, saying, "the book is a highly readable, accessible work of nonfiction (that) has a strong sense of America and deals with issues that are still relevant today." The Long Island librarians pointed out the local connection to the book—Steinbeck had begun and ended his trip in Sag Harbor, Long Island, where he had a home for the last two decades of his life. Librarians and readers even took a field trip to Sag Harbor so that readers could see Steinbeck's old haunts.

Given that Steinbeck covered 38 states on his ten-thousand-mile journey, librarians across America may be able to find their own local connection to the book. Many readers may also have memories of traveling across the United States—or at least a few of the same states that Steinbeck visited. If they brought along the family dog, so much the better! Book group members in their sixties and seventies will well remember what American life was like in 1960, while younger members can do a "then and now" comparison.

Steinbeck began his trip in September—a time when the weather was milder across the United States. This gives you a chance to dramatically open your discussion by saying, for example, "Forty-seven years ago this month, John Steinbeck took off with his poodle, Charley, on a road trip across America." (If you wait until 2010, you can do a 50th anniversary event!) Finally, as patrons settle back into their fall routines, this travelogue extends their summer vacation a bit, at least vicariously. Also at 214 pages in paperback, this is a quick read, which will be appreciated by all involved in the back-to-school rush.

HOW TO GET THIS BOOK

This book has been published continuously since 1962 and is available in a lot of different formats, including paperback, audio, and as a Library of Congress Talking Book for those with visual disabilities. If you are part of a larger library cooperative, you may be able to roundup enough copies through interlibrary loan. If you are going to buy copies, try the Penguin Books John Steinbeck Centennial Edition paperback (ISBN 0142000701). It contains a four-page originally proposed ending for the book which was omitted from previous publications. Or you can try the less expensive Penguin Books paperback version (ISBN 0140053204).

MATERIALS TO SUPPORT YOUR DISCUSSION

- A wall-size map of the United States to be used to trace Steinbeck's journey
- A book cart or display of other Steinbeck books and biographies of the author
- A book cart or display of other fiction or nonfiction "road trip" books. The NoveList discussion of *Travels with Charley* recommends the following travel memoirs: Jack

Kerouac's *On the Road* (1957), William Least Heat Moon's *Blue Highways* (1982), and Ernesto Che Guevara's *The Motorcycle Diaries* (1995 edition). But you can go back further in time with Cervantes' *Don Quixote de la Mancha*. And for readers interested in following up with some women on the road, you can include *The Last Secrets of the Silk Road: In the Footsteps of Marco Polo by Horse and Camel* by Countess Alexandra Tolstoy (2003) or the collection of short stories *Drive: Women's True Stories from the Open Road* edited by Jennie Goode (2002).

- Highbridge Audio's audiocassette of *Travels with Charley* narrated by Gary Sinise; (ISBN 0453008976). The narration is excellent and Sinise is able to convey Steinbeck's humor. Pick a five-minute section of the tape and play it for the group. One especially fun section to listen to is the part where Charley and Steinbeck encounter a vagabond Shakespearean actor in North Dakota.
- The Arts & Entertainment *Biography* series videocassette "John Steinbeck: An American Writer" (ISBN 0767017633). The biography does not focus on *Travels with Charley*, but instead focuses on Steinbeck's life. However, there are interviews with the author's third wife, Elaine, who is featured in the book.
- If you really have time, show off the reference capabilities of your library by including some books, sections of books, or articles on safe travel with pets.
- The Web site of the National Steinbeck Center in Salinas, California (www.steinbeck.org), which includes a picture of the camper, Rocinante.

Icebreaker: Ask all members of the group one by one: Have you ever taken a cross-country or multistate road trip? If so, where did you go, who did you go with, and how did you travel? Did you take a pet? If you've never been on a road trip, would you like to take one? Why or why not—and if yes, where would you want to go?

DISCUSSION QUESTIONS

1. In the first chapter, Steinbeck writes the following:

"Could it be that Americans are a restless people, a mobile people, never satisfied with where they are as a matter of selection? The pioneers, the immigrants who people the continent, were the restless ones in Europe. The steady rooted ones stayed home and are still there."

What is your reaction to this statement? Do you think that in this day and age, Americans are still a restless people? Or have we settled down more? Where are today's pioneers headed?

2. Steinbeck made his observations about American life in 1960. Let's take a look at a few of them and talk about whether they still hold true today. In some cases he made predictions. Were his predictions correct? Why or why not?

Here's what he said about American speech:

> One of my purposes was to listen, to hear speech, accent, speech rhythms, overtones and emphasis. For speech is so much more than words and sentences. I did listen everywhere. It seemed to me that regional speech is in the process of disappearing, not gone but going. Forty years of radio and twenty years of television must have this impact. Communications must destroy localness, by a slow, inevitable process . . . with local accent will disappear local tempo. The idioms, the figures of speech that make language rich and full of poetry of place and time must go. And in their place will be a national speech, wrapped and packaged, standard and tasteless.

Here's what he said about "junk" vs. "antiques":

> If I were a good businessman . . . I would gather all the junk and the wrecked automobiles and spray (them) with that stuff that the Navy uses to mothball ships. If the battered, cracked stuff and broken stuff our ancestors tried to get rid of now brings so much money, think what a 1954 Oldsmobile, or a 1960 toastmaster will bring— and a vintage Waring Mixer. . . . Things we have to pay to have hauled away could bring fortunes.

Here's what he said about road food:

> The restaurant accommodations, great scallops of counters with simulated leather stools, are as spotless as and not unlike the lavatories. Everything that can be captured and held down is sealed in clear plastic. The food is oven-fresh, spotless and tasteless; untouched by human hands. I remembered with an ache certain dishes in France and Italy touched by innumerable human hands.

3. Why do you think that Steinbeck got lost so often? How does his willingness to take chances and his reluctance to consult maps make for a more or less interesting read?

4. In August 1962, the year that the book was first published, a review by Edward Weeks in the *Atlantic Monthly* stated that in Steinbeck's passage of over 10,000 miles through thirty-eight states he was not recognized even once. Why do you think that no one recognized him? Do you think that was deliberate on Steinbeck's part? Do you think that a Nobel Prize–winning author who set out on the road today could travel unrecognized? (Note: You can get more 1962 reviews from *Book Review Digest* of that year.)

5. Throughout his trip Steinbeck benefits from the unexpected kindness and hospitality of strangers. He even suggests that this might be part of the American character. Do you think that this still holds true today? Or do you think that Americans were kinder a half-century ago?

6. As a witness to racial discrimination in New Orleans in 1960, where black children were harassed entering a previously all-white elementary school, Steinbeck writes, "I knew that I was not wanted in the South. When people engage in something they are not proud of, they do not welcome witnesses. In fact, they come to believe that the witness causes the trouble." Can you think of other examples, either in your own life or in America's political life, where this statement holds true?

7. Many travel memoirs are written by far younger men. Jack Kerouac comes to mind in *On the Road.* And even the more contemporary buddies in the book (turned popular movie) *Sideways* by Rex Pickett (2004) are in their thirties. But Steinbeck was fifty-eight years old and ailing when he wrote this book. How does that enhance or detract from the narrative?

8. What role does Charley play in this book? Do you think that he is an active or passive character? Tell us why? Do you think that he has his own personality or that Steinbeck is projecting a personality on to him?

9. Were you surprised by what happened when Charley sees the bears in Yellowstone Park? If you have a dog, is your relationship similar or different and why?

10. In the last chapter, Steinbeck writes, "My own journey started long before I left, and was over before I returned. . . . The reverse is also true, many a trip continues long after movement in time and space have ceased." What do you think he means by this? Can you recall your emotions when planning or returning from a trip?

OCTOBER

In Cold Blood: A True Account of a Multiple Murder and Its Consequences

BY TRUMAN CAPOTE

SUMMARY

On the Saturday night/early Sunday morning of November 15, 1959, intruders broke into the farmhouse of a wheat and cattle ranch in Holcomb, Kansas. They tied up the landowners, 48-year-old Herbert William Clutter, his 45-year-old wife, Bonnie, and their two youngest children, 15-year-old Kenyon and 16-year-old Nancy. Each was shot at close range by a rifle and their bodies were found in separate parts of the house by their neighbors, who became suspicious when the Clutters were late for church. Herbert Clutter's throat was slit before he was shot.

When the police investigators arrived the next morning, they could not determine a motive for the crime. About forty dollars in cash and a radio were missing but there were very few clues. The investigation was at a dead end until an unexpected tip from a prison inmate identified one of the killers. They were caught and convicted fairly quickly. But it was not until April 1965 that Richard Hickock and Perry Edward Smith—two drifters in their thirties with past criminal records—were hanged at Kansas State Penitentiary. *In Cold Blood*, written over a period of six years, details the crime and its aftermath and focuses on the personalities of the killers and their families, the victims, the investigators, and the townspeople of Holcomb.

AUTHOR BIOGRAPHY

Truman Streckfus Persons (1924–1984) was born in New Orleans, the son of Arculus Persons, a salesman and steamboat purser originally from Alabama. His mother, the former Lillie Mae Faulk, had been an Alabama beauty queen. Truman had an unstable home life with a father who struggled to make a living and a mother who was uninterested in raising a small child. As a result, he was sent back to Alabama to be raised by his mother's relatives in the small town of Monroeville. Many of Capote's early works were based on his childhood experiences. His best friend in Monroeville was the girl next door, Nelle Harper Lee, who grew up to write the Pulitzer Prize–winning novel *To Kill a Mockingbird*. She also traveled with Capote to Kansas to serve as his research and interviewing assistant on *In Cold Blood*.

In his teenage years, Truman's mother and father divorced and Lillie Mae moved to New York City with her new husband, Joe Capote. Truman moved there with them and took his stepfather's last name. He was a precocious student and was sent to several private schools but ultimately did not finish high school. When he was seventeen, he took a job as a researcher at *The New Yorker* magazine but it took him several years to establish himself as a writer. At 23, after having been published in magazines other than *The New Yorker* he wrote his first novel for Random House called *Other Voices, Other Rooms,* the story of a young New Orleans man sent to live with his mysterious father in rural Alabama.

By the age of thirty-five Capote was an established novelist and short story writer with eight major published works behind him, including the novella *Breakfast at Tiffany's*. Around this time he read a *New York Times* article about a chilling crime in rural Kansas. In a 1966 interview that appeared in the *New York Times Book Review* after *In Cold Blood* was published, Capote tells his colleague George Plimpton what happened next:

> After reading the story it suddenly struck me that a crime, the study of one such, might provide the broad scope I needed to write the kind of book I wanted to write. Moreover, the human heart being what it is, murder was a theme not likely to darken and yellow with time.
>
> I thought about it all that November day, and part of the next; and then I said to myself: Well, why not this crime? The Clutter case. Why not pack up and go to Kansas and see what happens? Of course it was a rather frightening thought—to arrive alone in a small, strange

town, a town in the grip of an unsolved mass murder. Still, the circumstances of the place being altogether unfamiliar, geographically and atmospherically, made it that much more tempting. Everything would seem freshly minted—the people, their accents and attitudes, the landscape, its contours, the weather. All this, it seemed to me, could only sharpen my eye and quicken my ear.

In the end, I did not go alone. I went with a lifelong friend, Harper Lee. She is a gifted woman, courageous, and with a warmth that instantly kindles most people, however suspicious or dour. She had recently completed a first novel (*To Kill a Mockingbird*), and, feeling at loose ends, she said she would accompany me in the role of assistant researchist. (Plimpton 1966)

Over the next six years, Capote "stayed on the story," writing a work which opened up a new literary form which he called the *nonfiction novel* and that others went on to call narrative nonfiction or "the new journalism." (Plimpton 1966)

Capote visited with and corresponded with the killers while they were on death row, forming a particularly close bond with Perry Smith. According to the Internet Movie Database, Capote was present at the executions and witnessed the carrying out of Hickock's sentence, but couldn't bear to watch Smith die, and left the room before he was brought in. Smith left most of his meager belongings, including books and drawings, to Capote (see http://www.imdb.com/title/tt0061809/trivia). *In Cold Blood* was serialized in four consecutive 1965 issues of *The New Yorker* prior to its publication as a book. Capote's long-sought-after celebrity status rose after the publication of *In Cold Blood*. In fact, in 1966, he made headlines not only for the book, but for a much-publicized masked ball that he held at the Plaza Hotel for five hundred of his "very closest friends."

In the last decades of his life, Capote began a biographical novel called *Answered Prayers*. Although he never finished the book, three stories from the novel appeared in *Esquire Magazine* in the 1970s and the unfinished book was published in 1986. Early reviews dismissed much of the writing as gossip and several of Capote's longtime socialite friends who were featured in the stories ended their friendships. *Music for Chameleons* (1981) was a collection of short pieces, stories, interviews, and conversations published in various magazines. Capote, who began drinking heavily, died in Los Angeles on August 26, 1984, of liver disease complicated by phlebitis and drug abuse at the home of Joanna Carson, ex-wife of the late talk-show host Johnny Carson.

WHY THIS BOOK IS A GOOD CHOICE FOR A BOOK DISCUSSION GROUP

The murders in this true crime story took place in the autumn under a full moon shining over a Kansas ranch. To be precise, the crimes took place in the month of November. However the setting and the frightening nature of the story make it a fitting read for Halloween. Posters for a book talk of *In Cold Blood* would certainly fit in with the Halloween theme and could be a centerpiece for a display of mystery/suspense/true crime books. If your library is in a small town or a rural town, there might be some discussion of "could it happen here today or might it have happened here in 1959." If your library is in a larger urban area, there might be more discussion of the randomness of certain violent acts.

Given that there were two teenagers in the Clutter family and that the impact of the murders on their young friends is described in detail, this book should be of interest to young adults. Adult readers may be especially interested in the family relationships that the killers had—especially the parent/child interactions. There are a lot of political issues to discuss here, too, since the issue of capital punishment is as controversial in America today as it was in 1965. Readers may wish to discuss whether this book altered their views in any way.

Finally, this book broke ground in a new field of writing which some call literary journalism or narrative nonfiction and which Capote himself termed the *nonfiction novel*. Group members may wish to analyze this style and talk about other books like it. They may also want to discuss whether they prefer to learn about current events through newspaper and television accounts, through books like this, or through a combination of media. As the library leader, you may wish to recommend some other examples of true crime nonfiction novels inspired by Capote's work. One good example is Norman Mailer's *The Executioner's Song,* which won the Pulitzer Prize in 1980. This book tells the tale of convicted Utah murderer Gary Gilmore, who made headlines when he fought to undergo the death penalty. Another true crime narrative now popular with book groups is *The Devil in the White City: Murder, Magic and Madness at the Fair that Changed America* by Erik Larson. This is a novelized, yet factua,l account of a serial murderer who ran amock at the Chicago World's Fair of 1893.

HOW TO GET THIS BOOK:

In Cold Blood, originally published by Random House in 1965, is available in hardcover, paperback, audiocassette (Books on Tape, ISBN 5557104739), and large print (G.K. Hall, 1993, c1965, ISBN 0816156646). It has also been translated into many different languages including Spanish (*A Sangre Fria*) and Japanese. People who are visually impaired can order the book through the Library of Congress's National Library Service (NLS) for the Blind and Physically Handicapped. If your library or library system does not already have copies, you may wish to purchase the Random House Vintage Books paperback edition (ISBN 0679745580).

MATERIALS TO SUPPORT YOUR PRESENTATION

- The movie version of *In Cold Blood* was released in 1967. Many audiences were surprised to see that it was filmed in black and white in film noir style. The screenplay stayed true to the book, although there was more focus on the pursuit of the killers, their trial, and execution and less on the Clutter family. According to the Internet Movie Database, the director Richard Brooks filmed in all the actual locations including the Clutter house (where the murders took place) and the actual Finney County courtroom in Garden City (six of the actual jurors were used). Even Nancy Clutter's horse, Babe, was used in a few scenes. The actual gallows at the Kansas State Penitentiary were used for filming the executions. The family photos seen in the rooms of the house are real photos of the Clutter family members. While the scenes of the actual murders are frightening, they are not gory or graphic but rather, as in Hitchcock style, more is left to your imagination. You might want to show a few parts of the film to give readers an idea of what the Kansas landscape and Clutter home looked like. Or you can run a book and film discussion on one or two evenings as was done by the Guilderland Public Library near Albany, New York. The DVD version of *In Cold Blood* is available from Columbia TriStar Home Entertainment, (ISBN: 0767871286). Dialogue is in English with optional soundtrack in French, and with optional subtitles in English, French, Spanish, Portuguese, Chinese, Korean and Thai; closed-captioning is available. The audiocassette (VHS) version of the film was released by Columbia/Tristar Studios on April 21, 1998 ASIN: 0800113268

In 2005, the film *Capote* was released by Sony Pictures starring Phillip Seymour Hoffman as Truman Capote and Catherine Keener as Nelle Harper Lee. The film was a fictionalized account of how Truman Capote came to write the book *In Cold Blood* and focused on his relationship with the convicted Clutter family murderers. As of late 2005 this film was not yet available on DVD.

- **The *Life* magazine story** The cover photo of the May 12, 1967, issue of *Life* magazine, taken in Kansas during the filming of *In Cold Blood*, shows Capote standing between actors Robert Blake, who played Perry Smith, and Scott Wilson, who played Dick Hickock. In 2005, the actor Blake was himself on trial and acquitted for the murder of his wife.
- **Truman Capote's correspondence**: In 2004, Truman Capote's authorized biographer Gerald Clarke (*Capote: A Biography*. New York: Simon and Schuster, 1988) released a collection of Capote's correspondence called *Too Brief a Treat*. (New York: Random House, 2004). In the section entitled "Four Murders and a Ball in Black and White," Clarke includes Capote's letters from the years 1959–1966, the time period during which he was writing *In Cold Blood*. Included here are Capote's letters to Perry Smith, and his correspondence with the Kansas detective in charge of the Clutter case, Alvin Dewey, and his wife, Marie.
- **Truman Capote interview by George Plimpton that appeared in the *New York Times Book Review* on January 16, 1966.** Entitled "The Story Behind a Nonfiction Novel," this interview with Capote was conducted by George Plimpton, then editor of the *Paris Review*. Plimpton, apparently inspired by Capote, also became well known for his narrative nonfiction articles. The entire interview deals with *In Cold Blood* and with Capote's creation of what Plimpton calls "a new literary art form." This interview is long (22 psges printed from the *New York Times Books Review* Web site), but you might want

to read it online before the discussion or at least scan it for interesting quotes. You can also refer readers to it for further study after your discussion.

- **Coverage of the crime from your hometown newspaper.** While this story begins and ends in Kansas, Dick Hickock and Perry Smith traveled cross-country to avoid being caught. As a result there are side trips to Las Vegas, and Miami, as well as rides through Nebraska and Iowa. If your library has newspaper records going back to the 1960s, it might be interesting to see how your community journalists covered the crime and how local people reacted to it.

DISCUSSION QUESTIONS

1. In a 1966 interview, Capote states that the first step in producing a nonfiction novel is to choose a promising subject that will hold readers' interest over the years. "If you intend to spend three or four or five years with a book . . . then you want to be reasonably certain that the material does not date," he said. (Plimpton 1966) As you read this book today, do you think that he succeeded? Why or why not?

2. In Part I of the book, entitled "The Last to See Them Alive," Capote recounts the last day on earth of the Clutter family. He brings them to life and re-creates their dialogue without ever having met any of them. What techniques does he use to do this?

3. Even today, tourists drive up the road of the Clutter farmhouse to see the site of the murders. Based on the descriptions in this book, did you admire the Clutter family? Which character or characters (if any) did you most identify with and why?

4. We learn little about the two surviving Clutter daughters—one married, the other away at college when the murders happened. Why do you think Capote chose not to tell more about them?

5. In prison, Perry Smith befriends two convicts—his ultimate partner in crime, the boastful Dick Hickock, and the thoughtful chaplain's clerk Willie-Jay. A few months after Perry is released from prison he takes a bus to Kansas hoping to meet one or the other. Do you think that Perry would have rejected Dick's offer to rob the Clutters if he had met with Willie Jay first? Why or why not?

Ice breaker: What, if anything, did you know about the Clutter case before you read the book? If you were unfamiliar with it, did you have any ideas about who might have done it before you learned the identity of the killers? For example, did you, like many of the townspeople, think that it was someone from the community or were you convinced that it was an outsider?

6. Describe the relationship between Dick and Perry. Do you think either of them would have been able to commit murder alone or that they needed to work as a team?

7. Did reading this book change your opinion of the death penalty? Why or why not? What do you think Capote's views are?

8. Many characters in this book recount their dreams/nightmares. Perry Smith often dreams of a yellow parrot that can rescue him and Inspector Dewey has a nightmare in which he sees the killers in a local café, but they jump through a plate glass window before he can catch them. How does the retelling of these dreams enhance or detract from the story? What do you think the yellow parrot symbolizes to Perry?

9. Capote himself never appears in the book. Why do or don't you think that this was an effective technique?

10. What effect did the investigation and trial have on Kansas Bureau of Investigation agent Alvin Dewey? What role does his character play in the book?

11. What did you think of the book's final scene in which Dewey meets up with Nancy Clutter's friend Sue Kidwell at Valley View Cemetery?

12. Thomas Dukes, an associate professor of English at the University of Akron, Ohio, says that the openly gay Capote established a writing style in both his fiction and nonfiction works that was both "closeted, in that it seldom dealt with overt homosexuality, and uncloseted, because its code for homosexual interpretations was so easily seen through." Do you agree with this analysis as it applies to *In Cold Blood*? Why or why not?

Source: http://www.glbtq.com/literature/capote_t.html (the Encyclopedia of Gay, Lesbians, Bisexual, Transgender and Queer Culture)

13. There are a lot of memorable quotes in this book. Describe your reaction to the following:

First line: The village of Holcomb stands on the high wheat plains of western Kansas, a lonesome area that other Kansans call "out there."

"Take ye heed, watch and pray, for ye know not when the time is"— passage on the silk bookmark in the Bible next to Bonnie Clutter's bed.

"By the way, do you know what tomorrow is? Nancy Clutter's birthday. She would have been seventeen"—Inspector Dewey as he ended a police interrogation with Smith.

Perry Smith: "I didn't want to harm the man. I thought he was a very nice gentleman. Soft-spoken. I thought so right up to the moment I cut his throat."

Dick Hickcock: "Well, what's there to say about capital punishment? I'm not against it. Revenge is all it is, but what's wrong with revenge? It's very important"

REFERENCES

Clarke, Gerald. *Capote: A Biography.* New York: Random House, 2004.

Dukes, Thomas. "Truman Capote." *An Encyclopedia of Gay, Lesbian, Bisexual, Transgender, and Queer Culture.* Chicago, Ill.: Glbtq., Inc. 2002. Available www.glbtq.com.com/literature/capote_t.html

Life magazine. May 12, 1967.

Plimpton, George. "The Story Behind a Nonfiction Novel" *The New York Times Book Review*, (January 16, 1966). www.nytimes.com/books/97/12/28/home/capote-interview.html.

"Truman Capote is Dead at 59; Novelist of Style and Clarity" *New York Times*, Obituary Section August 28, 1984.

NOVEMBER

The Namesake

BY JHUMPA LAHIRI

SUMMARY

The main character in this novel is Gogul Ganguli, the American-born son of parents who have recently emigrated from Calcutta, India, to Cambridge, Massachusetts. The story opens in 1968 when Gogol's father, Ashoke, begins a doctoral program in electrical engineering at the Massachusetts Institute of Technology (MIT). Ashoke is looking forward to a new life and career, but his wife, Ashima, has trouble adjusting. while she is pregnant with Gogol and will become a new mother without the help and support of the family that she left behind in India. She is also still getting to know her new husband Ashoke. Their marriage was arranged in India shortly before they left for the United States.

Ashoke does well in America and becomes a professor. He and his wife have a second child, Sonia, and move from Cambridge to a more distant Massachusetts suburb. Gogol grows up being part of both the Indian and American communities, but never feels completely connected to either one. He attends American high school and studies architecture at Yale and Columbia universities, legally changing his name to Nikhil along the way. His American and Indian worlds often collide, as seen when he brings an American girlfriend home to meet his parents for lunch or when he attends Indian celebrations of American holidays.

The surname Gogol is an unusual name for an Indian child. This becomes one of the major themes of the book, as well as the rationale for the book's title. Ashoke chooses the name Gogol for his son, in part because he admires the Russian author, Nikolai Gogol. Gogol learns as a teenager that the name was intended to be his nickname rather than his formal Bengali name, but the nickname sticks when a missive containing the formal name fails to arrive from his maternal grandmother in India.

The following passage from *Gale's Contemporary Authors Online* describes the themes of the book:

> *The Namesake* deals with identity, the importance of names and the effect the immigrant experience has on

family ties . . . While Gogol's parents followed the conventions of an arranged marriage, their son does not hold his family's cultural heritage in that high a regard, and wants more than his parents seem to have. Gogol's inner turmoil is also reflected in his unsuccessful romantic relationships. It is not until Lahiri's dissatisfied young protagonist comes to understand who his parents are that things begin to come together for him. (Gale's 2004)

AUTHOR BIOGRAPHY

Jhumpa Lahiri was thirty-two years old when she won the 2000 Pulitzer Prize for fiction for her first book, a short story collection called *Interpreter of Maladies,* published in 1999. The anthology focused on East Indian culture and domestic life, both in the United States and in India. *The Namesake,* published in 2003, is her first novel. Lahiri was born in London in 1967 to Bengali parents. The family moved to Kingstown, Rhode Island, when she was three years old. Her father, Amar, was a librarian at the University of Rhode Island and her mother, Tia, a teacher's aide at a Rhode Island elementary school.

A profile in the "Meet the Authors" section of the Barnes & Noble Web site states, "Like the rest of her family, Lahiri has a (private) 'pet name' and a (public) 'good name.' When she started school, her teachers decided that Jhumpa, her pet name, was the easier one to pronounce, and she has been called that in public ever since, something many of her relatives find odd." After graduating from South Kingstown High School, Lahiri went on to Barnard College, where she earned her Bachelor of Arts degree in English literature. She continued her studies at Boston University where she received three Masters of Arts degrees, one in creative writing, one in comparative studies, and one in literature and the arts. She also obtained her doctorate in Renaissance studies at Boston University. In her first jobs, Lahiri taught creative writing at Boston University and the Rhode Island School of Design. She also had an internship as a copywriter for *Boston Magazine.* In January 2001 Lahiri married American-born journalist Alberto Vourvoulias in a traditional Hindu ceremony at Singhi Palace in a suburb of Calcutta. Her husband is a former editor with Time Latin America and a Guatemalan-born American of Greek origin. Their son Octavio has learned to speak English, Bengali and Spanish.

Many of the themes and storylines in *The Namesake* were inspired by the author's own life or the lives of people she knows. For example, in 2003, Lahiri told a *Newsweek* interviewer about her father's cousin who, like Ashoke, was in a train wreck in India and had almost been given up for dead until a rescuer spotted something—perhaps, Lahiri speculated, sunlight glinting off his watch. This episode "captured Lahiri's imagination: what happens to a person whose very life depends on a random act?" (Kantrowitz 2003)

Part of the action in *The Namesake* take place in Calcutta as Gogol's family goes back to visit for weeks at a time. Lahiri told *Newsweek* that her descriptions of these visits were inspired by her own childhood trips back to India. There, surrounded by a vast extended family, she says that she got to see her parents in a setting where they were not foreigners and could just be themselves. She admits that she was never quite comfortable on those trips. "I've often felt," she says, "that I am somehow illegitimate in both cultures. A true Indian doesn't accept me as an Indian and a true American doesn't accept me as an American." She also notes that some reviewers in India gave the book bad reviews. These reviewers "were sensitive to the fact that the characters I wrote about were not very positive," she says, adding, "art is selective. Those were the characters and situations I felt I should write about." (Kantrowitz 2003)

WHY THIS BOOK IS A GOOD CHOICE FOR A BOOK DISCUSSION GROUP

Libraries and librarians are portrayed very positively in this book. Ashima takes Gogol to the public library for children's story hour and later as depicted in the following passage, enjoys spending time there when her son is at nursery school and her husband is at work:

> To avoid being alone at home she sits in the reading room of the public library, in a cracked leather armchair, writing letters to her mother, or reading magazines or one of her Bengali books from home. The room is cheerful, filled with light, with a tomato-colored carpet on the floor and people reading the paper around a big, round wooden table with forsythias or cattails arranged at its center. When she misses Gogol especially, she wanders into the children's room; there, pinned to a bulletin

board, is a picture of him in profile, sitting cross-legged on a cushion during story hour, listening to the children's librarian, Mrs. Aiken, reading *The Cat in the Hat.*

Later in the book, when Ashima is in her forties, she takes a part-time job at her local suburban Massachusetts library where her coworkers offer her advice on American family life and culture.

In a best case scenario for this particular book discussion, perhaps someone in your public library book group has come to the United States from another country and has joined your group to better connect with American life. Certainly, you will know library patrons who have done so even if they have not joined your book group. In the course of your book discussion, librarian leaders could take the opportunity to point out the services and resources that the library offers to new Americans including books that help people to prepare for citizenship tests and/or literary and language programs. If someone in your book group *is* from another country and *has* found the library to be helpful as a way to connect to American life, perhaps they would be willing to share some experiences. Even readers that have moved to your community from another town or state could offer an interesting perspective.

Many library patrons have had the experience of being newcomers and many do join public library book groups to feel a sense of connection to their new home. (Alternatively, people with long-standing community ties often join book clubs that meet at their friends' homes rather than the public library.) A discussion of *The Namesake* is a perfect opportunity to get some feedback on how the library has helped newcomers and explore what other services and resources might be needed. It is also a chance to promote services that members of your book club might not be aware of such as interlibrary loans with libraries that have books in other languages, or English as a Second Language (ESL) programs run at your library or elsewhere in the community. You might compile a book cart of materials aimed at American and international newcomers to your community.

This book is also a good choice for public libraries because it appeals to a wide range of ages. In her review of this book for *School Library Journal,* librarian Molly Connally, of Chantilly Regional Library in Virginia, writes, "This novel will attract not just teens of other cultures, but also readers struggling with the challenges of growing up and tugging at family ties." (Connally 2003) November is an appropriate month to discuss *The Namesake* because of the tie-in to the Thanksgiving holiday. There is a lot of discussion about how the Ganguli family adjusts to American holidays, and much of the plot in the book takes place each year between Thanksgiving and Christmas. Consider the following dilemmas that the family faces:

> Which was preferable, a live Christmas tree or an artificial one? They learn to roast turkeys, albeit rubbed with garlic and cumin and cayenne, at Thanksgiving, to nail a wreath to their door in December, to wrap woolen scarves around snow men, to color boiled eggs violet and pink at Easter and hide them around the house.

HOW TO GET THIS BOOK

Hardcover: Houghton Mifflin, 2003 (ISBN 0395927218)

Paperback: Mariner Books/Houghton Mifflin, 2004. (ISBN 0618485228)

Audiobook versions: Read by Sarita Choudhury. Books on Tape, 2003. CS, (ISBN 0736694269); CD, (ISBN 0736695303).

Spanish-language edition: *El Buen Nombre*. Planeta Publishing Corporation, 2004 (ISBN: 8495908778).

MATERIALS TO SUPPORT YOUR DISCUSSION

- Reader's Guide for *The Namesake* created by the publisher: Houghton Mifflin http://www.houghtonmifflin books.com/readers_guides/lahiri_namesake.shtml

  The guide includes ten discussion questions, an interview with the author, and suggestions for further reading. As of May 2005, the site also contained links and downloads to a twelve-minute "talking head" video of Lahiri reading from *The Namesake* and talking about how and why she wrote the book. Houghton Mifflin has also made free copies of the video available to book groups and public libraries upon request.

- A copy or copies of Russian writer Nikolai Gogol's classic short story "The Overcoat." If you do not have a collection of Gogol's works readily available, you might find this story in a Russian short story anthology or an international anthology.

Do you need to read the story in order to truly understand *The Namesake*? Here is what Jhumpa Lahiri said in an interview with *Publishers Weekly*:

PW: Would you advise someone to read Gogol's "The Overcoat" before or after reading your novel? Is there a key to your book in there somewhere?

JL: If you're moved to. I think it's an amazing story and anyone would be better for it. It's powerful and timeless. If the book does generate some new interest in Gogol, that would be great, a wonderful added consequence. I don't think the connection is as explicit. It's not like *The Hours*, where you should go back and read *Mrs. Dalloway*. It isn't such a strong presence, but it does inform the book in the same way (Nawotka 2003)

- A copy of "The Long Way Home," a personal essay about food and cooking that Jhumpa Lahiri published in *The New Yorker*, Sept. 6, 2004 v80 i25 p083 .

Here is an excerpt:

The first time I threw a dinner party, in a triple-decker in Somerville for my two housemates and two other friends, I prepared farfalle with olives, lemon rind, and sun-dried tomatoes, something that seemed quite exotic at the time. I did not make Indian food, not because I didn't like to eat it but because it remained my mother's territory. My new guides were Julia Child, Giuliano Bugialli, Marcella Hazan. My mother condescended toward Western cooking, which she believed was all either crudely boiled or baked. Some evenings, she'd call and ask what I was having for dinner. "Pasta," I'd tell her, in the process of making, say, a four-hour Bolognese. "Oh, pasta," she would reply, imagining me pouring Ragu from a jar over a plate of Ronzoni.

- A cart of materials that the library has to help new Americans and pamphlets and flyers advertising community programs. These could include guidebooks to citizenship, books, tapes and ESL programs and lists of community and social service organizations.
- Indian finger foods or snacks. Perhaps your library serves an Indian community or you have an adventurous cook in your book group. This is a chance to sample appetizers that can be eaten with fingers or toothpicks, such as

samosas or the spicy snack mix described at the opening of the book.

- A cart of materials about Indian culture and traditions. You might want to include a map of the country and some Indian cookbooks or Indian "Bollywood" films if you have some in your collection.

DISCUSSION QUESTIONS

1. In a video interview that Lahiri did for her publisher Houghton Mifflin, she says that when you grow up as the member of an immigrant family, "you have a private life with your family and a public life with the outside world." Do you think that this problem is faced just by immigrant families—or might it apply to kinds of families in the United States? Explain why.

2a. Did any members of your book group come to the United States from another country or have parents who did? Can you relate to the challenges that Gogol and his family members faced?

2b. What is your reaction to the following quote:
Being a foreigner, Ashima thinks "is a sort of lifelong pregnancy—a perpetual wait, a constant burden, a continuous feeling out of sorts. It is an ongoing responsibility, a parenthesis in what has once been ordinary life, only to discover that that previous life has vanished, replaced by something more complicated and demanding."

3. The following question comes from the Houghton Mifflin Guide:

> "When Gogol is born, the Gangulis meet other Bengali families with small children, and Ashima finds that with a new baby 'perfect strangers, all Americans, suddenly take notice of her, smiling, congratulating her for what she's done.' How, for all of us, do children change our place in the community, and what we expect from it? Have you ever connected with someone you may have otherwise never spoken to—of a different ethnic background or economic class—through his children or your own?"

4a. While, in general, *The Namesake* received glowing reviews, there were some criticisms. One review in *Publishers Weekly* noted:

Icebreakers: (All members of the group can answer these, one by one if they so choose.)

Identity icebreakers: In an interview with the Boston Herald, Lahiri said, *"Names speak as much about our parents as they do about us."* (Herbert 2003) Does your name reveal anything about your family history? How do you feel about the name that you were given? Have you changed it in some way or thought about changing it? Do you or did you have any nicknames?

Food icebreaker: The book opens with a very pregnant Ashima fixing herself a snack of Rice Krispies and Planters peanuts and chopped red onion in a bowl spiced with salt, lemon juice, and thin slices of chili pepper. She craves this as it is as close as she can get to a snack that she used to buy in newspaper cones from street vendors in Calcutta. Describe a food or snack from your childhood or hometown that you continue to turn to for comfort.

After the death of Gogol's father interrupts this interlude, Lahiri . . . jumps ahead a year, quickly moving Gogol into marriage, divorce and a role as a dutiful if a bit guilt-stricken son. This small summary demonstrates what is most flawed about the novel: jarring pacing that leaves too many emotional voids between chapters. (Nawotka 2003)

Do you agree with the reviewer? Why or why not?

4b. *New York Times* book reviewer Michiko Kakutani called the book "an intimate, closely observed family portrait," yet said "Ms. Lahiri's portraits of the women in Gogol's life are somewhat sketchy—Maxine and her parents, in particular, seem more like New York stereotypes than real individuals" (Kakutani 2003) Do you agree that the descriptions of the girlfriends are sketchy or superficial? Based on what *is* said about Maxine, do you think that Gogol gave her a fair chance? Do we fully understand why he broke off the relationship?

5. Were you surprised by Ashima's decision not to accompany Ashoke to his consulting assignment in Cleveland? Why or why not?

6. What did you think of Ashima and Ashoke's marriage? Do you think that they were happy together? Why or why not?

7. In what ways is Gogol like his father? In what ways is he different?

8. Gogol's parents socialize primarily with other Bengalis. But in Gogol's own brief marriage to an Indian woman, he and Moushumi socialize mostly with her American friends. How are these friends depicted? Why do you think that Gogol has so few friends of either nationality?

9. Jhumpa Lahiri chooses to make a male character the center of the book, and much of the story is told from Gogol's point of view. Much less is said about his sister, Sonia, although her experiences as the daughter of Indian immigrants are probably closer to Lahiri's personal experiences. Why do you think that Lahiri wrote much of the book from a male point of view? Do you think that she succeeded in presenting the male viewpoint?

10. By putting garlic, cumin, and cayenne on their Thanksgiving turkey the Gangulis combine Indian cooking traditions with American ones. Are there any food traditions that you observe at your own Thanksgiving that tie in to your individual family culture or heritage?

REFERENCES

Connally, Molly. "Lahiri, Jhumpa. *The Namesake: A Novel.*" *School Library Journal* 49 (November 2003), p. 172.

"Jhumpa Lahiri" in *Authors and Artists for Young Adults.* Vol. 56. Gale Group, 2004. (Reproduced in *Biography Resource Center,* galenet.galegroup.com/servlet/BioRC.)

Herbert, Rosemary. "Between Two Worlds. Indian-American author's novel explores culture's gray areas." *The Boston Herald* (9/11/2003), p. 48. Available at http://theedge.bostonherald.com/bookreviews/view.by?articleid=83&format=text.

Kakutani, Michiko. "From Calcutta to Suburbia: A Family's Perplexing Journey." *The New York Times* (9/2/03), p. E1.

Kantrowitz, Barbara. "Who Says There's No Second Act? *Newsweek* (August 2003), p. 61,

Lahiri, Jhumpa. "The Long Way Home." *The New Yorker* 80, no. 25 (September 2004), p. 83.

Nawotka, Edward. "Pulitzer winner finds much in a name." *Publishers Weekly* 250, no. 27 (July 2003), p. 49.

Pais, Arthur J. "What's in a namesake?" *India Abroad* (2003), p. M2.

DECEMBER

Holiday Book
Discussion Overview
Sample Selection

HOLIDAY BOOK DISCUSSION OVERVIEW

Some book groups decide to skip the December meeting because both library staff and readers are overwhelmed by holiday planning. On the other hand, people may be in the mood to celebrate and this could be a good time to foster the community spirit behind your book group. You might even want to turn your meeting into more of a holiday literary program and invite community members to perform brief readings. If you are lucky, you might even get readers in the holiday spirit to provide some donations for your library!

These days, in the interest of diversity and the many different religious beliefs held by readers, many libraries call their programs "holiday" or "winter" or even "winter solstice" programs, rather than using the word "Christmas." What do all of these programs have in common? The reading selections are short! This is not the time to take on *War and Peace;* in fact, you don't even have to assign any readings. Both adults and children love storytelling, so this is their chance to either perform or listen to performers. Some libraries have hosted abridged dramatizations of books and stories such as Charles Dickens' *A Christmas Carol* or the O. Henry short story "The Gift of the Magi." Some share the reading of the poem "'Twas the Night Before Christmas." You can hire a professional storyteller or actor, you can ask for volunteers from your local community theater or university drama department, or you can ask your book group members to do readings. What is important is not who does the reading but that the experience is shared.

At holiday time, adults may enjoy hearing or reading stories that they enjoyed as children so don't hesitate to include folk tales, fables, and poetry found in your library's children and young adults collections. If you use this kind of material, you might want to bill your holiday book group meeting as a family celebration. The Waterboro Public Library in Maine provides readers and librarians with some good choices in the section of the library Web site entitled Holidays and Seasons in Fiction, available at: www.waterborolibrary.org/bklists.htm#holwin

Here are some time-tested "old chestnuts" enjoyed by book groups at the holidays. You can read all or part of them or have a member or professional theatrical reader perform excerpts from several of them.

"A Child's Christmas in Wales" by Dylan Thomas.

"A Christmas Memory" by Truman Capote.

"The Good Shepherd" by Gunnar Gunnarsson.

"The Homecoming" by Earl Hamner. (*The Waltons* television series was based on his writing).

Carol of the Brown King: Nativity Poems by Langston Hughes.

LESS TRADITIONAL CHOICES:

Holidays on Ice (Back Bay Books, 1998) by David Sedaris is an anthology of short stories about the holiday season featuring social satire and dark humor. Many readers, especially young adults and those who favor contemporary fiction, find them to be hilarious. Still, if you have a senior or highly conservative audience, these stories may not be appealing so read these first to see if they might offend anyone. The Web site Barnes&Noble.com weighs in here with a review of the first story in the collection, "Santa Land Diaries," calling it "A laugh-out-loud-hysterical look at Sedaris's experiences working as an elf in Santa Land in Macy's. The story is a wickedly funny slicing-and-dicing of the holiday season and the good cheer that supposedly accompanies it. His dark humor is exactly what you need when you're getting sick of all the fuss about Christmas."

"The Loudest Voice" by Grace Paley is a short story dealing with Jewish cultural assimilation. In the 1930's, Shirley Abramowitz, a first-generation American, wants to participate in all things American, including the school Christmas pageant, but her parents don't want her to do it.

"Christmas Even" by Michael Connelly is a short story featuring Los Angeles detective Harry Bosch. In this case, Bosch, who is a jazz fan, is called out on Christmas day to investigate the death of a burglar during a break-in. While he's at the scene, Bosch notices a saxophone that had once belonged to a famous jazz musician. Bosch not only solves the crime—he tracks down the owner of the sax. (**Note:** This story can be found in a 2004 Signet Paperback anthology entitled *Murder and All That Jazz* edited by Robert J. Randisi; ISBN 0451213335.)

SELECTIONS THAT ARE POPULAR IN MULTICULTURAL PROGRAMS

Latino Holiday Stories

The Legend of the Poinsettia by Tomie dePaola (Putnam Juvenile, Reprint edition, 1997; ISBN 0698115678). This children's story, based on a legend from Mexico about the miraculous blooming of the first poinsettias, begins as a little girl named Lucinda and her mother attempt in vain to complete a woven new blanket for the Christmas procession Baby Jesus.

Too Many Tamales by Gary Soto, illustrated by Ed Martinez (Putnam Juvenile, 1996; ISBN 0698114124). This beautifully illustrated paperback features a Latino family's Christmas celebration and gathering. While Maria and her mother are making tamales for a holiday party, the daughter loses her mother's ring. Could it be in the tamales?

Noche Buena: Hispanic American Christmas Stories edited by Nicolas Kanellos (Oxford University Press, 2000; ISBN 01915135288). This is an anthology of holiday folk tales, stories, songs, and plays from Mexico, Colombia, Cuba, Puerto Rico, and the American Southwest.

Kwanzaa Stories

Kwanzaa, a seven-day cultural holiday that celebrates African American heritage, culture, and community is observed from December 26 through January 1. Although Kwanzaa commemorates an ancient African harvest ritual, it is a relatively new holiday in North America. Dr. Ron Karenga, an activist and director of the Black Studies department at the California State University, Long Beach, created the holiday in 1966. The name Kwanzaa comes from the Swahili phrase "matunda ya kwanza," which means "first fruits." Each of the seven days of Kwanzaa is dedicated to one principle. They are "Umoja" (unity), "Kujichagulia" (self-determination), "Ujima" (collective responsibility), "Ujamaa" (cooperation), "Nia" (purpose), "Kuumba" (creativity), and "Imani" (faith). The goal of Kwanzaa is to remind people to put the seven principles into daily practice.

Seven Candles for Kwanzaa by Andrea Davis Pinkney, illustrated by Brian Pinkney (Dial, 1993; ISBN 0803712928). This book explains the origins, language, and daily themes of the seven-day holiday.

Seven Spools of Thread: A Kwanzaa Story by Angela Shelf Medearis, illustrated by Daniel Minter. (Morton Grove, Ill.: Albert Whitman, 2000). In this children's story the seven Ashanti brothers are given the task of turning thread into gold. In order to achieve this task, they put aside their differences, learn to get along, and embody the principles of Kwanzaa.

The Complete Kwanzaa: Celebrating Our Cultural Harvest by Dorothy Winbush Riley (HarperCollins, 1995 ISBN 0060172150). A full explanation of Kwanzaa is provided in this volume with celebration ideas, poems, and readings.

Hanukah Stories

"Just Enough Is Plenty: A Hanukah Tale," by Barbara Diamond Goldin, illustrated by Seymour Chwast (Viking Children's, 1988; ISBN 0670818526. Paperback: Puffin Books, 1990; ISBN, 0140507876). In this fairy tale set in an Eastern European Jewish village, little Malka learns the true meaning of Hanukah as her family shares their meager celebration with a kind, yet mysterious stranger.

The Power of Light by Isaac Bashevis Singer, illustrated by Irene Libeblich (Farrar, Straus, and Giroux, 1990, ISBN 0374459843). Nobel Prize winner Singer, presents a collection of Hanukah-themed short stories set in Jewish communities in Ukraine and Brooklyn, New York.

"A Drugstore in Winter" by Cynthia Ozick. Although not specifically a Hanukah story, "A Drugstore in Winter" is about the issue of Jewish assimilation and the challenges of fitting into American society. It is included here, because librarians are portrayed in a wonderful light! In this autobiographical short story set in the 1940s, Ozick describes the traveling library that arrives in her Bronx neighborhood every other week, offering her books that helped her to escape the realities of her often difficult school days. Among her happy recollections are those of the librarians coming into her parents' pharmacy after their rounds to have a cup of hot coffee at the fountain. One of the many anthologies in which this story is available is *Ten on Ten: Major Essayists on Recurring Themes*. Robert Atwan, (1992 Paperbound ISBN 0312062362).

DECEMBER

"The Dead"

BY JAMES JOYCE

SUMMARY

James Joyce wrote "The Dead" in 1907 and it was the last and longest of the stories in his short story anthology called *Dubliners,* published in 1914. The main character in "The Dead" is Gabriel Conroy, a middle-aged professor and book reviewer who is attending a winter holiday party with his wife, Greta. The party is being given by his elderly aunts, the musically talented Morkan sisters, and Gabriel is their favorite nephew. Nevertheless, despite his education and the admiration of his aunts, the dialogue reveals Gabriel to be socially awkward and a bit condescending. At the end of the story he has a "wake-up call," known by Joyce scholars as an "epiphany," when his wife of many years reveals details about a romantic relationship that she had in her youth.

AUTHOR BIOGRAPHY

James Augustine Aloysius Joyce (1882–1941) was a novelist, short story writer, poet, and dramatist who also worked as a language instructor to make ends meet. He was born the oldest of eight children on February 2, 1882, in Rathgar, a suburb of Dublin, Ireland. His parents were John Stanislaus Joyce, a tax collector, and Mary Jane Murray Joyce, a pianist. From both parents Joyce inherited musical talent and, particularly from his father, a talent for playing with words and telling stories. Joyce began his childhood in fairly comfortable circumstances but his father squandered the family fortunes, and as a teenager, Joyce found himself a poor student, surrounded by wealthier ones.

Joyce was educated at Jesuit schools and between 1898 and 1902 attended University College in Dublin. Raised in the Roman Catholic faith, he broke with the Church while he was in college. In 1904 he met Galway chambermaid Nora Barnacle, the woman with whom he would spend the remainder of his life. At first, they lived together because Joyce did not believe in marriage. They eventually married in 1931 to preserve the inheritance rights of their two children, Giorgio and Lucia. Soon after they met, James and Nora left Ireland where Joyce began writing *Dubliners* and took a position as a Berlitz language instructor in Trieste, Italy. Although Joyce would return to Ireland briefly in 1909 and again in 1912, for the rest of his life he lived abroad while writing about Dublin.

A biographical entry published by the James Joyce Centre in Dublin explains some of the reasons for his exile:

> Originally well-to-do, his spendthrift father swept his large family into poverty, moving from lodging to lodging around the city. Joyce's home life stood in stark contrast to the comfort enjoyed by his schoolfriends at Clongowes and Belvedere and his colleagues at University College, and much of his youth was spent roaming the streets. His determination to escape was enhanced by what he saw as the introverted atmosphere of the Irish literary revival, which he denounced in a scurrilous broadsheet, The Holy Office, on the eve of his departure for the continent in 1904. . . . Joyce settled in Trieste with Nora Barnacle, the Galway girl who was to become his wife. Relations with Dublin were further strained when his book of short stories, *Dubliners*, caused a protracted argument between Joyce and his Dublin publisher, George Roberts. On Joyce's final visit to Dublin in 1912 Roberts destroyed the entire first edition and Joyce left the country for ever the next day. Disowned, as he felt, by Ireland, Joyce nevertheless acknowledged his Irishness throughout his exile.

James Joyce had a key year in 1914 as he began serial publication of the semiautobiographical *A Portrait of the Artist as a Young Man*, published in full in 1916. The fifteen stories in *Dubliners* were published in June 1914 and this was also the year that he began his novel *Ulysses*. The structure and some of the themes of this book were inspired by the tales of Homer. The storyline presents the events of a single day in Dublin, as told from the point of view of several characters. The day that was chosen, June 16 1904, has become known to Joyce fans as Bloomsday, named after the main character, Leopold Bloom, a middle-aged Irish Jewish ad salesman for a Dublin newspaper.

In 1920, Joyce moved to Paris, where he was befriended by a young American, Sylvia Beach, owner of the bookshop Shakespeare and Company. She agreed to bring out *Ulysses* under her own imprint. By the time the book appeared on February 2, 1922, Joyce and his family were firmly established in Paris and would remain in the city for the next twenty years. Early in World War II, when the Germans invaded France, Joyce and Nora moved to Zürich, Switzerland, where he died on January 13, 1941, from complications of a perforated ulcer.

HOW TO GET THE STORY:

One good source for the story is the Oxford World's Classics paperback edition (Oxford, 2002; ISBN 0192839993). The entire *Dubliners* collection, narrated by Malachy McCourt, is available in cassette format from Caedmon (2000; ISBN: 0694523003). The CD version offers several stories from *Dubliners* including "The Dead" and is narrated by Jim Norton (Naxos Audiobooks, 1999; ISBN 9626341831).

MATERIALS TO SUPPORT YOUR DISCUSSION

- **Music.** The Irish ballad that brings back memories of Greta's long-lost love is "The Lass of Aughrim." Although it might be hard to track down an audio recording of this, a version performed by Ewan McGregor and Susan Lynch is available on a soundtrack CD (Virgin Records, 1999) from the small independent film, *Nora* (2000). Sunphone Records has also issued a CD of music mentioned in several Joyce works including "The Dead" and has a Web site called "Music In The Works of James Joyce" (www.james-joyce-music.com). The song "Yes, Let Me Like a Soldier Fall" with music by William Vincent Wallace and words by Edward Fitzball is referred to in "The Dead" when Mr. Browne introduces the subject of an Italian tenor of bygone years who had once sung five encores to this song, "introducing a high C every time." You can order the CD by the same name from the Sunphone Web site

- **The film version of "The Dead" (1987).** This was the last film that John Huston directed, and his daughter, Angelica Huston, starred as Greta Conroy. It was filmed on location in Ireland and there are a lot of period details, as well as musical performances. You might want to show some excerpts from the film, especially the last ten minutes, which have been highly praised by critics. It is available on video (Lions Gate, 1992; ASIN 630113639X)

DISCUSSION QUESTIONS

1. What is the conflict between Gabriel Conroy and Lily the caretaker's daughter? How does Gabriel try to smooth over the situation? Does it help?

2. Gabriel relates the story of his grandfather's horse Johnny, much to the amusement of the crowd. What is the significance of this story to the plot as a whole?

3. Gabriel is a university professor and literary critic. Why do you think that Joyce chose to give him these professions?

4. Are there any women that you particularly admire in "The Dead?" How would you compare their occupations and social status to women's today?

5. Discuss Gabriel's treatment of his family.

6. Have someone read out loud the following description of the food at the Morkan sisters gathering:

> A fat brown goose lay at one end of the table and at the other end, on a bed of creased paper strewn with sprigs of parsley, lay a great ham, stripped of its outer skin and peppered over with crust crumbs, a neat paper frill round its shin and beside this was a round of spiced beef. Between these rival ends ran parallel lines of side-dishes: two little minsters of jelly, red and yellow; a shallow dish full of blocks of blancmange and red jam, a large green leaf-shaped dish with a stalk-shaped handle, on which lay bunches of purple raisins and peeled almonds, a companion dish on which lay a solid rectangle of Smyrna figs, a dish of custard topped with grated nutmeg, a small bowl full of chocolates and sweets wrapped

Icebreaker: This story shows how even someone who is married a long time may not be aware of the feelings of their partner. This is often a theme in literature, film, and drama. Can you think of other classic or not-so-classic works of film or literature where the plot revolved around longtime secrets kept by husbands and wives?

There is an Irish tradition of giving a toast at holiday and family occasions and Gabriel delivers a toast that honors his aunts, the hostesses, and recalls "those dead and gone great ones whose fame the world will not willingly let die." Do you have a tradition of toasts in your own family? Can you remember a toast that meant a lot to you or other family members?

in gold and silver papers and a glass vase in which stood some tall celery stalks. In the centre of the table there stood, as sentries to a fruit-stand which upheld a pyramid of oranges and American apples, two squat old-fashioned decanters of cut glass, one containing port and the other dark sherry. On the closed square piano a pudding in a huge yellow dish lay in waiting and behind it were three squads of bottles of stout and ale and minerals, drawn up according to the colours of their uniforms, the first two black, with brown and red labels, the third and smallest squad white, with transverse green sashes.

Does this make you hungry? What techniques does Joyce use to describe the food?

7. Discuss the role that music plays in this story in both providing entertainment, preserving traditions, and bringing back memories. Does music play a role in your own holiday celebrations?

8. The plot of the story ends with Greta's revelation to Gabriel that she has a long lost love. But because it ends at this point, we are not sure how the revelation will change their marriage, if at all. What kind of changes do you think there will be?

9. If you have read any novels by James Joyce (e.g., *A Portrait of the Artist as a Young Man* or *Finnegans Wake* or *Ulysses*), compare the writing style with the one that he uses in this short story. What themes are expressed throughout Joyce's work?

10. Have someone read the last paragraph of the book out loud:

A few light taps upon the pane made him turn to the window. It had begun to snow again. He watched sleepily the flakes, silver and dark, falling obliquely against the lamplight. The time had come for him to set out on his journey westward. Yes, the newspapers were right: snow was general all over Ireland. it was falling on every part of the dark central plain, on the treeless hills, falling softly upon the Bog of Allen and, farther westward, softly falling into the dark mutinous Shannon waves. It was falling, too, upon every part of the lonely churchyard on the hill where Michael Furey lay buried. It lay thickly drifted on the crooked crosses and headstones, on the spears of the little gate, on the barren thorns. His soul swooned slowly as he heard the snow falling faintly through the universe and faintly falling, like the descent of their last end, upon all the living and the dead.

What does snow symbolize here?

JANUARY

Friday Night Lights: A Town, A Team, and A Dream

BY H. G. BISSINGER

SUMMARY

Friday Night Lights is a nonfiction account of the 1988 football season played by the Permian Panthers, a West Texas high school team located in the boom and bust oil town of Odessa. The book opens with the preseason "Watermelon Feed," a standing-room-only booster event held at Permian High School, and ends with the team's final game of the season. Along the way, readers learn of the pressure that football players face from parents, teachers, coaches, and the town itself. In fact, many of these teenagers believe that winning a state championship is the most important thing that will ever happen to them.

The author, Pulitzer Prize–winning journalist H. G. "Buzz" Bissinger, moved from Philadelphia to Texas with his fiancée (now wife) Sarah Macdonald and their children in order to cover the 1988 Permian Panther football season. He had considered writing about high school football teams in several smaller towns in Georgia and Pennsylvania before finally choosing Odessa. Why Odessa and why Permian? Explains *Sports Illustrated*, "In the 1970s and '80s Permian won four state championships and never had a record worse than 7–2. The principal reason for this success was a fanaticism run amok. 'It's kind of a necessary evil,' acknowledged Chavez, the onetime Panthers tight end. 'You're not going to have a great team year after year unless you have all that craziness.'" (Bissinger 2004)

Odessa's spending habits at the time bear this out. Bissinger writes that team boosters would charter private jets to fly the team to "away games." And in October 2001, *USA Today* reported that season tickets were left to relatives in wills. (See www.usatoday.com/sports/preps/football/2001–10–25-top10-stadiums-permian.htm). Permian High spent more on physical education than on English language textbooks, and despite hard economic times, the town of Odessa spent $5.6 million to build the new Ratliff Stadium, which now seats 19,500 fans.

Without giving away the plot, 1988 was a challenging season for the team. For starters, their promising running back, Boobie Miles, suffered a knee injury that soon knocked him out of the game. Although Bissinger was with the team at every game and most practices during the season, he himself is not part of the story. Instead he uses his investigative journalism skills to describe (some might say, expose) the players, their coach, the people of small-town Odessa and neighboring towns, and their social lives and social values both on and off the field.

AUTHOR BIOGRAPHY

Harry Gerard Bissinger was born on November 1, 1954, in New York City. He attended the Dalton and Andover private schools and graduated from the University of Pennsylvania in 1976. Bissinger recalls that his interest in Texas high school football was sparked as a teenager when he read a *Sports Illustrated* story, "Pursuit of a Big Blue Chipper" (in the September 9, 1968, issue), about a Texas high school quarterback named Jack Mildren. Almost twenty years later, after winning a 1987 Pulitzer Prize as part of a team of *Philadelphia Inquirer* reporters investigating the Philadelphia court system, he packed up his family and moved to Odessa, Texas, for a year to cover high school football. The end result was the best-selling *Friday Night Lights*.

As indicated by the Pulitzer, Bissinger was already an established journalist when he wrote *Friday Night Lights*. He began his journalism career at the *Ledger-Star* in Norfolk, Virginia, where he worked as a reporter from 1976 to 1978. After that he worked as a reporter at the *St. Paul Pioneer Press Dispatch* in St. Paul, Minnesota. From 1981 to 1988 he wrote for the *Philadelphia Inquirer,* receiving a Nieman Fellowship to study at Harvard University during the 1985–1986 academic year. After publishing *Friday Night Lights* in 1990, he wrote a book about politics in Philadelphia called *A Prayer for the City,* published by Random House in 1997. In 2005, Houghton Mifflin published his latest sports book, *Three Nights in August,* a chronicle of the St. Louis Cardinals 2003 baseball season and their relationship with manager Tony La Russa.

Bissinger's teleplay and screenwriting work includes spending the 2000–2001 television season in Los Angeles as a coproducer and writer for *NYPD Blue*. Bissinger is also a contributing editor at *Vanity Fair* magazine, where his range of subjects has included

Pete Rose, the brutal killing of a gay soldier at an army barracks in Fort Campbell, Kentucky, and the first in-depth profile of Los Angeles police detective Mark Fuhrman in the aftermath of the O.J. Simpson trial. Another of his pieces for the magazine, "Shattered Glass," about young Washington journalist Stephen Glass, formed the basis for the highly acclaimed film *Shattered Glass,* which was released in 2003. *Friday Night Lights* was adapted as a film directed by Peter Berg, starring Billy Bob Thornton and released by Universal Pictures in 2004.

WHY THIS BOOK IS A GOOD CHOICE FOR A BOOK DISCUSSION GROUP

Friday Night Lights was on the *New York Times* best-seller list for fifteen weeks after it was first published in hardcover. It re-emerged on the *Times* nonfiction paperback best-seller list in the fall of 2003. Popular with teenagers and adults, it has even been taught in sociology and sports psychology classes. Many book reviewers and professors have noted that the human interest story is so strong that you don't have to be a football fan to appreciate the book. Regarding the popularity of the book, Bissinger admitted to *Sports Illustrated* in 2004, "When I first arrived in Odessa in 1988 to write about the influence of high school football in an American town, I had no idea, of course, that the book would cause a national sensation. It became a best-seller, and it still sells nearly 40,000 copies a year." "Andy Warhol talked about 15 minutes of fame," added Brian Chavez, the starting tight end for Odessa's Permian High School in 1988 who went on to Harvard and became a lawyer in Odessa, "Ours has lasted 15 years." (Bissinger 2004)

Friday Night Lights is the January selection because of the tie-in with Super Bowl Sunday and the opportunity to build buzz using that theme. If one of your state's teams is competing in the Super Bowl, you can work the reactions of fans into your book discussion whether pre- or post-game. In January, football will be on your readers' minds, whether they plan to watch the game, ignore the game, host a Super Bowl party, or work overtime that day delivering pizza. But this book could be presented at any time of year, and is, in fact, often assigned as summer reading at many high schools. Of course, you might encounter readers who are hesitant to attend because they don't know much about football.

But this really doesn't matter. Jack Foley, an English teacher and football coach at Burncoat High School in Worcester, Massachusetts, remarks,

> Students, whether athletes or not, can relate to the struggles of the players from Permian High School. These young men face pressure from themselves, from their teammates, their peers and their town to win football games. For some players the experience is fulfilling and rewarding while for others it is painful and traumatic. Reading about these experiences provides a fantastic springboard for discussions concerning self-image, persona and the importance of setting and accomplishing goals. (see www.fridaynightlightsbook.com/teachers).

If your library is located in a small town in which high school sports are important, the ideas presented here may resonate with parents, students, teachers, and fans. If your library is located in a larger city, where school sports play less of a social or economic role, then the book can be appreciated in terms of the pressures that young people face from their peers, parents, and teachers. Most of us have worked as part of a team, whether on a ball field, in the military, or on the job.

High school sports programs are often supported through collaborations between schools, local businesses, sporting good stores, and public and private athletic programs for kids and adults. As a result, you might want to use a book discussion about high school sports as an opportunity for community collaboration. For example, members of the same school team could be invited to attend this book discussion together, as could families in which one or more members are current or former athletes. Invite a local coach, athlete, or sportswriter to moderate the discussion or speak beforehand or afterwards. A local sporting goods store or local business that supports community teams might even be willing to sponsor refreshments or provide discount coupons. If the discussion attracts a lot of sports fans who might not otherwise come to the library, take the opportunity to let them know about other library materials that they might be interested in, including sports magazines, sports biographies, and even "how-to" videos that may help them to perfect their athletic skills.

HOW TO GET THIS BOOK

Friday Night Lights has been in print continuously since it was first published in 1990 and there are both hardcover and paperback editions. If you don't already have copies of this book in your collection, you might wish to purchase the tenth anniversary paperback edition (Da Capo Press, 2000; ISBN 0306809907). With an afterword by Bissinger that offers updates on the town of Odessa, Permian High School, and the players, this edition also contains fourteen book discussion questions, two of which are included in the question list that follows.

The *Friday Night Lights* Web site (www.fridaynightlights book.com) includes these discussion questions and details on how and where to purchase books and get group discounts.

A hard-to-get audiocassette versionof the book was narrated by Alex Karras (Publishing Mills, 1991; ISBN 0962718793). Used copies may be available from Amazon.com.

MATERIALS TO SUPPORT YOUR DISCUSSION

- **Sports books, etc.** While more women than men tend to participate in book discussions, this book may motivate more men to attend as well as more teenagers. As a result, you might want to take the opportunity to display more sports memoirs and biographies on book carts in or near the discussion area. Young adult books or action/adventure films might also appeal to your audience. One suggested title to display is an often overlooked contender in the category of nonfiction sports books that read like fiction, *Seabiscuit: An American Legend* by Laura Hillenbrand. This book is the story of the team that trained the unlikely, knobby-kneed champion racehorse that inspired downtrodden Americans in the 1930s. (See www.randomhouse.com/features/hillenbrand/about.html.) Another popular sports book is Madeleine Blais's book *In These Girls, Hope is a Muscle*, which follows the Amherst (Massachusetts) High girls basketball team, the Lady Hurricanes, through the 1992–93 season from the first game in December to the final game in March, when they face Haverhill in the state championship.

- **Show the film** (www.fridaynightlightsmovie.com). You also might want to show excerpts of the movie version of *Friday Night Lights,* released by Universal Pictures in 2004 and starring Billy Bob Thornton as Permian coach Gary Gaines. Rated PG–13, it is available on both VHS (ASIN B00061J5PW) and DVD (ISBN 1417011416). The movie was filmed on location in Odessa and West Texas and stuck to the basic story, although some details were modified for dramatic effect. For example, in the movie, Carter and Permian played for the state championship when they actually played in the state semifinal game. This game was played in front of ten thousand people in a heavy downpour at the University of Texas's Memorial Stadium in Austin, rather than fifty-five thousand in the Houston Astrodome.
- **Web-based materials.** Readers who want additional study questions and author and plot background can check out the Reading Group Guide section of the Book Report Network (www.readinggroupguides.com/guides3/friday_night_lights3.asp). Perseus Press also manages a site which focuses on the book (//www.fridaynightlightsbook.com).
- Follow-up materials. Since the book was first published, there have been many follow-up accounts of what has happened to the town of Odessa and the fate and fortunes of the 1988 team. One of the best accounts comes from Bissinger's October 2004 *Sports Illustrated* article. Here is an excerpt:

It's a trip I had thought about making for a decade, but I had always found an excuse to put it off. Too busy. No point in returning to the past. They were reasonable justifications, but I also felt a swirling apprehension, a queasiness—oh, what the hell, just come out with it: fear.

News of my possible return to the West Texas town of Odessa had once been greeted with threats of bodily harm. Since the publication of my book *Friday Night Lights* in 1990, dozens of people in town had accused me in the press of deception and betrayal, of wooing and then verbally raping them, of blaspheming the god of high school football and desecrating Odessa itself by depicting incidents of racism and misplaced educational priorities.

The recriminations had died down over the years, but

with a movie based on the book scheduled for release on October 8, they had appeared again in newspapers. I saw them, just as I saw a poll on an Odessa website in which 56% of respondents, asked if they would like me to come back, said, Hell, no!

But I am back, driving into town on a Monday in June. I have no impulse to turn around and go home, as I essentially did in 1990 when a visit to promote the book was canceled by my publisher because of threats phoned in to local bookstores. I am alone, unlike on the two trips I made to Odessa in the early '90s, when, fearing reprisals, I crept in like a church mouse for a day or two and then crept out. I feel a twinge in my stomach, but mostly I feel curiosity. I have time on my side: 14 years of it. Still, I know that grudges in West Texas, like the nubby mesquite bushes rising out of the pancake landscape, tend to last forever. (Bissinger, 2004)

DISCUSSION QUESTIONS

1. In a 2001 speech before the National Association of Independent Schools, Bissinger said:

> I come to you today as a proud product of all that you stand for and believe in as educators. I went to the Dalton School in New York City. Then to Andover. Then to Penn. I grew up in an atmosphere of privilege that, looking back on it, was almost embarrassing. So for me, the journey to Odessa represented something deeply personal, the idea of going to a place in the middle of nowhere and not treating it as nowhere but to listen to it, observe it, to not treat it with elitism and condescension.

What tone do you think that Bissinger took in this book? Do you think that he succeeded as an impartial observer? Why or why not?

2. In what ways does race influence the attitudes and behavior of Odessa's high school athletes, coaches, teachers, parents, and fans? What examples of, and explanations for, continuing racism in Odessa does Bissinger provide? Do you see similar examples in our own community? (from ReadingGroupGuides.com)

3. What do Bissinger's descriptions of classroom activity and

Icebreakers:
Ask for a show of hands: How many people have played on a high school sports team?

Ask those who raise their hands to tell the group, briefly, what their participation meant to them and if it influenced their choice of college and/or career?

Read this paragraph from Chapter 1: "In the absence of a shimmering skyline, the Odessas of the country had all found something similar in which to place their faith. In Indiana, it was the plink-plink of a ball on a parquet floor. In Minnesota, it was the swoosh of skates on the ice. In Ohio and Pennsylvania and Alabama and Georgia and Texas and dozens of other states, it was the weekly event simply known as Friday night."

Which, if any, high school sports do people in this community place their faith in? Are professional sports more or less important than high school sports in this town? Why?

teachers' behavior at Permian High School reveal about the role of education in the lives of the students and adults of Odessa? Why do you agree or disagree with Bissinger's statement that the school's "problems didn't make Permian a bad school at all, just a very typically American one"? (from ReadingGroupGuides.com)

4. What opportunities were there for the girls of Permian High School to participate in Mojo Madness? If you were the parent of a Permian High School girl, would you allow her to be a Pepette? Why or why not?

5. West Texans had been known to say that the town of Midland was where you went to raise a family, while the town of Odessa was where you went to raise hell. What techniques does Bissinger use to describe the differences and rivalries between the two cities? Can you describe any towns in this region or state that experience similar rivalries?

6. Based upon Boobie Miles' reactions and actions following his injury, what predictions might you make about his later life as an adult? Bissinger portrays Boobie as the victim of ruthless high school and college sports promoters. Do you agree? Why or why not?

7. After graduating from Permian, Panther's tight end, Brian Chavez, went to Harvard University (1990–93), where he graduated cum laude with a bachelor's degree in government. After graduation Chavez accepted a full scholarship to the Texas Tech Law School. He passed the bar exam and returned to Odessa to practice law with his father, Tony, and brother, Adrian. Based on the descriptions of Chavez in the book, are you surprised by this decision? Why or why not?

8. Describe the relationship that Odessa tailback Don Billingsley has with his father, a former Permian player. What are the dangers of parents trying to relive their glory days through their children? Why does the younger Billingsley say that he feels much older than seventeen?

9. If you lived in Odessa at the time and place depicted in the book, would you encourage your son to try out for the football team? Why or why not?

10. Have someone in the group read the last three paragraphs of the book out loud:

> On the far wall of their office was a depth chart. It had the names of each of the players on little magnets that could be constantly juggled, from first string to second string, from tackle to guard, from fullback to tailback, from offense to defense, or removed altogether.

They went to work immediately, because there was no time for sentiment, no reason to postpone it.

WINCHELL . . . MCDOUGAL . . . BILLINGLEY . . . CHAVEZ . . . CHRISTIAN . . . They and all the other seniors were placed in a neat little pile at the bottom, and suddenly there was no sign of them at all on the board, just black, empty spaces that would soon be filled by other magnets at quarterback and tailback and middle linebacker and all the other positions. The season had ended, but another one had begun.

People everywhere, young and old, were already dreaming of heroes.

What is your reaction to those closing lines and the image that the author creates? Do you think that this is an effective ending to the book? Why or why not?

REFERENCES

Bissinger, H. G. "Return to Odessa." *Sports Illustrated* 101, no.13 (October, 2004), p. 50.

FEBRUARY

Dreams from My Father: A Story of Race and Inheritance

BY BARACK OBAMA

SUMMARY

In November 2004, Democrat Barack Obama of Illinois became the third African-American popularly elected to the U.S. Senate. A few months earlier, he had gained national attention with a well-received, televised speech to the Democratic National Convention. Obama's memoir, *Dreams from My Father,* was published in 1995 long before he ran for public office. He originally was approached by several publishers because he had an interesting family background and was the first African-American president of the *Harvard Law Review*. Nine years later, when Obama emerged on the national scene as a politician, Three Rivers Press reissued a paperback edition of the book, this time including a new foreword and the text of the convention speech. It became a best-seller.

Dreams from My Father is a coming-of-age story focusing on the family life, education, and early community organizing career of a young man born to a white American mother and a black Kenyan father. Obama says in the preface to the 2004 edition that he wrote the book "with the belief that the story of my family, and my efforts to understand that story, might speak in some way to the fissures of race that have characterized the American experience." The book opens in New York City in 1982, when Obama, studying at Columbia University, learns of his father's death in an automobile accident in Kenya. He has only seen his father once since his parents divorced, and much of what he knows about his father is gleaned from the stories that his relatives tell.

The memoir then flashes back to Obama's childhood days in Honolulu, where his parents met as university students. Later he moves to Indonesia, when his mother marries another international student attending the University of Hawaii. At age ten,

Barack returns to Hawaii. The story continues with descriptions of his student and family life with his grandparents, including a brief visit from his father. The memoir describes young Barack's attempts to fit in first at prep school, then briefly at Occidental College in Los Angeles and ultimately at Columbia University. The narrative then continues with descriptions of his work in Chicago, where he moved in 1983 to work as a community organizer on the city's poverty-stricken South Side. He tries his best to help the people there to improve their housing and job opportunities but with mixed results.

The last part of the book details the trip that Obama made to Kenya, where, in attempt to find his roots and learn more about his father, he visited members of his extended family. He begins to separate the myths about his father from the realities but overall comes away from the trip bolstered by the love and support of his family. The memoir then skips over his years at Harvard Law School and ends with his wedding to Michelle, whom he had met in Chicago while working as a civil rights lawyer and law professor. Before the wedding, he had returned once again to Kenya to introduce Michelle to his extended family. The book ends with Obama expressing his pleasure that his African and American family members have been able to celebrate his wedding together.

AUTHOR BIOGRAPHY

Barack Obama was born on August 4, 1961, in Honolulu, Hawaii. His father, also named Barack, an African name meaning "blessing" in Swahili, was a black Kenyan exchange student. His mother, Ann Dunham, was a white woman from Kansas who had moved to Honolulu with her parents. Obama's mother and father met as students at the University of Hawaii. Barack Sr. won a scholarship to Harvard when his son was two years old. Since the scholarship wasn't large enough to support the whole family, he went to Massachusetts alone. After finishing his degree, he went home to Kenya and took a job as an economic planner for the country's government. The elder Obama continued to write letters to his son, and visited him once when he was ten, but his marriage to Obama's mother ended. She married an Indonesian oil company executive, and Obama lived in Indonesia between the ages of six and ten. His half-sister, Maya Soetoro-Ng, was born in Indonesia.

Convinced that he would receive a better education in the United States, Barack's mother then sent him back to Honolulu to live with his grandparents, while she and his sister remained in Indonesia. In Honolulu, Obama received a scholarship to attend Hawaii's top prep academy, the Punahou School. From there, Obama went briefly to Occidental College in Los Angeles and then on to Columbia University, where he became interested in community activism. After graduating in 1983, he moved to Chicago to spend three years as a South Side community organizer.

After a trip to visit with relatives in Kenya where he visited his father's grave, he attended Harvard Law School. At Harvard, he became the first African-American president of the *Harvard Law Review*. Upon his graduation (magna cum laude) in 1991, Obama practiced civil rights law in Chicago. He also took a position teaching constitutional law at the University of Chicago Law School, and soon became involved in politics. He married his wife, Michelle, in 1993 and they now have two daughters, Maila Ann, born in 2000, and Natasha, born in 2003.

Elected as a Democrat to the Illinois Senate in 1996, his work there included legislation to stop racial profiling and to expand medical coverage for uninsured children. In July 2004, as Illinois' Democratic candidate for the U.S. Senate, he gave a keynote speech at the Democratic Convention. He was elected to the United States Senate in November 2004, the third African-American U.S. Senator to be elected since the end of the Civil War.

WHY THIS BOOK IS A GOOD CHOICE FOR BOOK DISCUSSION GROUPS

In the preface to the 2004 edition of *Dreams From My Father*, Obama admits that sales of the first edition, published in 1995, were "underwhelming." But the rerelease sold well, making both the *New York Times* and Amazon.com best-seller lists. Given the renewed interest in the memoir and the man himself, this book has been chosen as the selection for February, which is Black History Month. The story of a young black man trying to make sense of his family history and heritage certainly fits in with this theme and will appeal to readers of all ages. It was written before Obama entered politics and possesses a candor and perhaps naiveté that would be absent if he wrote it today.

Given the ease with which libraries can now obtain the book in both paperback and audio book form and because of continued interest in Obama's political career, which many pollsters predict will include an eventual run for president, many people may be curious to learn more about him whether they agree with his politics or not. If your public library is in Illinois or Hawaii there may be special interest among readers because some may have a more personal connection to Obama or his family.

Obama, a strong supporter of libraries and literacy, was a keynote speaker at the American Library Association's annual meeting in Chicago in June 2005. He highlighted the importance of reading and literacy in his Democratic National Convention Speech, stating, "Children can't achieve unless we raise their expectations and turn off the television sets and eradicate the slander that says a black youth with a book is acting white." Later he added, "If there's a child on the South Side of Chicago who can't read, that matters to me, even if it's not my child."

HOW TO GET THIS BOOK:

This book was originally published in hardcover (Times Books, a division of Random House, 1995; ISBN 081292343X). Perhaps your library or library system already has a few copies. If not, the easiest way to get the book into readers' hands may be to distribute or order the newer paperback version (Three Rivers Press, ISBN 1400082773). The new version contains an updated preface and the text of Obama's 2004 Democratic National Convention speech. Random House Audio Publishing House, (2005, ISBN 073932100). An abridged CD version of the book, narrated by Obama, also includes his convention speech.

MATERIALS TO SUPPORT YOUR DISCUSSION

- **Black History Resources.** In his book, Obama mentions many black political leaders who influenced him, including Malcolm X and the late mayor of Chicago, Harold Washington. He also discusses the influence of his Kenyan father and great-grandfather. This could serve as a springboard for demonstrations of other black history resources in your library, ranging from book and video biographies of African-American political leaders, to materials about African culture, history, and family life.

- **Music.** If your library has a world music collection or you know someone who listens to African music, you might want to have a cassette or CD on hand so that patrons can listen to the kind of music that the Obamas in Kenya listened and danced to. In fact, Obama Sr. was known for his skill on the dance floor, and there is one moving scene in the book where his American family dances with him in their Hawaii apartment. Most likely, the music that the Obama family danced to, at least in Kenya if not in Hawaii, was *benga,* a fusion of jazz, rumba, and reggae styles, which originated among the Luo people of western Kenya in the 1950s. If you don't have this kind of music in your collection and you think there is enough interest, Amazon.com offers a benga CD called The Mighty Kings of Benga by a group called The Victoria Kings, (Globe Style Label, 1995: ASIN: B000000ZSO)
- **Map.** You may also wish to have a map of Africa or Kenya on hand.
- **Democratic National Convention Speech.** Obama's July 27, 2004, speech at the Democratic National Convention in Boston is eighteen minutes long and has been posted in audio and video form on many Web sites including the C-Net cable channel site (www.c-span.org). If you have the available technology or a large enough computer screen for your group to look at together, you might want to download it and watch it together before or after the discussion.
- **Web Sites** The "Librarian's Index to the Internet" contains a portal called "The African-American Experience: Resources related to Black History Month, and Beyond." (lii.org/bhmonth). You can check it out for additional programming ideas or refer patrons to it. Another excellent portal for black history information has been prepared by Bridgeport Public Library in Connecticut. (www.bridgeportpubliclibrary.org/Burroughs/Infoserv/HTML/bhistory.htm). Obama's Senate Web (obama.senate.gov/events) is also a good reference source.

Icebreaker:
Go around the room and ask: Based on what you have learned about Obama in this book would you have voted for him for U.S. senator? Why or why not? If he should decide to run for president one day, how do you think that this book will help or hurt his chances?

DISCUSSION QUESTIONS

1. Reviewer Lynn McKeown, a writer for an Illinois community newspaper, commented, "Much of the book tells a story of problems faced by an African-American — especially one who often felt an outsider in both worlds, black and white. Yet the tone of this memoir is seldom bitter." (See www.thezephyr.com/offtheshelf/obamafather.htm.) Did Obama sound bitter to you? Why or why not? Are there different tones at different points in his story? If so, what are they?

2. Obama had two very different grandfathers. Stanley Dunham was a white furniture salesman, who traveled from Kansas to Texas to Hawaii in search of greater personal and career opportunities. His African grandfather, Hussein Onyango Obama, was a "prominent farmer, an elder of the tribe, a medicine man with healing powers." Describe the impact that each of these men had upon his life.

3. When Obama was nine years old and living in Indonesia he read by chance a *Life* magazine article about an African American who'd tried to lighten his complexion. He states that it was only then that he discovered that being black was not a source of pride to everyone. "I suspect I was one of the luckier ones, having been given a stretch of childhood free of self-doubt," he writes. What family and social factors led Obama to maintain pride in his black heritage both as a child and as an adult? Are there ever times when he is ashamed of his father or of his family background?

4. When he moves to Chicago to become a community organizer, Obama notes how impressed he is by the personal connection that black people in Chicago appeared to have to Harold Washington, their city's first African-American mayor, who won two terms as mayor serving from 1983 until late 1987, when he died of a massive heart attack at his desk in City Hall. Obama writes,

> The woman so concerned with the cruder habits of her neighbors had a picture of Harold in her kitchen right next to the sampler of the Twenty-third Psalm. So did the young man who lived in the crumbling apartment a few blocks away and was trying to make ends meet by mixing records at dance parties. As it had for the men in Smitty's barbershop, the election had given both these people a new idea of themselves . . . Harold was something they still had in common: Like my idea of organizing, he held out an offer of collective redemption.

Have you ever had this kind of personal connection to a politician or community leader and if so, who?

Do any of you in the group remember reading about Harold Washington's election at the time? If so, what was your reaction?

5. As a community organizer in Chicago, Obama has mixed success in helping a group of public housing tenants to get the Chicago Public Housing Authority to remove asbestos from their apartments and make other repairs. What were some of the successful strategies that he and the tenants used to get the Housing Authority to pay attention to them? What mistakes did they make? What did Obama learn from the experience?

6. Have you ever been part of a community group that tried to improve your block or your building or your city? If so, what issues were at stake and what techniques did you use to try to change things?

7. Compare the feelings that Barack, who grew up mostly in America, has towards the father he had barely known with those of his half-brother, Mark, who grew up mostly in Kenya and did know his father. Compare the feelings that they each have about America and about Kenya. Why do you think that their reactions are so different? What role did each of their mothers have in shaping their son's opinions?

8. Obama thinks that he has heard the family land where his father and grandfather are buried referred to as *Home Square*. But he is corrected by his African relatives who tell them that the rural land that their ancestors farmed is known as Home-*Squared*. Here's how his sister Auma explains it:

> There's your ordinary house in Nairobi. And then there's your house in the country, where your people come from. Your ancestral home. Even the biggest minister or businessman thinks this way. He may have a mansion in Nairobi and build only a small hut on his land in the country. He may go there only once or twice a year. But if you ask him where he is from, he will tell you that that hut is his true home . . . it was home twice over, you see. *Home Squared*.

Is that concept less familiar in the United States? Why or why not? Does your own family have a place that it considers to be *Home Squared?*

9. Were you familiar with Kenyan politics, history, or culture before you read the book? What did you learn about Kenya that you did not know before?

10. In the preface to the 2004 edition, Obama says that his

mother died of cancer shortly after the book was first published. He adds that if he had known that she would not survive her illness, he would have written more about her in the book or maybe even focused the book on her rather than on his absent father. Do you think we got to know enough about his mother in this account? What, if anything else, would you have liked to know about her?

MARCH

Charming Billy

BY ALICE McDERMOTT

SUMMARY

"*Charming Billy* is a story about second- and third-generation Irish-Americans, most of whom are blood relations and live and love and laugh and drink and . . . confess and work for Consolidated Edison in the Queens part of New York City," writes John Goodspeed in a 1999 review in the *Baltimore Chronicle*, continuing, "The men have names like Dennis and Danny and Kevin, the women Maeve and Rosemary and Bridie. . . . they're proud to be descendants of Irish immigrants, and some still speak with a brogue. They're patriotic and conformist and voluble and entertaining."

The novel opens in April 1983 at a Bronx tavern where mourners have arrived for a late afternoon meal following the funeral of Billy Lynch, a charismatic, much loved alcoholic who has died in his sixties after wandering out into the street. At the tavern, friends and family recall Billy's life, mentioning his long-ago, tragic love affair. Through a series of conversations and anecdotes, readers learn about Eva, an Irish nanny that Billy met on a Long Island beach just after he returned from World War II. He was on Long Island that summer to help his cousin and best friend, Dennis, repair a summer cottage owned by Dennis's mother and stepfather. The beach and its surrounding mansions, ironically referred to as "cottages," became a dramatic backdrop for summer romance as Billy and Dennis court Irish sisters caring for the children of a wealthy family.

According to the accepted story, Eva had to return to Ireland in the fall. Billy sent her money and an engagement ring expecting that she would come back to New York and marry him. Allegedly, Eva died of pneumonia before she could return, and Billy's hard-earned money from a second job at a Queens shoe store was used to pay for her funeral. While the reader soon finds out what really happened to Eva, Billy does not discover it for another thirty years. In the meantime, he marries the plain steadfast Maeve, who is already caring for an alcoholic father. Still pining for Eva, but never mentioning her to Maeve, Billy works two jobs, charms his friends, and continues to drink.

The narrator of the story, never mentioned by name, is cousin Dennis's daughter. Critic John Goodspeed describes her as "a female baby-boomer who is a cousin-once-removed of the protagonist as well as (probably) the author's alter ego. She's tolerant and smart—she finishes college in two and a half years—but she's subtly critical of the pride and prejudice, racism, sexism, faith, and clannish behavior she observes in her elders." The narrator offers a more complex, yet clearer picture of the past including what was legend and what was real.

AUTHOR BIOGRAPHY

Like many of her characters, Alice McDermott grew up in a middle-class Irish-Catholic family on suburban Long Island. She was born in 1953, the third child and only daughter of Mildred Lynch McDermott, a secretary and homemaker, and William J. McDermott, who worked for the Con Edison electric utility company. Both of her parents were first generation Irish-Americans and both were orphaned in their youth. Though McDermott grew up never knowing any of her biological grandparents, she was part of a large Catholic community and she attended Catholic schools. McDermott remembers filling up notebooks with stories as a young girl as a way of expressing herself, while two brothers, who both became lawyers, dominated dinner table conversations.

In 1971 she went to college at the Oswego campus of the State University of New York, where she studied writing. After graduating in 1975, she went to work as a clerk-typist for Vantage Press, a vanity publishing house, but left to attend the graduate writing program at the University of New Hampshire, where she wrote several short stories for *Redbook, Mademoiselle,* and *Seventeen.* In 1978, after graduating with a master's degree, McDermott was hired by the university. While in New Hampshire, she also met and married her husband, David Armstrong, a neuroscientist.

Her first novel, *A Bigamist's Daughter*, was published in 1982 by Random House, and was based in part on the time that she spent at Vantage Press where she was basically paid for flattering self-published authors. Her second novel, *That Night,* was published in 1987 by Farrar, Straus and Giroux. The story of two star-crossed suburban teenage lovers, it was written in California where she briefly taught at the University of California at Davis while her husband worked at a lab in La Jolla. Farrar, Straus also published her third novel, *At Weddings and Wakes* (1991), a book that is also about Irish-Catholic families in New York City, and her most recent novel, *Child of My Heart* (2002). McDermott lives in Bethesda, Maryland, with her husband, and their three children. She teaches writing at Johns Hopkins University in Baltimore.

WHY THIS IS A GOOD CHOICE FOR A BOOK DISCUSSION GROUP

Charming Billy, with its focus on an Irish-American family is the March selection in honor of St. Patrick's Day. The characters presented, however, may resemble those in many working-class American families, especially those where the children are first and second-generation Americans.

This book should elicit some very interesting discussion. Readers learn about Billy through the stories that friends and family members tell about him, because storytelling remains a powerful way that family members make sense of each other and the world around them. The icebreaker discussion questions, encourages readers to briefly relate some of their own family "legends." Among the controversial themes included in the book are the role that religion plays in helping people to face life's uncertainties and the role that money plays in shaping our destinies. Some readers have noted that the observer/narrator's compilation of facts about Billy through collective anecdotes is confusing, while others have found it enchanting. Others have remarked that this is the way that they have learned about people in their own families. A discussion about the narrative style could raise a compelling debate.

HOW TO GET THIS BOOK

Charming Billy is available in paperback (Delta, 1998; ISBN 038533334X), hardback (Farrar, Straus and Giroux, 1997; ISBN 0374120803). There is a large print version (Wheeler, 1998; ISBN 1568956851), and unabridged audiocassette read by Roses Prichard (Books on Tape, 1999; ISBN 0736644253).

MATERIALS TO SUPPORT YOUR DISCUSSION

- **The poetry of Yeats.** Billy is known for quoting and carrying around a book of poems by the Irish Romantic poet William Butler Years (1865–1939). Toward the end of the book, having met Eva and learned about the lifelong estrangement between her and her sister, Mary, he reads Dennis the following Yeats line from the poem "The Stare's Nest by My Window" from the 1928 work *Meditations in Time of Civil War-VI*): "More substance in our enmities than in our love." The line is part of four stanzas that read:

  We had fed the heart on fantasies
  The heart's grown brutal from the fare
  More substance in our enmities than in our love.

Readers could discuss the meaning of this stanza as both an anti-war message and as a message about spurned lovers.

For readers interested in the work of Yeats, the *Collected Poems of William Butler Yeats* edited by Richard J. Finneran (Scribner, 1996) is recommended

- **Refreshments.** Authentic Irish soda bread, tea cookies, and well prepared Irish tea (steeped loose in a teapot rather than prepared using teabags) can go a long way toward setting the mood—especially if your book talk takes place around St. Patrick's Day. Ideally, you will have a talented baker in your group. Alternatively, perhaps you can find a local bakery that prepares these treats.
- **Irish folk music.** Billy returns from America to Ireland, fully expecting to visit the gravesite of his long lost love, Eva. This sad mission is much like that of the hero of the folk song "Danny Boy." In fact, Billy even sings this song as he drives to Eva's village in Ireland. There are many recorded versions of "Danny Boy," and if you have any Irish folk music in your library collection, chances are it will include this song. Better yet, perhaps someone in your book group or in your community might be a budding folk singer willing to give the tune a try.
- **A book cart featuring the works of Irish and Irish-American writers.** You can stick with fiction or include nonfiction, too. There are many wonderful Irish-American

journalists based in New York City including Pete Hamill and Jimmy Breslin, whose readers probably include folks like Billy.

In 2005, the Virginia cities of Richmond, Chesterfield, Hanover, and Henrico chose *Charming Billy* for a community-wide reading program, called "Go Read," which began in 2002 as an initiative to build a stronger community through reading and discussion. One book of literary fiction is chosen each year to be read and discussed over a three-month period ending with a residency by the featured author. Go Read programs are held in libraries, schools, and book discussion groups. Background material on *Charming Billy* and Alice McDermott can be found at the Go Read Web site archives (see www.goreadrichmond.com).

Here are some other sources for background information.

- The Public Broadcasting System Web site includes an interview with Alice McDermott (see www.pbs.org/ newshour/bb/entertainment/july-dec98/mcdermott_11– 20.html).
- Random House also issues a free Reader's Guide, (www.randomhouse.com/resources/bookgroup/charming billy_bgc.html#books). Call 1–800–323–9872 to order books or free Reader's Guides (available in packs of ten).
- John Goodspeed, "Charming Billy Captures the Irish in Prose" http://baltimorechronicle.com bkreview_charming_ mar99.html
- Christopher Cahill, ed. *There You Are* by Thomas Flanagan (New York Review, 2005; ISBN 15190171063).

Thomas Flanagan is an Irish novelist and literary critic best known for his trilogy of novels, starting with *The Year of the French,* which explores Ireland from the 1798 uprising to the civil war in the 1920s. This book is a collection of pieces on Irish and Irish-American cultural figures including American authors F. Scott Fitzgerald, John O'Hara, Mary McCarthy and William Kennedy.

> **Icebreaker:**
> In many families, small but significant incidents become legends through repeated storytelling. For example, there may be tales of everlasting or unrequited love, fortunes gained or lost, or arguments and reconciliations at family meals not to mention what was served at those meals. Relate (briefly) any family tales of unrequited love or dreams realized or failed, or even the adventures of a family pet, that have influenced or simply amused you.

DISCUSSION QUESTIONS

1. The story begins with a description of the mourners gathered for a meal at a Bronx tavern just after Billy's funeral. Here's how the narrator describes the food:

> The fruit salad was canned but served with a little scoop of lime sherbet, which was refreshing, everyone agreed. It cleared the palate. The rolls were nice. There was some soda bread in one of the bread baskets, someone must have brought it. "Not as good as mine, but then I prefer it with caraway seeds, the way my mother used to make it . . . "

What does this description tell you about the people eating the food? What does it tell you about the narrative style of the book?

2. At the mourner's meal, several minor female characters are introduced who add insights throughout the text into Billy's personality and the effect that he had on people. These characters include Billy's sisters Rosemary and Kate and their neighbor Bridie, who once had a crush on Billy. Some reviewers have said that these women function as a "Greek chorus" of sorts. Do you agree? Of these minor characters did you have a favorite or a woman that you particularly related to? Did they remind you of any of your own family or friends?

3. The narrator of *Charming Billy* is slow to reveal herself and never says her name. We know her as Dennis Lynch's daughter, a minor relation to Billy. Why is it that McDermott chooses this voice to tell Billy's story? What happens to the scope and focus of the novel when the narrator is an observer rather than a participant?

4. Billy had the endearing habit of sending spur-of-the-moment greeting cards to friends and family often from whatever bar or restaurant he happened to be at. In 1983, Bridie still has the one that he sent her on an Aer Lingus cocktail napkin from Shannon Airport in Ireland on his 1975 trip. It says, "Bridie: Just saw your face pass by on a twelve-year-old girl in a navy-blue school uniform. Said her name was Fiona. She was meeting her father's plane from New York. Your smile, your eyes, your very face at that age—second edition. Love, Billy." What does this note tell you about Billy? What does it tell you about his relationship to Bridie? Can you understand why she has saved this note on a cocktail napkin for eight years?

5. Why does Billy love the sight of the large houses in East Hampton, and what does that say about his character and circumstances? What class attitudes are held in common by this large extended family? Kate feels she has escaped her working-class background. Has she really? In what ways has she taken on the characteristics of the upper middle class, and in what ways is she rooted in her origins? (from the Random House Reader's Guide)

6. In November 1998, just after she won the National Book

Award, Alice McDermott told Elizabeth Farnsworth, a Public Broadcasting Service radio interviewer:

> I think *Charming Billy* ultimately is a novel about faith, and what we believe in, and above all, what we choose to believe in. And I think that Billy in this community is someone who the people around him have to believe a romantic tale about. They love him so dearly and are so fond of him and have—they've watched him destroy himself—and it's not enough for them to say, well, Billy's had an unfortunate life. They need to make something more of his life. And they do that by telling stories about him. They keep the faith that his life was valuable, even though on the surface it seems only pathetic.

What, if any, lessons did *you* learn from Billy's life? Did his life appear to be valuable to you, or did it seem pathetic? What lessons do you think that the narrator, Dennis's daughter, learned from Billy's life?

7. Some readers on Amazon.com and elsewhere have commented that they found McDermott's narration style confusing. For one thing, we never learn the name of cousin Dennis's daughter, who is an observer rather than an active character in this story. Rather than being straightforward, her tale is a compilation from the stories and recollections of many others. Here, in the same PBS interview mentioned above, is how McDermott, herself, justifies the narrative style:

> It seemed to me if you're telling a story about faith, you're also telling a story about telling stories, the things that we believe in—our stories that we hear and are told. And so it seemed to me that the entire novel needed to be told to someone, and that was where—the inevitability of that first-person voice telling a story that's not necessarily her own, but putting together, as women do, the various stories in her family and making something of it.

Do you think that she made a wise decision in telling Billy's story this way? Did you find the narrative style to be enlightening or confusing? Why or why not? What facts do we know about the narrator based upon both the details she actually reveals about herself and the observations that she makes?

8. Maeve and Eva are the two key women in Billy's life. Friends, family, and neighbors describe Maeve as the plain, long-suffering, steady wife and daughter, while Eva is remembered as the

beautiful love of his life who died tragically. Does our opinion of these women change as the novel continues? How does Billy's opinion change?

9. Do you think that Dennis should have told Billy the truth about Eva as soon as he found out? Would Billy's life have been any different had he known? Do you think he would have still married Maeve? Do you think that if he knew the truth, he would have drunk more or less?

10. Reviewers have compared Alice McDermott to other Irish writers, including Frank McCourt (*Angela's Ashes*), James Joyce ("The Dead"), F. Scott Fitzgerald (*The Great Gatsby*), and Roddy Doyle (*Paddy Clarke, Ha Ha Ha*). If you have read any of these other works, in what ways are they similar to *Charming Billy*? How do they differ? As they say in literature classes, "compare and contrast!"

APRIL

Nickel and Dimed: On (Not) Getting by in America

BY BARBARA EHRENREICH

SUMMARY

Nickel and Dimed is a nonfiction investigative account of the work done by American low-wage workers. Ehrenreich, a media critic, activist, essayist, and writer, went "undercover" between 1998 and 2000, taking on a series of minimum-wage jobs across the United States with breaks in between to return to her "regular life." As part of her investigation, she worked as a waitress in southern Florida, served as a nursing home aide and Merry Maid in Portland, Maine, and arranged clothing racks as an "associate" at a Wal-Mart near Minneapolis, Minnesota. She filled out applications for countless low-wage jobs, and underwent drug testing and personality/psychological testing. All in all she spent about three months working at these various jobs.

In the introduction to *Nickel and Dimed*, Barbara Ehrenreich explains why she decided to write the book:

> Lewis Lapham, the editor of *Harper's Magazine*, had taken me out for a $30 lunch . . . I was pitching him some ideas having to do with pop culture when the conversation drifted to one of my more familiar themes: poverty. How does anyone live on the wages available to the unskilled? How . . . were the roughly four million women about to be booted into the labor market by welfare reform going to make it on $6 or $7 an hour? Then I said something that I have since had many opportunities to regret: "Someone ought to do the old-fashioned kind of journalism — you know, go out there and try it for themselves." I meant someone much younger than myself, some hungry neophyte journalist with time on her hands.

But Lapham got this crazy-looking half-smile on his face and ended life as I knew it, for long stretches at least, with the single word, "You."

Ehrenreich began her job searches with some advantages that other low-wage workers might not have. She had cash reserves of about $1300 to cover the first month's rent and any emergencies that might crop up (and crop up, they did). She also had a car and a laptop computer. She lived alone, sometimes close to her job location and sometimes far away. Her goal was to pay for food, clothing, shelter, and transportation using only what she earned on the job. Living conditions ranged from hotel rooms, to cottages, to trailers. She ate a lot of fast food or food that could be easily prepared in poorly equipped kitchens. Her co-workers never knew her real identity unless she decided to tell them just before or just after leaving the job. Few were impressed by her revelation.

Ehrenreich worked all day at her job, sometimes taking two jobs at a time, and then spent her free time at her laptop recording her "field notes." At the end of each job, some lasting as long as a month, she wrote a chapter of the book while everything was still fresh in her mind. In *Nickel and Dimed*, she shares what she learned about working and living conditions of people earning minimum wages, and she offers some opinions about what the American government and employers could and should do to help.

AUTHOR BIOGRAPHY

Barbara Ehrenreich is a media critic, activist, essayist, and writer. Born in 1941 in Butte, Montana, to a working-class family, she attended Reed College, graduating with a B.A. in 1963, and in 1968 she graduated from Rockefeller University in New York City with a Ph.D. in biology. She has been married twice, first to co-writer John Ehrenreich in 1966, with whom she has two children, Rosa and Benjamin. After the marriage ended in divorce, in 1983 she married Gary Stevenson.

Ehrenreich began her career as a staff member of the Health Policy Advisory Center in Manhattan and then went on to work as an assistant professor of health sciences at the State University of New York College at Old Westbury between 1971 and 1974. She began working more and more as a writer and columnist in the mid-1970s and 1980s, serving as a writer for *Seven Days* magazine, an editor of *Mother Jones* magazine, and a columnist and essayist for *Time* magazine and the *Guardian* of London. She has also been an associate fellow at the New York Institute for the Humanities, a fellow of the Institute for Policy Studies, and cochair of the Democratic Socialists of America.

Ehrenreich received the Sidney Hillman Award for Journalism and a *Brill's* Content Honorable Mention for a chapter of *Nickel and Dimed* which appeared in *Harper's* in January 1999. A second essay entitled "Maid to Order," which grew out of her research for this book, was also published by *Harper's* (April 2000), where it generated so many letters that the magazine had to create a special section to accommodate them. Both articles drew widespread media interest. In 2002 she won both the Christopher Award and *Los Angeles Times* Book Award in the current interest category for *Nickel and Dimed*. Her most recent book, about white-collar workers facing layoffs and re-entry into the job market is *Bait and Switch: The (Futile) Search for the American Dream* (2005) published by Metropolitan Books. Here again, she went "undercover" disguising herself as a middle-aged recently laid off corporate job applicant with experience in public relations and marketing.

OTHER BOOKS BY BARBARA EHRENREICH:

Bait and Switch: The (Futile) Pursuit of the American Dream (Metropolitan Books, 2005)

For Her Own Good: Two Centuries of the Experts' Advice to Women (Anchor, 2005)

Global Woman: Nannies, Maids, and Sex Workers in the New Economy (Metropolitan Books, 2004)

Fear of Falling: The Inner Life of the Middle Class (Perennial, 1990)

WHY THIS BOOK IS A GOOD CHOICE FOR A BOOK DISCUSSION GROUP

Many readers have worked a minimum wage job or have a parent or child who worked one. As for those who have never had this experience, they certainly are served daily by minimum-wage workers, including retail workers, fast food workers, gas station attendants, house cleaners, and gardeners. These days big box stores such as Wal-Mart are a part of most American communities, and Wal-Mart management techniques and worker experiences have made headlines in daily newspapers. The challenges faced by minimum-wage workers go beyond the work environment—there are family challenges, health-care challenges, transportation issues, and housing problems. Many Americans disagree about how these problems could or should be solved and many disagree about what the government's role should be. All of this can lead to a stimulating book discussion. As a leader, however, you may find yourself in the midst of some heated political debates. As a result, you may have to work a bit harder at giving everyone a chance to speak and keeping the conversation civil.

HOW TO GET THIS BOOK

This book can be purchased in paperback (Owl Books, 2002; ISBN 0805063897) and hardcover (Metropolitan Books, 2001; ISBN 0805063889). A large print edition is also available (Wheeler Publishing, 2003; ISBN 1587243687) as well as a CD version narrated by Christine McMurdo Wallis (Recorded Books, 2004; ISBN 1419305077).

MATERIALS TO SUPPORT YOUR DISCUSSION

- **A book cart filled with books and articles by "muckrakers."** "Muckraker" was the term used in the late 1800s and early 1900s for investigative journalists and writers and filmmakers who "raked up muck," exposing social issues including political corruption, corporate crime, health care fraud, and substandard housing and consumer safety. If *Nickel and Dimed* is the first investigative journalism book that your readers have read, or the first that they have read in a while, this might be a good time to introduce them to some other writers—both past and present. Once upon a time Ralph Nader was known as more than just an unsuccessful presidential candidate. You might include his exposé of the auto industry, *Unsafe At Any Speed* (1965), on the book cart. You could go back further in time and include Upton Sinclair's *The Jungle* (1906), exposing unsanitary conditions in the meat-packing industry. More recently Eric Schlosser's *Fast Food Nation: The Dark Side of the American Meal* (2002) hit best-seller lists with a behind-the-scenes look at fast food restaurants, including sanitation and working conditions.

- **Films and Television Programs** In February and March of 2004, the Kalamazoo Public Library in Michigan chose *Nickel and Dimed* as the selection for a community-wide "Reading Together" program. You can read about the entire program at www.readingtogether.info/readingtogether2004. As part of the program, readers were invited to screenings and discussions of films and television programs about the working poor. The films included:

  Store Wars: When Wal-Mart Comes to Town (2001). A documentary account of how a small community in Ashland, West Virginia, tries to resist plans to open up a Wal-Mart in their town.

  "Wage Slaves: Not Getting by in America" (August 26, 2002). This segment of the A&E series *Investigative Reports* was based in part on *Nickel and Dimed*.

  Fast Food, Fast Women (2000). This comedy about a waitress in a New York City café shows the struggles of the young urban working poor.

  Roger and Me (1989). In this documentary, director Michael Moore pursues GM CEO Roger Smith to confront him about the harm he did to Flint, Michigan, with his massive downsizing. Viewers in Kalamazoo, Michigan, would especially relate to this film. There may be other documentaries or feature films with local connections to workers in your state or community.

- **Studs Terkel's 1974 book *Working: People Talk About What They Do All Day and How They Feel about What They Do.*** A paperback edition of this book was reissued by New Press in 1997 (ISBN 1565843428). In this book of a hundred interviews, Terkel speaks with waitresses, football coaches, dentists, actors, and other working people. Many of them take great pride in their jobs.

  This is a labor history classic and could be a good choice as a follow-up or earlier "compare and contrast" book to Ehrenreich's.

- **Online Study Guides**

  The Guthrie Theater in Minneapolis, which presented Joan Holden's play *Nickel and Dimed* based on the book, has a great study guide for the book as well as the play (www.guthrietheater.org/act_III/studyguide/toc.cfm?id_studyguide=15370100), while Ken Peterson, Professor of Economics at Furman University in Greenville, South Carolina, has posted his own online study guide with discussion questions (alpha.furman.edu/~kpeterso/peterson/

nickelanddimed.htm). The Barbara Ehrenreich Web site: (www.barbaraehrenreich.com) has author interviews with Ehrenreich, news about her appearances, and a separate Reader's Guide with discussion questions. The *Nickel and Dimed* Web site (www.nickelanddimed.net) has links to a number of articles, interviews, and resources related to the book.

The *Harper's* April 1, 2000 issue with Ehreinreich's original article "Maid to Order," and the June 1, 2000, issue that contained letters to the editor including the following:

Scenes from my life as a maid:
Climbing a ladder to change the kitty litter in an attic twice a week.

Bending over a stairway under the maid-service owner's supervision, sweeping the stairs with dustpan and broom, collapsing with asthma afterwards.

On my hands and knees polishing a tiled kitchen floor under the housewife's supervision. Polishing her bathroom floors likewise. Finding my jacket, which this woman had taken downstairs "to put away" for me, balled up in the bottom corner of the closet. The folds with a hollow where she'd punched it into place. (Her husband had one just like it, she'd said.)

Scrubbing a windowless bathroom, seven years' worth of mold off the shower doors, and reeling out past the glass afterwards, dizzy with unventilated ammonia fumes.

The weight and size of Kirby vacuum cleaners. The sheer weight of them. Lighter ones are universally said, by clients and supervisors alike, "not to clean."

Car in an underground car park, coffee from a thermos: lunch.

I was a maid in the early Eighties in the South Bay area of Los Angeles. . . . .

I worked for a company, not independently. All the clients were white.

The company charged $15 an hour; I got $5. By the time I got home I was often too tired to eat.

One of my supervisors was white, the other Latina. The owner of the business was Filipina. Inflicting the punishments of poverty on the poor is a game anyone can play. All it takes is money.

I will never hire someone to do my housework. I'll choke to death first.
Moira McAuliffe, Portland, Oregon.

DISCUSSION QUESTIONS

1. During the course of your day today, did you stop at the gas station or a fast food restaurant or discount chain store? While you were there did you notice the people who helped you? Did you experience any particularly good or bad customer service? If you are a regular customer, do you know any of these folks by name? What was your attitude toward the people who helped you.

2. As an investigative journalist, Ehrenreich was able to try on many different minimum-wage worker "roles." Still, she knew that she could return to her "real life" whenever she wanted to. Does this diminish the power of her story? How would this have been a different book if she had gone out and lived with and/or interviewed actual workers?

3. Why didn't the low-wage workers just switch to the higher paying jobs that Ehrenreich notes were available? What circumstances discourage low-wage workers from seeking out and taking the best paying job that they can find? (from Peterson online study guide)

4. What is meant by the term "mother's hours," a "benefit" offered by the maid service in Maine? Is this job trait likely to raise wages, lower wages, or leave wages unaffected? Should we think of this as a benefit? Can you think of other job characteristics that would be associated with higher or lower wages? (from Peterson online study guide)

5. Ehrenreich is white and middle class. She asserts that her experience would have been radically different had she been a person of color or a single parent. Do you think discrimination shaped Ehrenreich's story? In what ways? (from www.barbara ehrenreich.com)

6. Ehrenreich found that she could not survive on seven dollars per hour—not if she wanted to live indoors. Consider how her experiment would have played out in your community if you had to limit yourself to seven dollars per hour earnings or the current minimum wage. (from www.barbaraehrenreich.com)

7. In a review of *Nickel and Dimed* that appeared in the June 1, 2001, issue of *The Nation*, critic Steve Early writes:

> While often sad and grim, *Nickel and Dimed* is nevertheless sprinkled with the author's trademark humor. She is, for example, frequently struck by the oddity of her circumstances. Sitting alone in a cheap motel, eating takeout food after a hard day at Wal-Mart, she watches

an episode of *Survivor*. "Who are these nutcases who would volunteer for an artificially daunting situation in order to entertain millions of strangers with their half-assed efforts to survive? Then I remember where I am and why I am here."

What point is Ehrenreich trying to make here? Can you think other examples in the book, where Ehrenreich uses humor to make a point? Does her humor work for or against her as a teaching tool?

8. While *Nickel and Dimed* clearly takes a position of government support for minimum-wage workers—including an increase in the minimum wage and improvements in benefits such as health insurance—not everyone in the United States agrees. Many voters and businesses don't want the government to be able to tell employers how to treat workers. Still others don't think that people earning minimum wage should get more money because they don't yet have the marketable skills and experience that employers value.

Did reading this book change your views of social or government responsibility in any way? How did you feel about this issue before you read the book? Did the book change your opinion? Why or why not?

9. In her review of *Nickel and Dimed* in the *New York Times* on May 13, 2001, critic Dorothy Gallagher wrote:

> We have Barbara Ehrenreich to thank for bringing us the news of America's working poor so clearly and directly, and conveying with it a deep moral outrage and a finely textured sense of lives as lived . . . she is now our premier reporter of the underside of capitalism.

Do you agree with this review or do you think that the critic is over-exaggerating Ehrenreich's achievements? Do you view Ehrenreich as a heroine or as a troublemaker?

Can you think of other fiction or nonfiction writers that you have read who have made you more aware of social or political issues either in this country or elsewhere in the world? Can you think of other writers who have sympathized with or identified with low-wage workers?

10. If you were to go undercover to investigate a social issue what issue would you pick? If you were to tackle the same subject as Ehrenreich and learn about the experiences of low-wage workers, is there anything that you would do differently in your undercover operations?

MAY

Snow Flower and the Secret Fan

BY LISA SEE

SUMMARY

This historical novel, set in the remote Hunan province of China in the nineteenth and early twentieth century, opens in 1903 as Lily, a wealthy and amazingly long-lived eighty-year-old widow, looks back on her family life, her friendships, and her rise from poor farm girl to wealthy landowner. Lily's memories center on her relationship with Snow Flower who became her friend when both girls were seven. The girls were paired in a traditional life-long social arrangement in which girls born in the same year under a series of similar auspicious circumstances become sworn sisters known as *laotongs,* meaning "old sames."

Given that in nineteenth-century China, wives and daughters had their feet bound and lived in almost total seclusion, these friendships were very intense and provided much-needed social and emotional support. In fact, the women in Hunan county developed their own secret code for communication: a thousand-year-old language called *nu shu* or "women's writing." Female relatives, friends, and *laotongs* painted these letters on fans, embroidered messages on handkerchiefs, and composed stories in which they shared their hopes, dreams, and accomplishments. The language was then either read silently or read aloud in a sing-song call-and-response as the women did embroidery or weaving.

Snow Flower and Lily's friendship begins when Snow Flower, who comes from a distinguished family whose fortunes have declined, sends Lily a *nu shu* poem inscribed on a silk fan. Over the years Lily's fortunes have increased, in part because her high arches and tiny feet have made her attractive to a wealthy suitor.

Lily and Snow Flower's changing fortunes challenge their strong friendship, a relationship that sustains them through their arranged marriages and bolsters them as they are constantly told that women are worthless except for their ability to give birth to sons. Snow Flower and Lily communicate in person and via secret *nu shu* messages as their villages face a typhoid fever epidemic and they must flee for three months to the mountains during the Taiping Rebellion. Although their friendship helps them to survive this ordeal, a misunderstanding that arises over a message that Snow Flower sends suddenly threatens to tear apart their lifelong friendship.

AUTHOR BIOGRAPHY

Lisa See was born in Paris in 1955, the daughter of anthropologist Richard Edward and novelist Carolyn See. Her family soon moved back to Pasadena, California, where she grew up in the back room of the F. Suie One Company, a Chinese antiques business founded by her paternal great-grandparents. As a young girl, Lisa spent a lot of time there and in Los Angeles's Chinatown. She graduated from Loyola Marymount University in West Los Angeles in 1979 and has worked as a writer ever since.

Lisa See's autobiography, *On Gold Mountain: The One Hundred Year Odyssey of My Chinese-American Family*, was a national best-seller and a *New York Times* Notable Book of 1995. The book traces the journey of Lisa's great-grandfather, Fong See, who overcame obstacles at every step to become the hundred-year-old godfather of Los Angeles's Chinatown and the patriarch of a sprawling family. While collecting the details of her family history for *On Gold Mountain,* See developed the idea for her first mystery/detective book, *Flower Net*, which was published by Ballantine in 1997. It was followed by *The Interior* (HarperCollins, 2001) and *Dragon Bone*s (Random House, 2003). In each of these mysteries, set in China, an American FBI agent, David Stark, teams up with a Chinese woman agent, Liu Hulan, to investigate murders that span both countries. Although the stories take place in modern times, each of these books incorporates Chinese history and traditions into the story line.

In addition to writing books, Ms. See was the *Publishers Weekly* West Coast correspondent for thirteen years. Her freelance articles have appeared in *Vogue, Self, New York Times Book Review, The Los Angeles Times Magazine, The Washington Post Book World*, and *TV Guide*. In 2002, See traveled to Jiangyong County, a remote region of China where few Westerners have ventured, to research *Snow Flower and the Secret Fan,* which was published by Random House in 2005. In her author's note to the book, See discusses her discovery of the secret women's calligraphy known as *nu shu*, and her interviews with ninety-six-year-old Yang Huanyi, the last surviving original *nu shu* writer. Here's what she told the *L.A. Weekly* about her motivations for writing the book:

> What I've been trying to do with this work overall is to write about one-fourth of the world's population and get beyond the stereotypes and misconceptions and preconceptions that people have about China and the Chinese. I'm not trying to say this is how it is; I'm just trying to open a window and let people look through. This book is more about people, about these two Chinese women, but it could be any two women. The circumstance and particulars are different, but these are people who have mothers and fathers, all the human emotions, the love and desire, regret, and the ancestral feelings that transcend culture, time, country.

Ms. See was honored as National Woman of the Year by the Organization of Chinese-American Women in 2001 and was also the recipient of the Chinese-American Museum's History Makers Award in Fall 2003. She lives in Los Angeles with her husband, an international lawyer, and two sons.

WHY THIS BOOK IS A GOOD CHOICE FOR A BOOK DISCUSSION GROUP

As the newest book on the reading list, I have not used *Snow Flower and the Secret Fan* in a book group yet, nor have I seen it used. So a leap of faith is required to predict that it will work in the public library setting. Although this book may appeal to men as well as women, most readers would consider it a "woman's story." The book is chosen for May as a Mother's Day pick and my hope is that mothers and daughters will participate in the discussion. The book presents a variety of mother/daughter relationships worth exploring and is certainly a starting point for how mother/daughter relationships have changed over the years both in the United States and internationally.

If your book group attracts people from different nationalities and cultures, this could also stimulate discussions about how different cultures approach marriage. Readers in your group with a Chinese cultural heritage may recall stories that their grandparents told them or talk about how the culture has changed. You could also invite a guest lecturer in Chinese culture or history or present a slide show since this book includes many vivid images (e.g., carriages that Snow Flower and Lily travel in, and the houses that they lived in). This is also an opportunity to serve some Chinese foods—perhaps a version of the taro custard that Snow Flower and Lily enjoyed. At the very least, you might serve Chinese tea.

This book provides an opportunity to showcase a lot of your library's resources. You could display books on Chinese culture and history or books on women's history or fiction selections by other Asian-American authors including Amy Tan and Gish Gen. If your library is in an area with a large Chinese community, you may already have books and tapes available in Chinese. If you decide to bring in a guest speaker, this could be an opportunity to do outreach to Chinese community members. Speakers could be invited, from a wide range of disciplines: historians, calligraphers, women's history professors, or even the local orthopedic surgeon or foot doctor talking about the mechanics of foot binding.

HOW TO GET THIS BOOK

To date, there is only a hardcover version of this book available (Random House, 1995; ISBN 1400060281), however a paperback version should be out in 2006. The book is also available as an abridged audio CD narrated by Jodi Long, (Random House Audio, 2005; ISBN 0739319817). Random House has also made this book available as a downloadable audiobook and as an eBook.

MATERIALS TO SUPPORT YOUR DISCUSSION

- **The Chinese Animal Zodiac.** Many characters in this book are described in terms of their Chinese zodiac/animal signs. Snow Flower and Lily, for example, are born in the year of the horse while Lily's husband is born in the year of the tiger. Snow Flower's husband is born in the year of the rooster and her mother-in-law is born in the year of the rat. In fact, Snow Flower writes in a note to Lily, "My mother-in-law was born in the year of the rat. Can you imagine anyone worse for someone born in the year of the horse? The rat believes that the horse is selfish and thoughtless, though I am not. The horse believes that the rat is scheming and demanding, which she is." If you can get one, post a chart of the Chinese animal zodiac in the room and describe the characteristics of the people who are born under different signs. You can sometimes find paper zodiac placemats or postcards at Chinese restaurants and stores which you could give to everyone in the group. A chart and information about the Chinese Zodiac is available at the Web site run by San Francisco's Chinese Cultural Center: (www.c-c-c.org/chineseculture/zodiac/zodiac.html).

- **Nu shu.** See's author notes and acknowledgments at the back of the book explain more about the history of *nu shu* writing and the research that went into preparing the book. Your book group could read the first three pages of the notes out loud or you could play this section of the audiotaped version of the book. There are also images of *nu shu* writing available on the Internet. Using the Google search engine, put the words "nu shu" in the search field and click on the "images only" option. Finally, if you have the budget for it, you could obtain the film on *nu shu* distributed by a nonprofit media arts organization called Women Make Movies (www.wmm.com).

  Nu Shu: A Hidden Language of Women in China
  A Videotape by Yue-Qing Yang. 1999 59 minutes Color, VHS Canada/China Subtitled
  Rental VHS $75 VHS Sale: $250 Order# W00655
  Women Make Movies
  462 Broadway Suite 500WS
  New York, NY 10013
  212–925–0606
  212–925–2052 (Fax)
  info@wmm.com (for general information)
  orders@wmm.com (for film and videotape orders
  In *Nu Shu: A Hidden Language of Women in China*, the following poem is translated:
  For sister, the attic
  For brother, the great hall and study
  We embroider a thousand patterns
  Younger brother reads a thousand books

- Random House Reading Group Guide (www.reading groupguides.com/guides3/snow_flower1.asp#discuss).
- Lisa See Web site (www.lisasee.com).

DISCUSSION QUESTIONS

In a book review that appeared in the *Wichita Eagle* on August 14, 2005, reviewer Victoria R. Brownworth of the *Baltimore Sun* wrote:

> Lily evolves as a character with whom the reader (of either gender) can feel a deep affinity, for Lily's quest is irrespective of era or geography or even isolation. See makes her audience feel what Lily feels, to identify with her desperate desire to be touched at that place we call "soul," to exorcise the alienation she feels through one passionate connection with another.

1. Do you agree with the reviewer? Were you personally able to relate to Lily even though her life circumstances were far different than yours? Why or why not?

2. Do you agree with the reviewer that readers of either gender will be able to feel a deep affinity for the character? Or is this a "woman's book" or even what used to be referred to as "an Oprah book"?

3. The book opens with an eighty-year-old widowed Lily looking back on her life. Why do you think that the author chose this way to tell the story? Can you think of other novels or films that begin this way?

4. Who do you think Lily wants to tell this story to? Who do you think the author wants to tell this story to?

5. If Lily is writing her story to Snow Flower in the afterworld, what do you think Snow Flower's response would or should be? (from ReadingGroupGuides.com)

6. Lily's life was far better than her mother's. How much of this was luck and how much of this was by design? What did Lily's mother do to ensure a better life for her daughter? What were the drawbacks to her mother's counsel and attitude?

7. In a society completely dominated by men, Lily's mother-in-law offers her the advice "Obey, obey, obey, then do what you want." How does Lily follow this advice? Do you think that this still applies to roles in marriage today? Why or why not?

8. Snow Flower says that she enjoys having sexual relations with her husband, while Lily sees it as a duty. What effect does this have on their marriages? What effect does this have on the women's relationship with each other?

9. Is the miscommunication in the fan the *only* factor that causes the great rift in Snow Flower and Lily's friendship? What, if any other factors, contribute to the break?

10. Of all of the women described in the book, who do you think is the most independent? the most dependent?

REFERENCES

Kinsella, Bridget. "Seeing China." *Publishers Weekly* 252, no. 27 (July 2005), p. 28.

Huneven, Michelle. "Female Trouble: Lisa See On Women's Friendship and the Secret Hidden Language at the Heart of Snow Flower and the Secret Fan." *L.A. Weekly*, (July 8, 2005). Available at http://laweekly.com/ink/05/33/books-huneven.php.

JUNE

The Kite Runner

BY KHALED HOSSEINI

SUMMARY

Khaled Hosseini's debut novel, *The Kite Runner,* set in Afghanistan, Pakistan, and Northern California, spans a time period of almost forty years. The story begins in Afghanistan in the mid-1960s and ends in Northern California in March 2002. In terms of the history of Afghanistan, the story begins before the coup which toppled King Zahir Shah in 1973. The action then continues as the main character, Amir, and his father flee their home country of Afghanistan during the Russian occupation in the 1980s. Amir later revisits the country in 2001, during the reign of the Taliban.

The narrator of the story is Amir, who is born in 1963 in Kabul, Afghanistan. Amir's mother has died in childbirth and he is the only child of a wealthy businessman. Amir's daily needs are met by his father's servant, Ali, and Ali's son, Hassan, who is just a year younger than Amir. Hassan, too, appears to be an only child, who was abandoned by his mother after he was born. Although of a different servant class, he becomes a loyal friend to Amir. Amir, who loves to read and write stories, is very different in temperament from his bold, aggressive father, whom he calls Baba. Though Amir is constantly seeking Baba's attention and approval, he believes that he has disappointed and at times even disgusted Baba. On the other hand, both Ali and Baba admire Hassan. Although Hassan can neither read nor write as a child, he often appears to be more clever and resourceful than Amir. All of these factors lead Amir and Hassan to form a complex friendship of love, jealousy, class differences, and, ultimately, betrayal.

Striving to impress his father, Amir competes in a kite running tournament, a contest in which participants must cut down the kites of their competitors with their kite strings sharpened with ground glass. The fallen kites are then tracked down and displayed as trophies by players known as kite runners. With Hassan serving as kite runner, Amir wins the tournament. Yet his victory is embittered by a tragedy that occurs on the same day as his victory. As he searches for Hassan who has collected the last fallen kite, Amir passively witnesses Hassan being attacked and raped by the leader of a group of local toughs who have threatened both boys before. In the past, Hassan has stood up to the bullies, but Amir does nothing to help his friend. Throughout his life, Amir remembers this moment with great guilt, harboring bad memories even when moving to California where he marries and becomes a writer. Decades later, in June 2001, he is called back to Afghanistan by a dying family friend who offers him a chance to redeem himself.

AUTHOR BIOGRAPHY

Khaled Hosseini was born in Kabul, Afghanistan, in 1965, the oldest of five children. His father was a diplomat who worked for the foreign ministry and his mother taught Farsi and history at a large girl's high school in Kabul. In 1970, the foreign ministry sent the Hosseini family to Tehran, where their father worked for the Afghan embassy. They lived in Tehran until 1973, at which point they returned to Kabul. In July of 1973, on the night Hosseini's youngest brother was born, the Afghan king, Zahir Shah, was overthrown in a bloodless coup by the king's cousin, Daoud Khan. At the time, Hosseini was in fourth grade and was already drawn to poetry and prose; he read a great deal of Persian poetry as well as Farsi translations of novels ranging from *Alice in Wonderland* to Mickey Spillane's Mike Hammer series.

In 1976, Khaled's family was relocated to Paris, France, where his father was assigned a diplomatic post in the Afghan embassy. The Hosseini family was going to return to Afghanistan in 1980 when the assignment ended. By then, however, Afghanistan had already witnessed a bloody communist coup and the Soviet invasion. In response, Khaled's father asked for and was granted political asylum in the U.S. So the family moved to San Jose, California, in 1980 and lived on welfare and food stamps for a short while, having lost all of their property in Afghanistan. Their father took multiple jobs and managed to get his family off welfare. Hosseini graduated from high school in 1984 and enrolled at Santa Clara University, where he earned a bachelor's degree in biology in 1988. The following year, he entered the University of California-San Diego's School of Medicine, where he earned a Medical Degree in 1993. He completed his residency at Cedars-Sinai Hospital in Los Angeles.

Hosseini, a practicing internist since 1996, is married and has two children, a boy and a girl, Haris and Farah. *The Kite Runner* is Hosseini's debut novel and the first Afghan novel to be written in English. It was published to much critical acclaim, including designation as the "Best Book of the Year" by the *San Francisco Chronicle,* and was a recipient of a 2004 Alex Award as an adult book that appeals to teen readers. According to the Penguin Press biography, Dr. Hosseini's first love has always been writing. This biography states

> Hosseini has vivid, and fond, memories of peaceful pre-Soviet era Afghanistan, as well as of his personal experiences with Afghan Hazaras. One Hazara in particular was a thirty-year-old man named Hossein Khan, who worked for the Hosseinis when they were living in Iran. When Hosseini was in the third grade, he taught Khan to read and write. Though his relationship with Hossein Khan was brief and rather formal, Hosseini always remembered the fondness that developed between them. (www.penguinputnam.com/nf/Author/AuthorPage/0,,0_1000060668,00.html?sym=BIO).

In March 2003, having completed *The Kite Runner*, Hosseini returned to Afghanistan for the first time in over twenty-five years. He described that trip in an article for the *San Francisco Chronicle* ("Following Amir—A Trip to Afghanistan in Which Life Imitates Art," August 10, 2003). Here are some excerpts:

> With the novel proofread and in production, I found myself tracing my protagonist's footsteps, sitting in the window seat of an Ariana Airlines Boeing 727 headed toward Kabul. Like Amir, I had been gone a long time, almost 27 years, in fact; I was an 11-year-old, thin-framed seventh-grader when I left Afghanistan. I was going back now as a 38-year-old physician residing in Northern California, a writer, a husband and father of two. I gazed out the window, waiting for the plane to break through the clouds, waiting for Kabul to appear below me. When it did, a few lines from *The Kite Runner* came to me, and Amir's thoughts suddenly became my own: The kinship I felt suddenly for the old land surprised me. I thought I had forgotten about this land. But I hadn't. Maybe Afghanistan hadn't forgotten me either. The old adage in writing is you write about what you've experienced. I was going to experience what I had already written about.

The emotional impact of finding my father's house would have been even more intense if I hadn't written *The Kite Runner*. After all, I had already been through this. I had stood beside Amir at the gates of his father's house—now overtaken by murderous Taliban soldiers—and felt his loss. I'd watched him set his hands on the rusty wrought-iron bars, and together we'd gazed at the sagging roof and crumbling front steps. Having written that scene took some of the edge off my own experience. Call it art stealing life's thunder.

You can read the entire article and learn more about Hosseini's life at the author's Web site: (www.khaledhosseini.com).

WHY THIS BOOK IS A GOOD CHOICE FOR A BOOK DISCUSSION GROUP

The review of this book that appeared in *Library Journal* notes that "Hosseini, now a doctor in California, is possibly the only Afghan author writing in English (who) . . . provides a vivid glimpse of life in Afghanistan over the past quarter century." Many public libraries throughout the United States have used this book in community-wide reading programs. "This novel invites readers to peer through a window into Afghanistan before the Russian occupation and imagine what it would be like to grow up during troubled times," said Carol Jago, Santa Monica High School's English department chair and a member of the Citywide Reads Advisory Committee which chose *The Kite Runner* as its 2005 selection. In a press release announcing the choice, she added, "The author offers no simple solutions but rather a heartbreaking story of friends caught up in history. After reading this novel, media coverage of the region took on new meaning. Fiction can sometimes teach us every bit as much as news reports."

Some libraries have run *Kite Runner* book discussions at which Islamic religious leaders, diplomats, and scholars are invited to speak. Some libraries have offered Afghan cooking lessons, and others have even sponsored kite building workshops. Many of these libraries have put up Web sites related to *Kite Runner* reading programs or have added links to their library sites. To find these sites, do a Google search: "Kite Runner" and "libraries." Many of the libraries sponsoring community-wide reading programs have posted great activity and speaker ideas and discussion questions. Some of these libraries and their activities are mentioned in this guide.

HOW TO GET THIS BOOK

The Kite Runner is available in paperback (Riverhead Books, 2003; ISBN 00594480001), and hard cover (Riverhead Books, 2003; ISBN 1573222453). A large print edition (Center Point Large Print Publishers, 2003; ISBN 1585473634), and audio versions are available. There is an audiocassette collection (Simon & Schuster Audio, 2003; ISBN 0743530233) read by the author as well as an unabridged CD. (Audioworks, 2005; ISBN 0743545230).

MATERIALS TO SUPPORT YOUR DISCUSSION

- **Films.** In 2005, *The Kite Runner* was the fiction selection for "United We Read," a community-wide reading program coordinated by the Kansas City Metropolitan Library & Information Network and libraries throughout the Kansas City Metropolitan Region. The program was sponsored by an advisory board of local librarians, teachers, bookstores, and community agencies. Modeled after Chicago's successful "One Book, One Chicago" project, "United We Read" involves libraries, cities, counties, media outlets, colleges, senior/retirement centers, universities, high schools, businesses and book clubs. One of the reasons that Kansas City chose *The Kite Runner* was because the selection committee believed that it would appeal to people of all ages. The Web site for the program has a wide range of supporting materials for *The Kite Runner.* (www.kcmlin.org/UnitedWeRead/2005/introduction.htm).

  It also links to a list of multimedia resources about Afghani culture compiled by Andrea Kempf, Reference Librarian at the Johnson County Community College Billington Library in Overland Park, Kansas. (library.jccc.

net/reference/guides/afghanfiction.html). Here are some of the films that she recommends:

Daughters of Afghanistan 2004
ASIN: B0002ZA1HA **List price**: $99.95
This is a documentary chronicling the struggle for women's rights in Post-Taliban Afghanistan. Award-winning journalist and UNICEF representative Sally Armstrong witnesses heroic women fighting for the cause, and the powerful forces that threaten their freedom.

Kandahar Journey into the Heart of Afghanistan [DVD] (2001)
Run Time: 81 min
ASIN: B000089RTN **List price**: $29.95
This film is a fictionalized story of Nafas, an Afghan-born Canadian journalist who returns to her homeland. She goes back in a desperate attempt to reach her sister, who, overcome with grief after being injured by a landmine and despairing over the Taliban's oppression of women, has vowed that she will commit suicide at the time of the next solar eclipse, only three days away.

Osama [DVD] (2003)
Run Time: 83 min
ASIN: B0001IXTDG **List price**: **$14.95**
The first feature film made in Afghanistan in the post-Taliban era, *Osama* chronicles the true story of a young girl in Taliban-ruled Afghanistan who must disguise herself as a boy to save her family from starvation.

- **The Shahnamah (Book of Kings) in translation.** Ali read to Hassan from the *Shahnamah*, the tenth-century epic of ancient Persian heroes. The two boys had a favorite story, "Rostam and Sohrab," the tale of the great warrior Rostan and his fleet-footed horse, Rakhsh. Rostam mortally wounds his valiant nemesis, Sohrab, in battle, only to discover that Sohrab is his long-lost son. Hassan later gives Ali a new copy of the *Shahnamah* as a birthday gift and later names his son Sohrab. Book group readers may be interested in further exploring this epic poem in translation, although it might be difficult to find a copy in English at your neighborhood bookstore or library. However, in March 2006, Viking Press is planning to release an American translation of the book (ISBN 0670034851), translated by Dick Davis, professor of Persian at Ohio State University and a Fellow of the Royal Society of Literature.

  Here is the description of this ancient work from the Amazon.com Web site:

Among the great works of world literature, perhaps one of the least familiar to English readers is the *Shahnameh: The Persian Book of Kings*, the national epic of Persia. This prodigious narrative, composed by the poet Ferdowsi between the years 980 and 1010, tells the story of pre-Islamic Iran, beginning in the mythic time of Creation and continuing forward to the Arab invasion in the seventh century.

As a window on the world, *Shahnameh* belongs in the company of such literary masterpieces as Dante's *Divine Comedy*, the plays of Shakespeare, the epics of Homer—classics whose reach and range bring whole cultures into view. In its pages are unforgettable moments of national triumph and failure, human courage and cruelty, blissful love and bitter grief.

In tracing the roots of Iran, *Shahnameh* initially draws on the depths of legend and then carries its story into historical times, when ancient Persia was swept into an expanding Islamic empire.

(The original author of the work) Abolqasem Ferdowsi was born in Khorasan in a village near Tus in 940. His great epic, *Shahnameh*, was originally composed for the Samanid princes of Khorasan. Ferdowsi died around 1020 in poverty.

You can also read an English translation online at the Web site of the Shahnamah project, put together by a group of international scholars (shahnama.caret.cam.ac.uk/index.php).

- **The Penguin Press Reader's Guide.** There are a lot of commercially prepared reader's guides available for modern fiction paperbacks, but Penguin Press does a particularly good job with its guides, including this one for *The Kite Runner* which is available on the Internet in a printer-friendly version at (www.penguinputnam.com/static/rguides/us/kite_runner.html).
- **A map of Afghanistan.** By providing readers with a map, they can see the strategic proximity to Pakistan, Iran, and the former Soviet Union and see the size of the country.
- **Other recent novels set in Afghanistan.** These days, inspired both by the commercial success of *The Kite Runner,* and by overall increased interest in the country and its people, more publishers are offering books about contemporary Afghanistan. If your book group members want to follow up *The Kite Runner* with related selections, here are some others that book groups have been reading:

The Swallows of Kabul by Yasmina Khadra; translated by John Cullen (Anchor, 2005; ISBN 1400033764).

This novel describes the tragic trajectory of two couples, a jailer and his wife, and a middle-class Afghani and his wife, as oppression and religious fanaticism bring them together. Khadra is the pen name for Algerian army officer Mohamed Moulessehoul (In the Name of God; Wolf Dreams), who describes the effects of political repression and religious rule on a pair of Kabul couples—a jailer and his wife and a middle-class Afghani husband and wife.

The Warlord's Son by Dan Fesperman (Vintage, 2005; ISBN 140003048X).

This espionage thriller, features Stan Kelly, a former war correspondent, now covering town meetings for a midwestern daily. Five weeks after 9/11 he is given another chance to get back into war-zone journalism, on a journey into Afghanistan. The plot thickens when he hires a local guide with a dangerous past.

Parvana's Journey by Deborah Willis (Groundwood Books, 2003; ISBN 0888995199).

This novel was written with a young adult audience in mind. Disguised as a boy, a twelve-year-old girl named Parvana sets off from Kabul in search of her missing mother and siblings in Taliban-era Afghanistan. When war breaks out, she bands together with other displaced children. Royalties from the sale of the book go to Women for Women, a relief organization benefiting women in Afghanistan.

The Breadwinner by Deborah Willis (Groundwood Books, 2001; ISBN 0888994168). Here is the description of this young adult novel from Amazon.com

In the wily Parvana, Ellis creates a character to whom North American children will have no difficulty relating. The daughter of university-educated parents, Parvana is thoroughly westernized in her outlook and responses. A pint-sized version of Offred from Margaret Atwood's *The Handmaid's Tale*, Parvana conceals her critique of the repressive Muslim state behind the veil of her chador. Although the dialogue is occasionally stilted and the ending disappointingly sketchy, *The Breadwinner* is essential reading for any child curious about ordinary Afghans. Like so many books and movies on the subject, it is also eerily prophetic. "Maybe someone should drop a big bomb on the country and start again," says a friend of Parvana's. "'They've tried that,' Parvana said, 'It only made things worse.'"

- Recent nonfiction about Afghanistan

    The Bookseller of Kabul by Asne Seierstad (Back Bay Books, 2003: ISBN 0316159417).

    A thirty-one-year-old Norwegian journalist describes middle-class life in Afghanistan immediately after the fall of the Taliban as she lived for three months with a bookseller and his extended family in Kabul.

    The Sewing Circles of Herat: A Personal Voyage Through Afghanistan by Christina Lamb (Perennial; February, 2004; ISBN 0060505273).

    Award-winning British journalist Lamb, who covered Afghanistan during the Russian occupation, returns to the country after 9/11 and interviews politicians, teachers, religious leaders, and average citizens focusing on life under the Taliban.

- **A list of the major characters.** Because their names are unfamiliar to American readers, you might want to write down the following list of names of the major characters on a blackboard or poster easel:

    Amir—the narrator
    Baba—Amir's father
    Ali—Baba's long-time servant
    Hassan—Amir's servant, friend, and son of Ali
    Assef—a neighborhood bully
    Sanaubar—Hassan's mother
    Soraya—Amir's wife
    Sohrab—Hassan's son

Icebreaker:
Although we hear about Afghanistan on the news, many of us knew very little about the country and its people—especially prior to September 11, 2001. Some people who have read this book have said that they were surprised to learn that it snows in Afghanistan—picturing it as a more desert-like nation. Let's begin by asking each person in the group to share what they knew about the culture of Afghanistan before reading the book and what they learned afterward.

DISCUSSION QUESTIONS

1. Hosseini writes a lot about bullies, both in our neighborhood and in the world, starting with a vicious German/Afghani teen, Assef, who happens to admire Adolf Hitler. Who are the other bullies in this book? Who gets the chance to redeem themselves?

2. Consider the following paragraph—especially the highlighted part:

"One time, a bratty Hindi kid whose family had recently moved into the neighborhood, told us that in his hometown, kite fighting had strict rules and regulations . . . Hassan and I looked at each other. Cracked up. The

> Hindi kid would soon learn what the British learned earlier in the century—and what the Russians would eventually learn by the late 1980s—that Afghans are an independent people. **Afghans cherish custom but abhor rules. And so it was with kite flying. The rules were simple: No rules. Fly your kite. Cut the opponent's. Good luck."**

How does this compare with American and European cultures and philosophies? How does this philosophy help to explain conflicts in the Middle East? Can customs coexist with rules?

3. In a 2003 interview on National Public Radio, Hosseini describes the traditional father/son relationship in Afghanistan.

> It's a patriarchal society, and fatherhood, particularly, is a revered institution . . . The dynamics between fathers and sons are based on esteem and respect and etiquette and so on. You know, Dad is not somebody who, you know, slaps you on the butt when you hit a triple, you know? You have your mother's love, but you earn your father's. And Amir feels that in a very difficult way.

Do you agree with Hosseini that many Americans have less formal, more unconditionally loving father/son relationships? What kind of father/son relationships do you observe in your own family and/or your culture or country of origin?

4. As Amir remembers an Afghan celebration in which a sheep must be sacrificed, he talks about seeing the sheep's eyes moments before its death. "I don't know why I watch this yearly ritual in our backyard; my nightmares persist long after the bloodstains on the grass have faded. But I always watch, I watch because of that look of acceptance in the animal's eyes. Absurdly, I imagine the animal understands. I imagine the animal sees that its imminent demise is for a higher purpose." Why do you think Amir recalls this memory when he witnesses Hassan's tragedy in the alleyway? Amir recollects the memory again toward the end of the novel when he sees Sohrab in the home of the Taliban. Discuss the image in the context of the novel. (from www.penguinputnam.com/static/rguides/us/kite_runner.html)

5. When Amir and Baba move to the States their relationship changes, and Amir begins to view his father as a more complex man. Discuss the changes in their relationship. Do you see the changes in Baba as tragic or positive? (from www.penguin putnam.com/static/rguides/us/kite_runner.html)

6. After Soraya tells Amir about her past, she says, "I'm so

lucky to have found you. You're so different from every Afghan guy I've met." How do Afghan women fare in America? Are they any better off than they were in Afghanistan before the Taliban seized power? There is a noticeable absence of women in the novel. How is this significant? (from a discussion guide prepared for the Cincinnati Public Library "On the Same Page" community reading program)

In the fall of 2005, the community of Edina, Minnesota, chose *The Kite Runner* for their community-wide reading program. The Web site is www.edinareads.com. The following two questions come from the site.

7. Amir and Baba come to America as immigrants. Do you think their experiences were typical of new immigrants? Was anything about their life in America unique to their being from Afghanistan?

8. How does Amir's confrontation with Assef at Wazir Akar Khan (chapter 22) represent a turning point in the story?

9. Some critics have said that the last third of the book read more like an action/adventure screenplay and that the coincidences were hard to believe. Do you agree? Why or why not? Did you enjoy the last part of the book in which Amir rescues Sohrab? Discuss the symbolism of the slingshot in the fight scene with Assef. What did you think of Hossein's decision to depict the villain Assef as a homosexual?

10. What did you think of the ending of the book? Did you find it hopeful? What kind of life do you imagine for Sohrab as he grows up?

Part IV

Resources for Book
Discussion Groups

RESOURCE A: ANNOTATED BIBLIOGRAPHY OF BOOKS AND MAGAZINES FOR BOOK GROUPS

Gelman, Judy and Vicki Levy Krupp. *The Book Club Cook Book: Recipes and Food for Thought from Your Book Club's Favorite Books and Authors.* New York: Tarcher/Penguin Press, 2004.

Authors Gelman and Krupp, both members of several book clubs, decided that instead of organizing a cookbook around the foods and recipes mentioned in particular books, they would start instead by choosing the one hundred favorite books of book clubs from around the country. Once the books, including fiction, non-fiction and memoirs, were identified, the authors asked members about the meals and food served at these discussions. Each book listed is accompanied by a brief summary, including comments from book club members, and a recipe for an appropriate dish. For example, for Frank McCourt's *Angela's Ashes*, there is a recipe for Irish Soda Bread and for Sue Monk Kidd's *The Secret Life of Bees*, there's honey cake.

Jacobsohn, Rachel W. *The Reading Group Handbook: Everything You Need to Know to Start Your Own Book Club.* New York: Hyperion, 1998.

This Chicago-based author has been a professional reading group leader for over twenty-five years and the strength of this book is her discussion of group dynamics. Her chapter on food is fun to read, too; she notes that popcorn and chocolate are favorite snacks, and that madeleines are good when discussing Proust. Here's some of her advice on opening the discussion:

> Usually I let the book dictate how the discussion begins. A new author may need introduction. An unfamiliar genre may need background. The setting of the book (the time and place in which it was written) may need explanation. These procedures are leader-directed. But turnabout is fair play, so many times a discussion simply needs a kick-start question such as "So, what did

you think of this?" or . . . "Did we like the book?" to become member-directed. Sometimes asking, "Is there anyone who didn't like this book?" creates the perfect entree into a controversial discussion on its merits. "Has anybody been to?" elicits member's verification of the novel's place. And we go from there.

Kennedy. *Exxon Mobil Masterpiece Theatre Book & Film Club II: A Guide for Libraries.* Boston: WGBH Educational Foundation, Fall 2004.

Masterpiece Theatre produces many television dramatizations based on classic works of literature. Some of the productions have included Tolstoy's *Anna Karenina*, Shakespeare's *Othello*, and *Almost a Woman*, Esmeralda Santiago's memoir of her teenage years in New York City. This guide, produced by the outreach department of Boston public television and radio station WGBH, features ideas for library-based book/movie clubs centered on *Masterpiece Theatre* productions. However, there are plenty of ideas here for public librarians who run book groups that are not based on these programs. You can order the free pamphlet from WGBH, Educational Outreach, 125 Western Avenue, Boston, MA 02134. There are also materials for book groups at the Public Broadcasting System (see www.pbs.org/wgbh/masterpiece/learningresources/bookclub.html).

Laskin, David, and Holly Hughes. *The Reading Group: The complete guide to starting and sustaining a reading group with annotated lists of 250 titles for provocative discussion.* New York: Plume, 1995.

Laskin and Hughes are freelance writers who belonged to the same monthly New York City book group for fourteen years. Eventually the group fizzled out, but the authors were sorry to see it go. So when they wrote this book, they did research on what they might have done differently to keep their group going. The result is an excellent chapter on troubleshooting which looks at issues including attendance problems and what to do when lots of members don't have time or don't bother to finish the book. Here's a suggestion I may follow when my group tackles Steinbeck's *East of Eden* in 2004: "If you've chosen a really long book that few members have finished, discuss the first half at one meeting and then schedule a second meeting to wrap things up." Trivia and history buffs will also enjoy the chapter "A Brief History of the Reading Group in America."

Moore, Ellen and Kira Stevens. *Good Books Lately: The One Stop Resource for Book Groups and Other Greedy Readers.* New York: St. Martin's Griffin, 2004.

The authors are English professors at the University of Denver who are studying the cultural phenomenon of book groups. They also run a book group consulting business. Their book has a list of suggested book group selections and anecdotes from book groups across the United States. Related resources for book groups are available at their Web site, www.goodbookslately.com.

Nelson, Sara. *So Many Books, So Little Time: A Year of Passionate Reading.* New York: Berkley 2003.

Nelson, a voracious and varied reader who is now editor in chief of *Publishers Weekly,* describes a year of reading choices ranging from classics—"the homework I didn't do in college"—to current books that "everyone is talking about." Along the way, she describes how what she is reading intersects with her personal life.

Pearl, Nancy. *Book Lust: Recommended Reading for Every Mood, Moment and Reason.* Seattle: Sasquatch Books, 2003.

Seattle public librarian Nancy Pearl created the program, "If All of Seattle Read the Same Book," which became a model for "One Book One City" programs. This book is a good starting point for creating reading lists because Pearl has well-honed professional instincts for recognizing quality literature with broad appeal. Book group leaders will appreciate her historical context for different genres including the experiences of different ethnic groups in America, and a list of one hundred good reads, decade by decade for the twentieth century. Imagine immersing your book group in one book for each decade over the course of a year. Book group leaders may also appreciate her section on Companion Reads, books that can be linked sequentially to broaden the understanding of each. For example, she suggests "moving memoirs about growing up Hispanic in America: *Down These Mean Streets* by Piri Thomas, and *When I Was Puerto Rican* and *Almost a Woman* by Esmeralda Santiago. There's also a list of books about Elvis for those so inclined. One caveat: Some of the books that she recommends are now out of print but could be obtained via interlibrary loan.

Pearl, Nancy. *More Book Lust: Recommended Reading for Every Mood, Moment and Reason.* Seattle: Sasquatch Books, 2005.

This is a sequel to *Book Lust,* offering another thousand recommended titles. Reading suggestions and booklists are organized into nearly 150 eclectic categories, including "Plots for Plotzing" (highly unusual storylines), "The Autobiographical Gesture" (memoirs about complex lives), "Child Prodigies" (child characters who are called on to perform great and sometimes heroic acts), "Nagging Mothers, Crying Children" (true tales from the frontlines of parenting), and "Libraries and Librarians."

Note: Nancy Pearl also edits a monthly "Reader's Shelf" column in *Library Journal* in which a different guest author makes recommendations for a group of fiction or nonfiction books on a very specific genre (e.g., books about the state of Florida or books about breast cancer).

***Slezak, Ellen, ed. The Book Group: A Thoughtful Guide to Forming and Enjoying a Stimulating Book Discussion Group.* Chicago Review Press, 2000.**

This is a collection of essays written by book group participants and leaders across the United States and Canada. Each talks about the challenges and rewards of participating in their particular groups. Reading lists for each group are provided at the back of the book which is really helpful if you find an essay about a group that sounds a lot like yours. The book focuses on privately run book discussion groups but there are four well-written essays by public library group leaders in Illinois, Iowa, and Pennsylvania. The quality of writing is excellent. Some of the essays about how people's lives were changed by their groups are narrative nonfiction at their best. You might even want your book group to read an essay or two!

MAGAZINES

New magazines aimed at book lovers rather than book buyers often have a very short shelf life. Many have come and gone in the past few years, although book review sections in online literary and cultural magazines like *Salon* (www.salon.com) and *Ruminator* (www.ruminator.com) are thriving.

Book group members and library book group leaders often peruse book reviews, author interviews, and book excerpts that appear in longtime hard copy subscription magazines, including *The New Yorker, Harper's Magazine,* the *Atlantic Monthly,* and The *New York Review of Books.* And librarians continue to rely on the book reviews in *Kirkus Reviews, Library Journal,* and *Publishers Weekly* for both acquisition and readers advisory activities.

Here are three lesser known but equally well regarded magazines/newsletters that library book group leaders recommend:

Bookmarks. This relatively new magazine has been around since 2002 in both hard copy and online versions (http://bookmarksmagazine.com). It is published six times a year and actually features a book group in each issue. Editorial offices are in Chapel Hill, North Carolina. Hundreds of books are reviewed in each issue with mini-reviews formatted to include comments from a number of book reviewers around the United States. The works of classic authors are also featured, running the gamut from F. Scott Fitzgerald to Kurt Vonnegut, Jr. The September/October 2005 issue had an overview of works by John Updike and a list of definitive books about ancient Greece. In addition to the reviews of new books contained in each issue of *Bookmarks,* concise summaries of reviews from a number of newspapers are also included. *Bookmarks* is published by Phillips and Nelson Media, Inc. and hard copies are distributed only in the United States.

Book Sense. Since *Book Sense* is a national marketing campaign of the independent bookstores of America you can often find hard copies of the *Book Sense* newsletter distributed for free at your local independent bookstore. In fact, the *Book Sense* bestseller list runs in more than a dozen newspapers as well as monthly in *U.S. News and World Report* and on CSPAN. *Book Sense* "Picks" is a monthly pamphlet with summaries and recommendations of eclectic new books chosen by independent booksellers in the United States and Puerto Rico. You can see some of the monthly Booksense picks online at www.booksense.com.

Reverberations: News Journal of the Association of Book Group Readers and Leaders (ABGRL). This monthly newsletter is published by Rachel Jacobsohn, who wrote the *Reading Book Handbook*. The subscription fee, which includes membership in the organization, is twenty dollars. ABGRL does NOT advertise and maintains a membership of approximately one thousand members, almost all of whom belong to at least one book group, if not more. People can join by sending the $20 annual membership fee to: ABGRL, P.O. Box 885, Highland Park, IL 60035.

RESOURCE B: ONLINE TOOLS FOR CHOOSING AND EVALUATING BOOKS

In Chapter 3, "Choosing the Right Books," you'll find a wide range of online resources for book selection. Here are a few more general interest and specialty sites recommended by librarians across the United States:

GENERAL INTEREST SITES

- **The Books Section of the National Public Radio Web Site (www.npr.org/templates/topics/topic.php?topicId=1032)**
  Here you'll find book recommendations, author interviews, news about publishing, and commentary by Nancy Pearl, the Seattle librarian who founded the "One Book One City" program. There are also audio links so that readers can listen to recorded interviews and stories.
- **The National Book Critics Circle Web Site (www.bookcritics.org)**
  The National Book Critics Circle, founded in 1974, consists of over seven hundred active book reviewers. Each year NBCC members vote on book awards in five categories: fiction, general nonfiction, biography/autobiography, poetry, and cultural and literary criticism. The Web site has a section entitled "Useful Book and Criticism Related Links" (www.bookcritics.org/page13.html) that will link you to the homepages of newspapers and magazines that have book sections or directly to the book section. There are also links to the British Broadcasting Company (BBC) books Web site (www.bbc.co.uk/arts/books) and the book section of the CNN Web site (www.cnn.com/books/reviews).

SPECIAL INTEREST SITES

- **African-American Voices from the New York Public Library** (www.nypl.org/branch/books/index2.cfm?ListID=221)
  Here are well-reviewed recent fiction and nonfiction titles by and about African-Americans. The library updates this list each year.
- **Gay and Lesbian Pride from the New York Public Library** (www.nypl.org/branch/books/index2.cfm?ListID=236)
  Here are well-reviewed fiction and nonfiction books by and about gay people. The library also updates this list each year.
- **Novedades**
  Written in Spanish, this monthly listing, includes new popular American books that have been translated into Spanish.
- **Index of Native American Book Resources on the Internet** (www.hanksville.org/NAresources/indices/NAbooks.html)
  This comprehensive Web site is maintained by one woman who is helped by hundreds of volunteers. You'll find reviews of fiction and nonfiction books for children as well as adults. While there are author profiles of mainstream writers like Sherman Alexis and Louise Erdich, there are also profiles of lesser-known authors, including traditional Native American storytellers. This site includes links to Native American social, cultural, and educational organizations.

LIBRARY SITES FOR BOOK GROUP LEADERS

- **Montgomery County Public Library in Maryland** (www.montgomerycountymd.gov/content/libraries/index.asp)
  Montgomery County Library has some great reader's advisory material on its Web site, including lists of books by international authors that have been translated into English. The library's "Readers Café" (www.montgomerycountymd.gov/apps/Libraries/readerscafe/index.asp) contains special sections such as Latin American and U.S.

Latino Writers (www.montgomerycountymd.gov/lrctext.
asp?url=/content/libraries/readerscafe/lawriters.asp).
- **The Waterville Public Library in Maine (www.waterville.
lib.me.us)**
  The Waterville Public Library has a Reader's Services
  section on its Web site that lists book sites by genre
  (www.waterville.lib.me.us/ReadersServices.htm). You'll
  also find links that can provide you with the entire text of
  books that you can read online, including free storybooks
  for children, and links to sites with information on graphic
  novels (books with lots of pen-and-ink illustrations forming the storyline), mysteries, gay and lesbian literature,
  and genre author lists.

AWARD SITES

- **The Man Booker Prize Web Site (www.themanbooker
prize.com)**
  This annual prize is awarded to the best work of fiction written in the United Kingdom. A special section of
  the Web site designed for librarians includes promotional
  ideas, competitions, and activities for libraries that choose
  the prize winners for displays and discussion programs.
  (www.themanbookerprize.com/librarians).
- **The National Book Award Web Site (www.national
book.org/nba.html)**
  The National Book Awards are given yearly to recog-
  nize American achievements in four categories: Fiction,
  Nonfiction, Poetry, and Young People's Literature.
  The site also contains study guides for the works of
  the award-winning authors and finalists in fiction, nonfiction, and poetry. Authors include John Updike, Gloria
  Naylor, Joyce Carol Oates, and J. Anthony Lukas.
  (www.nationalbook.org/authstudyguides.html)
- **The PEN-Faulkner Award Web site (www.penfaulkner.org)**
  The PEN/Faulkner Award is the largest annual juried
  prize for fiction in the United States in which writers are
  evaluated by their peers. The award is named for William
  Faulkner, who gave away his 1950 Nobel Prize money to
  establish a fund to support and encourage new fiction
  writers.

RESOURCE C: PROFESSIONAL ORGANIZATIONS/ SUBCOMMITTEES: SUPPORT FOR LIBRARIANS WHO RUN BOOK GROUPS

The American Library Association Public Programming Office (ALA-PPO) (www.ala.org/template.cfm?Section=ppo)

50 E. Huron Street

Chicago, IL 60611

Fax: (312) 944–2404

E-mail: publicprograms@ala.org

Director's Office: 312–280–5057

The mission of the ALA Public Programs Office (PPO) is to promote cultural programming including book and literature discussions in all types of libraries. The PPO provides leadership, resources, training, and grant opportunities that help thousands of librarians nationwide develop and host cultural opportunities for adults, young adults, and families. For example, between October 2002 and December 2005, the PPO cosponsored a traveling exhibition entitled "*Frankenstein*: Penetrating the Secrets of Nature," which encouraged audiences at eighty libraries to read and discuss Mary Shelley's novel, *Frankenstein*. Participating libraries also hosted interpretive and educational programs that helped audiences examine how the novel uses scientific experimentation as metaphor to comment on cultural values, especially the importance of exercising responsibility toward individuals and the community in all areas of human activity, including science. "*Frankenstein*: Penetrating the Secrets of Nature" was developed by the National Library of Medicine (NLM) in collaboration with the ALA Public Programs Office. It was funded by major grants from the National Endowment for the Humanities (NEH), Washington, D.C., and the National Library of Medicine, Bethesda, Md. Check the Web site regularly or contact the office to see which programs may benefit your book group readers and your library as a whole. Pay special attention to the PPO's offers of small grants and offers of free books for book discussion programs that meet certain themes and guidelines.

The Center for the Book (www.loc.gov/loc/cfbook/ctr-bro.html)
Library of Congress
101 Independence Ave., SE
Washington, DC 20540–4920
Telephone: 202–707–5221
Fax: 202–707–0269

The Center for the Book was established in 1977 by the Library of Congress to promote books, reading, libraries, and literacy. The Center, structured as a partnership between the government and the private sector, is funded by tax-deductible contributions from corporations and individuals. It runs projects, publications, and events aimed at both the general public and scholars. Its major themes and interests are reading and literacy promotion, the role of books and reading in today's society, the international role of books, the recognition and celebration of America's literary heritage, and the history of books and print culture. The Center for the Book has affiliated centers for the book in all fifty states and the District of Columbia, a reading promotion partners program that includes more than eighty national civic and educational organizations, and a broad network of national and international organizations and programs that promote books, reading, and libraries including several centers for the study of the history of the book located in academic or research organizations. Be sure to check out the affiliated center in your state. The Center For the Book is also the clearinghouse for "One Book" Reading Promotion Projects. These community and statewide reading programs, initiated by the Washington Center for the Book in 1998, now take place across the United States of America and around the world. The national Center for the Book Web site contains a state-by-state listing of past and current "One Book" projects listed by author and community (www.loc.gov/loc/cfbook/one-book.html).

RESOURCE D: PARTNERSHIP STRATEGIES: CHECKLIST FOR GETTING HELP FROM BOOKSTORES, SCHOOLS, AND COMMUNITY GROUPS

CHOOSING PARTNERS

1. Think through your program goals and objectives.

Who is the program for? What do you hope to achieve with the program? Which of your organizational strengths will help you achieve your goals, and which of your weaknesses might stand in your way? How could a program partner build on your strengths and compensate for your weaknesses?

2. Think about what you want from a program partner.

Do you want your partner to be actively involved in organizing the program and guiding its direction? Or do you want them only to publicize and create awareness of a program that you design and create? If you are trying to bring under-served constituents into the library, consider partnering with an organization that serves the constituents you are trying to attract. If you have trouble publicizing your programs, you might choose to partner with a media organization such as a local newspaper, radio, or television station to help create awareness of the program. Be clear about what you want from your potential partner before you approach them.

3. Think about the benefits you can provide for your program partner.

A successful working relationship will benefit both parties, and any potential partner will want to know how they will benefit from the time and resources they give to the program. Think about the ways in which working on the program might benefit your program partner. For example, will the organization's constituents benefit from participating in the program or becoming more aware of the library? Will the organization receive valuable publicity by partnering with you? Will an ongoing relationship with the library be of benefit to your potential partner?

4. Researching the organization.

Make sure you have up-to-date information about the organization you plan to contact. Know who they are, what they do, who they serve, and what their achievements are. Talk to other people who have previously worked in partnership with the organization. Find out if you have a friend or colleague in common with the person you plan to contact so that you don't have to cold-call. If you can get a recommendation, or an "in," making the contact will be much easier.

5. Making a preliminary contact.

During the first communication with your potential partner, let them know quickly and concisely who you are, why you are calling or e-mailing, and what your proposal for them is. Be prepared to answer questions at this time, and to follow up if they ask you questions that you can't immediately answer. Find out if you are talking to the right person—the person who can help you the most. Once you have established who the best person to talk to is, arrange to have a more in-depth conversation at a mutually convenient time.

6. Meeting with a representative of the partnering organization.

Before you meet, send background information about the library and the program to the person you are meeting with. Take supplementary materials to the meeting—for example, a program fact sheet and your business card. At the meeting, discuss your program goals and objectives, your reasons for choosing this organization as your potential partnering organization, and the mutually beneficial results you anticipate coming from the partnership.

WORKING WITH A PARTNER

7. Establish the terms of the partnership.

Clarify the expectations you have of each other and of the program. Once you have agreed on terms and expectations, do your best to keep to them. If you find that you cannot meet some of the expectations outlined at the beginning of the partnership, talk to your partner about this as soon as possible.

8. Communicate effectively with your partner.

Create and maintain a positive working relationship by regularly talking to your partner and listening to what they have to say. Be sure to show appreciation for their effort. Create opportunities for you and your partner to express and work through problems, challenges, or dissatisfaction.

9. Communicate effectively with the members of your organization.

Ensure that your staff feel comfortable about working alongside representatives of the partnering organization. Talk to them about the partnership and discuss with them any apprehensions and concerns they might have. Involve them in the process of choosing a program partner.

ONCE THE PROGRAM IS OVER

10. Follow up.

Publicly acknowledge and thank your partner for the work they have done to make your program a success. Put them on your mailing list and ensure they receive regular updates about library activities. Keep up to date with what they're doing. If the program was a great success for both of you, start planning another program together!

REFERENCES

Joint Ventures: The Promise, Power and Performance of Partnering. Sacramento, Calif.: California State Library, 2001.

Winer, Michael, and Karen Ray. *Collaboration Handbook: Creating, Sustaining, and Enjoying the Journey*. Saint Paul, Minn.: Amherst H. Wilder Foundation, 2000.

Created by the California Center for the Book September 2002, The California Center for the Book is supported by the U.S. Institute of Museum and Library Services, under the provisions of the Library Services and Technology Act, administered in California by the State Librarian.

INDEX

A

Absalom, Absalom!, 93
Aesop's Fables, 87
African-American literature, 5, 15, 33, 232
   See also Kwanzaa
Alaska, 12
Albom, Mitch, 32, 39
Alcott, Louisa May, 33, 87
Ali, Monica, 34
Alice in Wonderland, 95
All Over But The Shoutin', 35
All the Pretty Horses, 12
Allende, Isabel , 8, 13
Almost A Woman, 226
Alvarez, Julia, 7
Amazon.com. 86, 181, 193, 216–217
American Library Association, 44, 182
   Office for Information Technology Policy, 60
   Public Programming Office, 235–236
   Young Adult Library Services, 40
Americans With Disabilities Act, 50
Anaya, Rudolfo, 12
Angela's Ashes, 34, 225
Angelou, Maya, 34
Anna Karenina, 53, 226
Anson, Alison, 25
Answered Prayers, 141
Armstrong, Karen, 6, 34
Arts & Entertainment Biography Series (A&E), 136
Arts & Entertainment Investigative Reports (A&E), 199
Asian-American authors, 206
Association of Book Group Leaders and Readers, 229
At Weddings and Wakes, 189
Atlantic Monthly, 228
Atticus, 109
Atwan, Robert, 162
Atwood, Margaret, 218
Author events, 103–112
AuthorYellowPages.com., 86
Ava's Man, 35

B

Bait and Switch, 197
Baldwin, James, 33
Baltimore Chronicle, 187
Banks, Russell, 12
Beach, Sylvia, 165
Beacon Press, 89

The Bean Trees, 96
Beecher, Suzanne, 125
   See also DearReader.com
Behr, Alan, 103
Bel Canto, 96
Benga (African music), 183
Berendt, John, 40
Best-seller selection criteria, 39
Big Russ and Me, 91
A Bigamist's Daughter, 188
Bissinger, H.G. (Buzz), 169
   Biography, 170–171
Black and Blue, 8
Black History Month (February), 15, 181–183
Blais, Madeleine, 173
Bless Me, Ultima, 12
Block, Marta Segal, 14
Blogs (defined), 117–118
Bloomsday, 165
Blue Shoe, 82
The Bondwoman's Narrative, 15
Book Awards
   Edgar Awards, 42
   Hugo Awards, 45
   Macavity Award, 43
   Man Booker Prize, 233
   National Book Award, 192, 233
   Nebula Awards, 45
   Nobel Prize for Literature, 8, 47
   PEN-Faulkner Award, 233
   Pulitzer Prize, 46, 142, 150, 169, 170
The Book Club Cookbook, 225
Book Discussion Kits, 95–100
The Book Group: A Thoughtful Guide to Forming and Enjoying A Stimulating Book Discussion Group, 228
Book Lust, 227
Book Report Network, 86, 174
Book Review Digest, 138
Booklist, 90
Bookmarks Magazine, 39–40, 228–229
BookPage, 40
Books On Tape, 153
The Bookseller of Kabul, 219
Booksense, 40, 229
Bookspot.com, 40
Bookstores, 21, 41, 52, 62, 105
   Barnes & Noble, 58
   Murder Ink, I and II, 42

Shakespeare and Company, 165
Something Wicked, 41
Space-Crime Continuum, 41
BoucherCon, 42
Boyle, T.C., 13
Bradbury, Ray, 46
Bragg, Rick, 35
The Breadwinner, 218
Brick Lane, 34
The Bridge of San Luis Rey, 58, 59, 70
The Bridges of Madison County, 39
British Broadcasting Company (BBC), 231
Brown, Dan, 39, 83, 103
Bush, Barbara, 108
Butler, Octavia, 46

C

Cable News Network (CNN), 221
Caedmon Audiobooks, 165
Caldwell, Bo, 61, 64
California Center For the Book, 239
Canada, Geoffrey, 90
Cane River, 8
Cannery Row, 134
Capote, Truman, 42, 87, 160
   Biography, 140–141, 144
Carol of the Brown King: Nativity Poems, 160
Carson, Rachel, 6
Carter, James Earl, 84
Cather, Willa, 33, 87
The Center for the Book, 236
   See also Library of Congress
Center Point Large Print Publishers, 215
Cervantes, 136
Charles, John, 44
Charming Billy
   Ready-made book discussion, 187–194
Chautauqua Literary and Scientific Circle 6, 18
Child of My Heart, 189
A Child's Christmas In Wales, 160
China Boy, 11, 14, 16
Chiochios, Linda, 52
A Christmas Carol, 31, 159
Christmas Even, 160
A Christmas Memory, 160
Church of Dead Girls, 96
Chwast, Seymour, 162
Cisneros, Sandra, 13
The City of Falling Angels, 40

Clancy, Tom, 103
Clark, Candace, 44
Clarke, Arthur C, 46
Clarke, Gerald, 144, 147
Classic Fiction Selection Criteria, 30–32
Clinton, William J., 34, 35, 83, 108
Cohen, Fran, 92, 101
The Color of Water, 14
Columbia Tristar Home Entertainment, 144
Columbia University, 7
The Common Review, 14
Community partnerships checklist, 237–239
Community-wide reading programs, *See* "One-Book"
   programs.
*Complete Kwanzaa: Celebrating Our Cultural Har-
   vest,* 162
Connally, Molly, 152, 157
Connelly, Michael, 160
Contemporary Authors, 32 *See* Thompson Gale
   Publishers
Copyright issues, 60
The Corrections, 9
The Count of Monte Cristo, 32
Cozies, 41
Craft, Hannah, 15
Craigslist, 23
Creedon, Cynthia, 51
Crystal, Billy, 40
Cullen, John, 218

D

The Da Vinci Code, 39, 83, 103
Daughter of Fortune, 8
Daughters of Afghanistan (film), 216
Dead White Males, 7, 11
De Paola, Tomie, 161
"The Dead"
   Ready-made book discussion, 163–167
Dean, Deborah, 54
DearReader.com, 115, 117, 124–125
   See also Suzanne Beecher
The Deep End of the Ocean, 7
Desperadoes, 109
Detecting Men, 44
Detecting Women, 44
The Devil In the White City, 142
The Diary of Anne Frank, 86
Dibdin, Michael, 44
Dickens, Charles, 7, 31, 159

Difficult readers, *See* problem personalities
Distant Land of My Father, 61
Dobyns, Stephen, 96
Doctorow, E.L., 40
Don Quixote de la Mancha, 136
Dos Passos, John, 33
Double Helix, 35
Doyle, Arthur Conan, 31
Doyle, Roddy, 194
Dragon Bones, 205
Dreams From My Father
    Ready-made book discussion, 179–186
Drive: Women's True Stories From the Open Road,
    136
"A Drugstore In Winter", 162
Dubliners, 163, 164
Dumas, Alexandre , 32

E

Early, Steve, *201*
East of Eden, 53, 69,133, 226
Edgar Awards, 42
Edinger, Monica, 94–95, 101
Ehrenreich, Barbara
    Biography, 195–197
Eliot, T.S. 43
Ellis, Deborah, 218
Emerson College (Boston), 8
Encyclopedia of Murder and Mystery, 44
Endurance: Shackleton's Incredible Voyage, 12
Espada, Martin, 7
Esquire Magazine, 141
Evanovich, Janet, 39
Evans, Sherry, 24, 28
The Executioner's Song, 142

F

Fahrenheit 451, 15, 45
Farrar, Straus and Giroux, 90, 188
Fast Food Nation, 34, 198
Faulkner, William, 93
Fear of Falling: The Inner Life of the Middle Class, 197
Fesperman, Dan, 218
Finnegan's Wake, 31, 167
Fist, Stick, Knife, Gun, 90
Fitzgerald, F. Scott, 31, 194
Flyers, 58–61
Follett, Ken, 42
For Her Own Good, 197

Ford Foundation, 33
Francis, Dick, 42
Franzen, Jonathan, 9
Fraser, Laura, 108, 110–111
Free-range librarian, *See* Karen Schneider
Frey, James, 9
Friday Night Lights
    Ready-made book discussion, 169–177
Friedman, Thomas, 34
Friends of the Library, 21, 67, 104–105

G

Gaines, Ernest, 12–13
Garrison, William Lloyd, *5*
Gaudy Night, 41
Gay, Lesbian, Bisexual and Transgender Literature,
    146, 232
Gelman, Judy, 225
Gen, Gish, 206
Germain, Carol Anne, 63, 77
Gisonni, Debbie, 108
*Global Woman: Nannies, Maids and Sex Workers in
    the New Economy*, 197
The Goddess of Happiness, 108
Gogol, Nikolai, 153
Goldin, Barbara Diamond, 162
Good Books Lately, 227
The Good Shepherd, 160
Goode, Jenny, 136
Goodspeed, John, 187–188
Google, 86, 214
Grafton, Sue, 39
The Grapes of Wrath, 83, 134
Great Books, 6–7, 9–11, 14
The Great Gatsby, 31
Green, Hardy, 9, 18
Guardian of London, 196
Guevara, Ernesto Che, 136
Gunnarsson, Gunnar, 160
Guthrie Theater (Minneapolis), 199

H

Hammer, Earl, 160
The Handmaid's Tale, 218
Hansen, Ron, *109*
Harper Collins Reader Resources, 89
Harper's, 197, 200, 228
Harry Potter series, 45, 89
Harvard Law Review, 181

Hausladen, Gary J., 44
Hawthorne, Nathaniel, 32
Heising, Willetta L., 44
Herbert, Rosemary, 44, 157
Hermann, Carrie, 96
Highbridge Audio, 136
Hijuelos, Oscar, 7
Hillenbrand, Laura, 35, 173
Hillerman, Tony, 42
Hispanic Literature, *See* Latino Literature
Hitler, Adolf, 4, 5, 219
Holes, 12
Holiday programming, 159–167
    Christmas 159–161; Latino Christmas, 161
    Halloween, 142
    Hanukah, 162
    Kwanzaa 161–162
    Mother's Day, 205
    St Patrick's Day, 189
    Superbowl Sunday, 171
Holidays on Ice, 160
The Homecoming, 160
Homer, 31
Hosseini, Khaled, 11, 34
    Biography, 212–214
    Web site, 214
Houghton Mifflin Publishers, 153, 155
The Hound of the Baskervilles, 31
An Hour Before Daylight, 84
The House of Spirits, 13
The House on Mango Street, 13
Hughes, Holly, 226
Hughes, Langston, 160
Hugo Awards, 45
Huston, Angelica, 166
Huston, John, 166
Hutchins, Robert M, 10
Hutchinson, Anne, 4, 9

I

I Know Why the Caged Bird Sings, 34
Icebreakers, 81–85
The Iliad, 31
In Cold Blood, 42
    Ready-made book discussion, 139–147
In These Girls, Hope is A Muscle, 173
Independent Mystery Booksellers Association, 42
Infopeople, 50, 54
Intel, 87

The Interior, 205
Internet Movie Database, 141, 143
Internet Public Library, 86–88
Interpreter of Maladies, 150
Irish-American writers, 191, 194
Islam: A Short History, 6, 34
Isn't It Romantic, 109
An Italian Affair, 108, 110, 111

J

Jacobsohn, Rachel W, 225
    See also Association of Book Group Leaders and
    Readers
Jaffe, Rachel, 113
Jago, Carol, 214
Janes, Joe, 62
Johnson County Community College Billington Library
    (Kansas), 215
Joyce, James, 30, 31
    Biography, 163–165
Junger, Sebastian, 35
The Jungle, 198
Just Enough Is Plenty: A Hanukah Tale, 162

K

Kakutani, Michiko, 156, 157
Kandahar Journey Into the Heart of Afghanistan,
    (film), 216
Karenga, Dr. Ron, 161
Karras, Alex, 173
Kempf, Andrea, 215
Kempf, Becky, 55
Kentucky Post, 55
Kerouac, Jack, 136, 138
Kessler, Jane, 63,77
Khadra, Yasmina, 218
Kidd, Sue Monk, 225
King, David, 122
King, Ross, 84
King, Stephen, 20, 108
King Lear, 91
The Kingdom of the Golden Dragon, 13
Kingsolver, Barbara, 8, 96
Kirkus Reviews, 228
The Kite Runner, 11, 34
    Ready-made book discussion, 211–221
Kleim, Richard, 5, 18
Knowmobile, 62
Kofmel, Kim G., 45, 48

Koskinen, Pat, 54
Krupp, Vicki Levy, 225

L

La Mott, Anne, 82
LA Weekly, 204, 209
Lahiri, Jhumpa, 149–151, 157
Lamb, Christina, 219
Lansing, Alfred, 12
Lapham, Lewis, 195
Larson, Eric, 142
Laskin, David, 226
Latino Literature, 232
Latino National Conversation, 7
Laws, David, 69, 112
Lee, Chang Rae, 14
Lee, Gus, 11, 14, 16
Lee, Harper, 31, 83, 140, 141
The Legend of the Poinsettia, 161
Leon, Donna, 44
A Lesson Before Dying, 12
Librarian's Index to the Internet, 183
Library Journal, 30, 39, 45, 48, 77, 90, 127, 157, 214,
    228
Library of America, 32
Library of Congress, 14, 135, 236
Lieblich, Irene, 162
Life magazine, 144, 184
The Little Prince, 31
Locus Magazine, 45
Lolita, 31, 89
Long Island Reads, 134
The Lord of the Rings trilogy, 45
Los Angeles Times, 39
Losing It: False Hopes and Fat Profit in the Diet
    Industry, 110
The Loudest Voice, 160
The Lovely Bones, 84

M

Macavity Award, 43
Mailer, Norman, 142
Man Booker Prize, 233
The Man Who Mistook His Wife For A Hat, 35
The March, 940
Mariette in Ecstasy, 109
Masterpiece Theatre Book and Film Club, 226
McCarthy, Cormac, 12
McCourt, Frank, 34, 194, 225

McDermott, Alice
    Biography, 188–189
McGlinn, Sharon Hilts, 114, 120–121
McKeown, Lynn, 184
Mechanics Institute Library (San Francisco), 113
Medearis, Angela Shelf, 162
Mein Kampf, 4
Melville, Herman, 31
Menlo Park Almanac, 63, 64
Metropolitan Books, 197
Metropolitan Community College Library (MI), 49
Michelangelo and the Pope's Ceiling, 84
Michener, James, 33
Midnight in the Garden of Good and Evil, 40
The Mighty Kings of Benga, 183
A Million Little Pieces, 9
Minter, Daniel, 162
Mitchard, Jacquelyn, 8
Moby-Dick, 31, 93
Monk Kidd, Sue, 96, 225
Moore, Ellen, 227
More Book Lust, 227
Morrison, Joanna, 44
Morrison, Toni, 8, 87
Mother Jones Magazine, 196
The Motorcycle Diaries, 136
Muckraker (defined), 198
Munro, Alice, 87
Murder and All That Jazz, 161
Murphy, Bruce F., 43
Music for Chameleons, 141
Mystery Readers Advisory: Librarians Clues to Murder
    and Mayhem, 44
Mystery Readers Journal, 42
Mystery selection criteria, 41–44

N

Nabokov, Vladimir, 31, 89
Nader, Ralph, 198
Nafisi, Azar, 34
The Namesake
    Ready-made book talk, 149–157
The Nation, 201
National Book Award, 192, 233
National Book Critics Circle, 231
National Endowment for the Humanities, 33
National Public Radio, 220, 231
Nonfiction selection criteria, 33–38
Native American Literature, 40, 232

Native Speaker, 14
Nebraska, 104
Nebula Awards, 45
Nelson, Sarah, 227
New journalism, 141
New York Review of Books, 228
New York Times, 39, 156, 171, 181, 205
New York Times Book Review, 140, 144, 204
The New Yorker, 140, 141, 154, 228
Newmark, Craig, 23
Nickel and Dimed
    Ready-made book discussion, 195–202
Nobel Prize for Literature, 8, 47
Noche Buena: Hispanic American Christmas Stories,
    161
Nonfiction novel, 141, 142
Novedades, 232
NoveList, 90
Nu shu writing, 203–205, 207

O

Obama, Barack,
    Biography, 180–181
    Senate Web site, 183
The Odyssey, 31
Old Possum's Book of Practical Cats, 43
The Oxford Companion to Crime and Mystery Writ-
    ing, 44
On Gold Mountain, 205
On the Road, 136, 138
Once Around the Fountain, 103
"One Book" Programs, 11–16, 125, 231, 236
    (a.k.a. "One City One Book" Programs)
    Chicago, (IL), 215
    Edina, Minnesota, 221
    Indianapolis, (IN) 15
    Kalamazoo (MI), 199
    Kansas City (Missouri), 215
    New York City, 14
    Pasadena (CA)14
    Richmond (VA), 191
    San Francisco, 16
    Santa Ana (CA), 14, 16
    Santa Monica (CA) , 214
    Seattle (WA), 11–13
Online Book Discussion Groups, 113–127
Online Book Page, 126
Osama (film), 216
The Other Side of Eden, 92

Other Voices, Other Rooms, 140
Our Town, 33
The Overcoat, 153
Ozick, Cynthia, 162

P

Paddy Clarke, Ha, Ha, Ha, 194
Paley, Grace, 160
Paretsky, Sara, *42*
Paris Review, *144*
Patchett, Anne, 96
The Pearl, 17
Pearl, Nancy, 11, 41, 48, 227–228, 231
Pearlman, Mickey, 85
PEN-Faulkner Award, 233
Penguin Press, 225
    Readers Guide, 217
The Perfect Storm, 35
Perseus Press, 174
Peterson, Ken, 199
Pinkney, Andrea Davis, 161
Places for Dead Bodies, 44
Planeta Publishing Corporation, 153
Plimpton, George, 140, 144, 145
Poe, Edgar Allan, 42
Poisonwood Bible, 8
A Portrait of the Artist As A Young Man, 164, 167
The Power of Light, 162
A Prayer for the City, 170
Press releases, 62–64
The Prizewinner of Defiance, Ohio, 35
Problem personalities, 91–95
    Readers who talk too little, 94–95
    Readers who talk too much, 92–93
Proust, Marcel, 20, 30
Publishers Readers Guides, 85–90
    See also individual publishers
Publishers Weekly, 45, 90, 154, 155, 204, 227,228
Public Libraries
    Albany Public Library (CA), 11
    Alderney Gate Public Library (Halifax, Canada,
        Nova Scotia) , 114, 122
    Austin Public Library (TX), 12
    Belmont Public Library (CA), 52
    Bettendorf Public Library (IA), 74–76
    Boone County Library (KY), 55, 71–73, 96–100
    Bridgeport Public Library (CT), 183
    Chantilly Regional Library (VA), 152
    Downer's Grove Public Library (IL), 36

Fremont Public Library (CA), 11
Glendale Public Library (IN), 15
Greater Cincinnati Library Consortium (OH), 96
Guilderland Public Library (NY), 143
Halifax (Nova Scotia, Canada) Public Library System, 123–124
Hennepin County Public Library (MN), 114–115
Indianapolis Marion County Library (IN), 15
Kalamazoo Public Library (MI), 199
Kansas City Metropolitan Library and Information Network, 215
Kansas City Public Library (Missouri), 122
Live Oak Public Libraries (GA), 26
Lodi Public Library (CA), 54
Menlo Park Public Library (CA), 11, 59, 61, 67–70, 111–112
Montgomery County Public Library (MD), 232
Multnomah County Library (WI), 86
New York Public Library, 232
Pasadena Public Library (CA), 14
Portola Valley Public Library(CA), 36
Portsmouth Public Library (NH), 24
Roselle Public Library (IL), 115–116, 123
San Carlos Public Library (CA), 25
San Francisco Public Library (CA), 11
Scottsdale Public Library (AZ), 44
Seattle Public Library (WA), 11–13
Shasta County Library (CA), 49–50, 54
Shrewsbury Public Library (MA), 51
Thompson Nicola Regional District Library System (Kamloops, British Columbia, Canada), 45
Tippecanoe Public Library (IN), 118–120
Vermont Department of Libraries, 86
Waterboro Public Library (ME), 160
Waterville Public Library (ME), 233
Pulitzer Prize, 46, 142, 150, 169, 170

Q

Quindlen, Anna, 8

R

Random House Publishers, 143, 204, 206
　Audio Publishing, 182, 206
　Reader's Guides, 86, 89, 192, 208
　Vintage Books, 143
Reader's Robot, 45
Reader's Guides
　See individual publishers
Readerville, 126

The Reading Group, 226
ReadingGroupGuides.com, 86
The Reading Group Handbook, 225, 229
*Reading Lolita in Te*hran, 34
Ready-made questions, *See* Publisher's Reader Guides
Recruiting Survey, 27
Reverberations Magazine, 229
Rice, Anne, 20
Riley, Dorothy Winbush, 162
Rodriguez, Richard, 7
Rooney, Kathleen, 8–9, 11, 18
Rowling, J.K., 32, 89
Ruminator, 228
Russell, Carrie, 60, 77
Russert, Tim, 91
Ryan, Terry, 35

S

700 Sundays, 40
Sachar, Louis, 12
Sacks, Oliver, 35
Saint-Exupery, Antoine de, 31
Salon, 228
Salzman, Mark, 14
San Francisco Chronicle, 104, 213
San Jose State University, 56
Santiago, Esmeralda, 226
Sasquatch Books, 227
Sayers, Dorothy, 41
The Scarlet Letter, 32
Schlosser, Eric, 34, 198
Schneider, Karen, 117
School Library Journal, 90, 127, 152
Scifi.com; 46
Science Fiction and Fantasy Selection Criteria, 45–46
Science Fiction and Fantasy Writers of America, Inc., 45
Science Fiction Museum and Hall of Fame (Seattle), 46
The Sea Around Us, 6
The Sea of Cortez, 134
Seabiscuit: An American Legend, 35, 173
Seattle Reads. *See* "One Book" Programs-Seattle
Sebold, Alice, 84
The Secret Life of Bees, 96, 225
Sedaris, David, 160
See, Lisa
　Biography, 204–205
　Web site, 208
Seierstad, Anne, 219
Seniornet, 126

Seven Candles For Kwanzaa, 161
Seven Spools of Thread, 162
The Sewing Circles of Herat, 219
Shader, Robin, 26, 28
The Shahnamah (Book of Kings), 216–217
Shakespeare, William, 7, 20, 32, 87, 91, 226
Shared inquiry method, 7
Shattered Glass, 171
Sinclair, Upton, 198
Singer, Isaac Bashevis, 162
Singh, Carolyn, 49–40
Sinise, Gary, 136
Sisters In Crime, 42
Slezak, Ellen, 3, 18, 228
Smiley, Jane, 91
Smith, Sandy, 54
Smokler, Kevin, 113, 127
Snacks, 53–54, 155
Snow Flower and the Secret Fan
    Ready-made book discussion, 203–209
Sodowsky, Kay, 49
*So Many Books, So Little Time: A Year of Passionate
    Reading*, 227
Somers, Denise, 114, 122
Song of Solomon, 8
Sony Pictures, 144
Soto, Gary, 161
SparkNotes, 32, 89
Speculative fiction, 45
Spielberg, Steven, 46
Sports Illustrated, 169, 170,171, 174–175, 177
Starkey, Neal, 120
A Stay Against Confusion, 109
Steele, Danielle, 39
*Steinbeck Country: Exploring the Settings For the
    Stories*, 112
Steinbeck, John. 13–14, 17, 53, 69, 82–83, 92
    biography, 133–134
    National Steinbeck Center (Salinas), 136
Steinbeck, John IV, 92
Stegner, Wallace, 20
Stevens, Ellen, 227
Stuhlman, Daniel, 56, 77
Sula, 8
Sun Microsystems, 87
Sunphone Records, 165
The Swallows of Kabul, 218
The Sweet Hereafter, 12

T

2001 Space Odyssey, 45
Tademy, Lalita, 8
Tales of the South Pacific, 33
Tan, Amy, 206
Ten on Ten: Major Essayists on Recurring Themes, 162
Terkel, Studs, 199
That Night, 188
Thomas, Dylan, 160
Thompson, Sandra, 14, 18
Thompson Gale Publishers
    Authors and Artists For Young Adults, 157
    Contemporary Authors, 32, 134, 149–150
    *Nineteenth and Twentieth Century Contemporary
    Literary Criticism*, 32
Thoreau, Henry D., 31
Thorn, Patti, 8, 18
A Thousand Acres, 91
Three Nights In August, 170
Three Rivers Press, 179
Time magazine, 196
Time Warner Books Reading Guides, 89
To Kill a Mockingbird, 13, 31, 83, 140, 141
Tolkien, J.R.R., 32
Tolstoy, Countess Alexandra, 136
Tolstoy, Leo, 52, 226
Too Many Tamales, 161
The Tortilla Curtain, 13
Travels with Charley, 92
    Ready-made book discussion, 133–138
Tuesdays with Morrie, 32, 39
Twain, Mark, 31, 87

U

Ulysses (Homer), 30
Ulysses (Joyce), 164, 165, 167
University of Albany (NY), 63
University of Chicago, 7, 10
University of Michigan at Ann Arbor School of Library
    and Information Science, 86–87
University of Washington Information School, 62
Unsafe at Any Speed, 198
USA Today, 169

V

Victoria Kings, *183*
Viking Press, 216
Vita's Will, 108

Vonnegut, Kurt, 87

W

Waller, Robert James, 36
The Warlord's Son, 218
Washington Center for the Book, 11–13, 41
Washington Post, 39, 204
Watson, James D., 35
WBGH Educational Foundation, 226

Wharton, Edith, 20
Wilder, Thornton, 33, 58, 59, 70
Winfrey, Oprah, 4, 7–12, 18, 31, 33, 39, 85
The Wizard of Oz, 95
World Science Fiction Society, 45
Worldcon, 45

Y

Yeats, William Butler, 190

ABOUT THE AUTHOR

LAUREN ZINA JOHN is a librarian, writer, and book group leader who has led literature discussions in New York City, Boston, and the San Francisco Bay area.

She currently works as a librarian and book group leader at two very different kinds of libraries: 1) The private Town and Country Club library housed in a historic women's club in San Francisco and 2) Menlo Park Public Library in the heart of Silicon Valley. She also leads children's story hours in Menlo Park.

Born and raised in Queens, New York, she received her B.A. in English literature from New York State's Binghamton University, her master's degree in library science from St John's University in Jamaica, New York, and her master's degree in journalism from Boston University.

Her book reviews have appeared in *Library Journal* and *Publishers Weekly* and her commentary on public libraries has been heard on San Francisco's National Public Radio station KQED.